JEWISH
Heroes & Heroines of
America

151 True Stories of Jewish American Heroism

by Seymour "Sy" Brody

Frederick Fell
Publishers, Inc.
Since 1943

Frederick Fell Publishers, Inc.
2131 Hollywood Blvd., Suite 305, Hollywood, FL 33020
Phone: (954) 925-5242   Fax: (954) 925-5244
Web Site: www.FellPub.com

Frederick Fell Publishers, Inc.

2131 Hollywood Boulevard, Suite 305

Hollywood, Florida 33020

954-925-5242

e-mail: fellpub@aol.com

Visit our Web site at www.fellpub.com

Library of Congress Cataloging-in-Publication Data

Brody, Seymour.
  Jewish heroes & heroine of America : 151 true stories of Jewish
American heroism / by Seymour "Sy" Brody.
      p. cm.
  ISBN 0-88391-026-8 (pbk.)
1. Jews--United States--Biography. 2. Jewish women--United
States--Biography I. Title: Jewish heroes and heroine. II. Title.
  E184.37A132 2003
  920'.0092924073--dc21

                        2003002256

10 9 8 7 6 5 4 3 2 1
Graphic Design: Chris Hetzer

ENDORSEMENTS

"Jewish Heroes tells the stories of the heroic role of Jews in America."
—**The Jewish Ledger, Rochester, New York**

"Sy Brody's book on Jewish heroes and heroine could well be for assignments in Jewish and non-Jewish schools for strengthening the pride of our youth."
—**B'Nai Brith Life, New York, New York**

"Sy Brody's book on Jewish heroes and heroine carefully documents the heroism and sacrifices of American Jewish men and women fighting in our country's wars."
—**The Jewish War Veteran Magazine,**
Jewish War Veterans of the USA, Washington, D.C.

"Brody's book factually destroys the myths and lies that Jews never did anything for our country."
—**Texas Jewish Post, Dallas, Texas**

"Ex-Marine's book combats the misconceptions about American Jews."
—**Star Ledger, New Jersey**

"Jewish youth learn about their heroes from Brody's book."
—**Jewish News of MetroWest, Whippany, New Jersey**

"Brody's book factually traces the history and heroism of American Jews in our country's wars, from colonial times to the present."
—**Stars and Stripes, Washington, D.C.**

"The role and contribution of Jews in America is carefully documented in Brody's book on Jewish heroes and heroine."
—**American Jewish Times, Lakewood, NJ**

"Sy Brody's book on Jewish heroes and heroine is a rebuttal to the lies that Jews didn't fight in our country's wars."
—**The News Bee, Morris Plains, New Jersey**

"Sy Brody's book on Jewish heroes and heroine makes for top reading in the Morristown area."
—**The Journal, Morristown, New Jersey**

"Jewish heroes and heroine in America are saluted in Sy Brody's book."
—**Joan Barbato, Daily Record, Parisppany, New Jersey**

"The best kept secret in America is revealed in Sy Brody's book on Jewish heroes and heroine in America."
—**Jewish Community News, Clifton, New Jersey**

"Sy Brody's book on Jewish heroes and heroine in America is a must for every home."
—**Jewish Reporter, Trenton, New Jersey**

TABLE OF CONTENTS

DEDICATION

This book is dedicated to my wife, Ruth, who in my eyes is
the personification of a Jewish heroine. She has given me
encouragement, support and strength in writing this book.
She has devoted herself to the family, Judaism and the
community. This dedication and my love is only a part of
the greater recognition that she deserves.

Foreword

America is a vibrant spectrum of many different ethnic, racial, and religious people—not one better than the other and all seeking to work together, with dignity, for a better and more meaningful life. A recognition of that diversity of pride and identity is the ingredient that provides an enrichment quality to American life and the American being.

With such recognition, Sy Brody has added immeasurably to that enrichment by relating the contributions of Jewish men and women to the American purpose—contributions that reflect the fact that Jews have been an integral part of the American whole. Many may ignore, forget or seek to minimize the Jewish contribution to America's growth and stability. Sy's book, Jewish Heroes and Heroine of America, shall not allow that to happen.

Many of the following stories has appeared in many newspapers and magazines throughout the country. Sy has put them together in exhibition form and displayed them in public libraries, community centers and elsewhere for all to see and read. The stories regale us with great, but meaningful, simplicity in telling how the Jewish contribution is, in fact, an American contribution. Each of the stories—an appetizer—teases us with a desire to learn more about the person or the event.

I, for one, applaud this book and look forward to Sy's future articles and his next book, since all of that will enhance my Jewish pride and my Jewish identity as an American.

—**Bob Zweiman**
Past National Commander, JWV
Past President, National Museum of
American Jewish Military History

SPECIAL NOTE

Every religious and ethnic group has its "Mother" and the Jewish people have their "Yiddishe Mama." She has instilled in her daughters and sons the need for education, devotion, charity and service to the community and the nation. As a result of this training and upbringing, Jewish women and men have contributed to the defense and welfare of our nation.

They have fought in every war in defense of our country, from colonial times to the present. In defending our nation, many Jewish men and women have given their lives and others have been recognized with medals for their bravery. In peace time, Jewish women and men have made outstanding contributions in philanthropy, arts, science, sports, industry and medicine.

The National Ladies Auxiliary of the Jewish War Veterans of the USA is another part of this Jewish contribution. Their voluntary work in helping veterans, senior citizens, the sick and disabled, in caring for the graves of deceased veterans and in helping battered women is another part of the greater role of Jews in America.

Seymour Brody's book documents the contributions and sacrifices that Jews have made in America to help make it number one in the world.

He highlights the role of Jewish women in war and in peace, who alongside of the Jewish men, have helped to defend and create a better America. Seymour Brody's book refutes the lies that Jews never did anything for our country. Jewish Heroes and Heroine is a must for every Jewish home and library.

—**Sophie Ruderman, Past President**
National Ladies Auxiliary
Jewish War Veterans of the USA

X

PREFACE

I congratulate Sy Brody for his outstanding contributions to the literature of Jewish patriotism in America. The Jewish War Veterans of the USA is celebrating over a 100 years of continuous service.

The Jewish community continues to be enriched by the work of Sy Brody as he seeks further to establish the Jewish American as an integral and important part of our country's diverse makeup. His works have brought out those individuals that fill the gaps of our history; these are some of the people who have fought in the trenches, served in the public offices, worked in their communities.

Sy Brody's works have helped to deepen the Jewish community's understanding of its own role in the development of our country.

We all owe Sy Brody a great deal of gratitude for his untiring work to bring to light the patriotism and heroism of Jews in America.

—**Col. Herb Rosenbleeth, USA (Ret)**
National Executive Director
Jewish War Veterans of the USA

Introduction & Acknowledgments

Jews in America have been maligned, slandered and attacked about their participation in American affairs, patriotism and involvement in America's wars, from colonial times to the present. These false accusations by the anti-Semites, bigots and distorters of the truth belie the facts that Jews have fought in every major skirmish, battle, war and military campaign that the United States has been involved in. Jews have given the best years of their lives, dying, being wounded and receiving recognition and medals for their bravery in defense of our country.

There are seventeen Jewish Congressional Medal of Honor recipients. In World War I more than 250,000 Jews served, 3,500 were killed, 14,000 were wounded and they received 1,135 decorations for bravery. In World War II, 550,000 Jews were in the military; 11,000 were killed, 40,000 were wounded and they received over 52,000 medals and decorations for bravery.

Jewish civilians contribute in peace-time and in times of war, always in support of our country. They are politicians, scientists, producers of merchandise, entertainment, philanthropists, etc. They give of themselves in support of our country and many of them receive recognition for their activities.

 Jews have never shirked their responsibilities in helping America become the greatest nation in the world.

This book documents the many notable contributions and sacrifices made by Jewish men and women, in war and in peace. This book refutes the lies and distortions of truth regarding the Jew in America. It is hoped that the readers of this book will use it to combat any lies about Jews and that it will arouse your curiosity to investigate further about these and other Jews who have so notably given of themselves to our country.

I wish to express my love and gratitude to my wife, Ruth, for her sacrifices, patience and understanding on being left alone when I did my research and writing. She has also been a pillar of strength and encouragement during this period.

My special thanks is for one of the best illustrators in the publishing industry, Art Seiden. His illustrations have given a living dimension to the stories in the book through his professional animated artistic drawings.

I want to thank the library staff of Florida Atlantic University, where I spent much time doing research. They extended themselves in helping me find the information that I needed.

I want to thank the Jewish War Veterans of the United States of America and the National Museum of American Jewish Military History (the only accredited veterans museum in the country) for their inspiration and, at times, for the information that I needed.

I hope that this book will inspire you to go forward in the quest for further knowledge about our American Jewish men and women and their role and contributions in helping to build and develop our country.

—Seymour "Sy" Brody
Delray Beach, Florida

1

Jacob Barsimson

Paved the Way for Full Citizenship Rights

The first Jewish settler who came to New Amsterdam, later to be called New York, was Jacob Barsimson, a Hollander who arrived on August 22, 1654. He was soon followed by others. Jews who came from the West Indies and Brazil because they were disillusioned with the religious and political situations that existed there.The Jews settling in New Amsterdam were seeking the equality of free men in a land of liberty where they could freely worship and have equal opportunities and obligations alongside the Christian citizens.

Jacob Barsimson and the other Jews found that New Amsterdam was no different from where they came. Governor Peter Stuyvesant treated them as separate citizens. They couldn't engage in retail trade, practice handicrafts, hold public position, serve in the militia or practice their religion in a synagogue or in gatherings.

Barsimson and the other Jews presented a petition to Governor Stuyvesant for the right to buy a burial plot, which was denied because there was no immediate need for it. Later under pressure from Holland's Amsterdam Jews, Stuyvesant gave them the right to buy a burial plot.

Stuyvesant imposed many restrictions on the Jews in the colony. One of these was that Jews would be exempt from general training in the militia and guard duty on the walls of the fort on the condition that each male over 16 and under 60 years of age would contribute 65 stivers each month.

On September 22, 1654, Stuyvesant wrote to the Amsterdam Chamber of Commerce to complain about the presence of Jewish refugees from Brazil who had recently arrived in New Amsterdam. He felt that they were blasphemers of the name Christ and that they would infect the colony with trouble.

Portuguese Jews, who escaped the Inquisition, had arrived in Holland in 1593. Some of them were investors in the West India Company which controlled New Amsterdam. They petitioned the West India Company to allow Brazilian Jews to remain in New Amsterdam as they would not be a burden.

In the meantime, Barsimson, Asser Levy, Abraham de Lucena, Jacob Cohen Henricques and other New Amsterdam Jews kept putting pressure on Stuyvesant for full citizenship rights. They insisted on the right to serve in the militia and do guard duty on the walls of the city to protect the settlers and cattle, which were kept inside the walls at night, from the raids and attacks of the Indians and the New England settlers. They continued their petitions and pressure until the Governor finally granted them full citizenship.

Barsimson and the other Jews proudly did their guard duty on the walls of the colony alongside of the Christian militia men. When the British conquered New Amsterdam and changed its name to New York, the Jewish settlers continued to have full citizenship.

This tiny group of Jews displayed courage and bravery, under the leadership of Jacob Barsimson, to obtain citizenship for all Jews coming to the New World for the next three hundred years.

2

Gershom Mendes Seixas

The First Native-Born U.S. Rabbi

Gershom Mendes Seixas was the first native-born rabbi in the United States. He was one of seven children of Rachel and Isaac Seixas. He was born in New York City on January 15, 1746. His father had emigrated from Lisbon, Portugal, to New York in 1730, where he went into the mercantile business.

Gershom Seixas studied with Rabbi Joseph Pinto. He was appointed to be the rabbi of Congregation Shearith Israel, a Spanish and Portuguese synagogue in New York City, in 1768. Seixas was the father of fifteen children from his first wife, Elkay Cohen, who died in 1785, and eleven by his second wife Hannah Manuel, whom he married on November 1, 1789.

Seixas also served the religious needs of other Jews in the outlying areas of New York. He was the teacher of Hebrew, literature and law for the community.

He and most of his congregation left New York City in 1776, when the British were approaching during the American Revolutionary War. He went to Stamford, Connecticut, while most of the congregation went to Philadelphia. Four years later, he joined the others in Philadelphia where he helped found a new synagogue, Mikveh Israel. He was its rabbi for two years.

Seixas returned to New York to serve the Jewish community in 1784. He was the leader in helping to save the Jewish cemetery in Chatham

Square from obliteration. He helped establish the Kalfe Sedeka Matten Besether, in 1788, and the Hebra Hased Va-Amer, in 1792. Both were charitable organizations.

He was the first rabbi in America to give his sermons in English. He gave sermons which dealt with Jewish participation in the life of the state and made appeals for support of the American Revolution and against the British-Indian raids in the Northwest Territory. When the council members of Philadelphia made eligibility for an assembly seat dependent on professing the divine origin of the New Testament, he and other Jews fought against this unconstitutional religious test.

Seixas was in communication with the Jews in Europe and in other parts of America. He frequently consulted with the Beth Din (Court of Judgement) of the London synagogue on religious problems. He helped raise funds to build synagogues in other American cities. He served as trustee of Columbia College and often exchanged pulpits with other New York Clergymen.

Seixas' brothers were also active in the life and development of the United States. Abraham Mendes was an officer in the Revolutionary Army who fought the British in the southern states. Benjamin was a founder of the New York Stock Exchange. Moses Mendes was one of the organizers and the first cashier of the Bank of Rhode Island. He was also the president of the Newport Jewish Congregation.

David Seixas, a son, established the Deaf and Dumb Institute of Philadelphia. He was one of the first to discover ways of burning anthracite coal. He also helped to introduce daguerreotypes (a photograph made by an early process on a light-sensitive silver-coated metallic plate and developed by mercury vapor) in the United States.

Gershom Seixas died on July 2, 1816. He is buried in New York City's New Bowery Cemetery of the Shearith Israel Congregation.

16

3

Francis Salvador

Became the "Paul Revere of the South"

rancis Salvador was the first Jew to die in the American Revolution—on August 1, 1776—following the signing of the Declaration of Independence by the colonies. He was killed leading a little army of 330 men who were defending the frontier settlers against the Cherokee Indians, who had been incited by the British.

The battleground was near his plantation along the Keowee River in South Carolina. His exploits as an officer quickly earned him the title of the "Paul Revere of the south."

Salvador was the son of a wealthy London family who grew tired of living the life of a "dandy." In 1773, he decided to set sail for the colonies and he settled in South Carolina. His ability for leadership was quickly recognized and he was elected a delegate for his area to the first South Carolina Provincial Congress.

Salvador, serving as a delegate in Charleston, earned the esteem and friendship of such eminent colonials as Edward Rutledge,

Patrick Calhoun, and Charles Pinckney, who later uttered the imperishable words "Millions for defense, but not one cent for tribute!"

In his brief life, Salvador acquired many honors, which included a commission to sign and stamp South Carolina currency, serving as financial adviser to the Assembly, participating in reorganizing the courts and the selection of magistrates and serving as adviser to the Assembly election procedures. He also participated in drafting South Carolina's Constitution.

Salvador was only 29 years old when he was killed, but he had already established himself as a soldier, statesman, and leader.

He was the forerunner of the many Jews who would fight and, if necessary, be killed in defending the United States from its enemies. His brief life gave abundant nourishment to his beloved South Carolina and to the roots of our great nation.

4

Mordecai Sheftall

Acquired the Reputation of the "Great Rebel"

ordecai Sheftall was a leader in the Revolutionary movement against the British in Georgia and was recognized as
an important outstanding citizen in Savannah. He quickly
acquired the reputation of being a "great rebel" and the British were
very anxious to capture him.

His reputation and abilities were used for the war effort when
the Revolutionary Government named him Commissioner General of
Purchases and Issues to the Militia of Georgia. When supplies were
needed and money scarce, Sheftalll advanced his own funds to buy
the provisions for the Revolutionary troops. A year later, his leadership was extended by American General Robert Howe to service the
troops of both Georgia and South Carolina.

While he was awaiting confirmation from Congress, he was captured by the British. On December 29, 1778, a force of 3,500 soldiers,
consisting of two battalions of Hessians and British Redcoats, landed in
the early morning at Brewton Hill, two miles below Savannah. The

invading force encountered very little opposition and, by three o'clock, they had captured the city.

Sheftall and his 15-year-old son, Sheftall Sheftall, tried to escape the enemy with about 186 Revolutionary officers and men across Musgrove Creek. The British encircled them and, after a brief skirmish, Mordecai, his son and the others surrendered. He was treated very badly on a prison ship and, after several months, he and his son were transferred to a British garrison in Savannah. He managed to escape, but the British soldiers dogged him for many miles, finally overcoming and returning him to the garrison prison.

Sheftall had difficulties while in prison and he was finally freed when the British and Americans exchanged prisoners of war. After his release, he went to Philadelphia. There, he engaged in "legalized piracy" by selling shares in a privateering vessel. This ship would join other patriotic privateers in playing havoc on British commerce in the Atlantic Ocean.

These ships ransacked and destroyed many British commercial ships, which started to hurt their owners in their pocketbooks. These acts of piracy pressured the English businessmen to favor an end to hostilities. Sheftall was very active in his newfound role until the war ended.

Visitors to Savannah can view the old Jewish cemetery on Broughton Street, which was donated by Mordecai Sheftall in 1773. It was declared an historic landmark by the commission in 1850.

5

Haym Salomon

Financier of the Revolutionary War

Haym Salomon was a hero and a fervent patriot whose love of liberty and business acumen combined made him a vital force for the War of Independence. Born in Poland, in 1740, he was forced to flee for his life due to his fight for freedom alongside Pulaski and Kosciusko, who later became military heroes in the American Revolution.

After Salomon landed in New York, he immediately became a successful broker because of his education and his remarkable talents. He married Rachel Franks, who came from a famous American Jewish family.

While New York was the seat of British power, and he was doing business with the wealthy loyalists, Salomon joined the Sons of Liberty, a group of revolutionary patriots. When the Revolutionary War started in 1776, the British arrested him and flung him into prison as a spy.

The British recognized his linguistic abilities—he could speak 10 languages-and put him to work as an interpreter. He was finally

Jewish Heroes & Heroine of America

released and went back into business, aiding the Colonists with his mounting fortune.

Salomon was arrested again for his pro-revolutionary activities. This time he was tortured and condemned to be hanged. With the aid of his friends, he managed to escape to Philadelphia, where he arrived penniless. Salomon quickly returned to business, using his profits to buy food for the starving Colonial Army. Generals Washington, Lafayette,Von Steuben and others often came to him for food and material aid.

Salomon negotiated many loans for the Colonies from France and Holland, but never took a commission for himself. According to legend, General Washington's appeal for funds with which to maintain his ragged army came to Salomon on Yom Kippur. Devoutly religious, Salomon recognized that love of country was an aspect of his religion. So he turned to the congregation and suspended services to secure pledges for the necessary funds. Only after he obtained the necessary amount needed in pledges did he proceed with the solemn holiday observances.

It became a regular practice—the Revolutionary leaders' diaries testify to this—"that when money was needed for the Revolutionary War, you went to Haym Salomon."

6

Solomon Bush

Is Remembered as a Soldier and Citizen

L ieutenant Colonel Solomon Bush was the highest-ranking Jewish officer in the Continental Army and was decorated for his bravery in action. The son of Mathias Bush, a merchant, he was born in Philadelphia in 1753.

His first duty in the War of Independence was as deputy adjutant general of the Pennsylvania State Militia. At Brandywine, the militia encountered the British Army. Bullets and cannon balls flew through the air as the two armies intensified their battle. Captain Lewis Bush, the colonel's brother, was mortally wounded.

Colonel Bush was deeply involved in the battle and he received a near-fatal wound that affected him for the rest of his life. Although he survived the battle, he was captured when the British took Philadelphia. He was later freed in an exchange of prisoners between the British and the Americans.

Upon his release, he applied for rations and back pay, and the Supreme Executive Committee of the Continental Army reviewed his request and his records. The review disclosed the distinguished and brilliant service that Colonel Bush had rendered in and out of battle, especially during the winter of 1776, "when the service was critical and hazardous." The Supreme Executive Committee presented him with a special citation.

After the war, Colonel Bush went to England seeking better medical care for his war wound. While he was there, he again found himself in a position to serve his country.

The British, still smarting over their loss in the Revolutionary War, were pursuing a policy that finally led to the War of 1812. The British were seizing and searching American ships and conscripting their sailors into the Royal Navy.

In England, there was no American Consul or Ambassador present to intervene, so Colonel Bush took it upon himself to act on behalf of his fellow citizens. He reported his efforts to President George Washington, whose answers contained warm commendations for the Colonel's successful interventions.

When he returned to America, Colonel Bush applied for the position of Postmaster General, which had recently been vacated. He was the first Jew known to have been considered for a Cabinet rank in the government. He failed to get this appointment and his unhealed war injury hastened his death in 1796. Prior to his death, however, Colonel Bush contributed toward a new building for the Mikveh Israel Congregation in Philadelphia. He will long be remembered for his service to his country as a soldier and a citizen.

7

Aaron Lopez
Merchant King Who Kept
The Revolutionary Army Supplied

Aaron Lopez was a major factor in the Colonies' ability to continue to revolt against the British in their quest for freedom. He is said to have owned, whole or in part, 30 transoceanic ships and more than 100 coastal vessels that became an important delivery arm for supplying sorely needed supplies to the Revolutionary Army.

Despite the pressure put on his ships by the British to prevent them from supplying the Colonial Army, his ships managed to deliver the materials needed for the Revolution.

Lopez was a power in Newport, Rhode Island, for years, when the port city was described as a shipping center that "New York can never hope to rival." One of the reasons for this was Rhode Island's great religious liberalism, which attracted a substantial community of well-educated and able Jews, the most affluent in the Colonies.

Lopez, who was born in Portugal in 1731 and died in Newport in 1782, was one of the most outstanding Jews. He was described by Ezra Styles, Christian pastor and president of Yale, as "a merchant of first eminence; for honor and extent of commerce probably surpassed by no merchant in America." Newport's shipping industry was most important to young America's growing strength and power that enabled it to revolt.

Lopez was also recognized as a promoter of friendly relations between the faiths. He was respected by Christians and Jews alike, and no ship ever left his dock on either's Sabbath, Lopez personally laid the cornerstone of Touro Synagogue in Newport, which is now a Federal Shrine.

In strong sympathy with the Revolutionary patriots, Lopez fled Newport when the British attacked. Although Newport was ruined in the war, he did attempt to return when peace was won, but he was killed in an accident on the way.

8

Uriah P. Levy
A Naval Hero Who
Ended the Practice of Flogging

riah P. Levy was a naval hero who served his country from the War of 1812 to 1862. He was the first Jew to obtain the rank of commodore in the United States Navy, which is the equivalent of an admiral.

On April 22, 1793, Levy left his home in Philadelphia, at the age of 14, to sign up as an apprentice seaman aboard a merchant ship. At 15, he became the mate of the brig *Polley and Betsy*, and at 20 he became master and part owner of the brig-of-war *Argus*, which ran the British blockade to France.

On her return voyage to the United States, the *Argus* destroyed 21 British merchant ships and captured a number of vessels, which Levy armed for battle against the British men-of-war. When he met the heavily armed British frigate *Pelican*, Levy fought an unequal battle until the *Argus* was sunk and he was taken prisoner. He spent 16 months in Dartmoor Prison in England.

Levy was one of the first naval officers to recognize men for their ability and not by their ethnic roots, religion or social standing. When he was commander of the U.S.S. *Vandalia* during the War of 1812, he fathered a law that would place his name in history. The law abolished flogging in the Navy.

Because there was no Naval Academy to train and guide the young officers, Levy wrote and published the "Manual of War," the first printed guide that detailed all aspects of a young officer's duties aboard a ship. This manual was in three volumes and included the "new age of steam."

When Levy was promoted to lieutenant in 1817, he was confronted by a large group of anti-Semitic officers who slighted, rebuffed and discriminated against him. At one point, he was forced to fight a duel and killed the man. He was court-martialed and found guilty six times. On appeal, however, each case was overturned by a higher board of inquiry.

The anti-Levy feelings were so great that his enemies managed, in 1855, to get Congress to set up a board of inquiry to purge him from the Navy. Levy and the board received many letters of sympathy and support. Once again the anti-Semites lost and Levy remained in the Navy. It was after this event that Levy was promoted to the rank of commodore and given command of the Mediterranean Squadron.

Levy was a devoted admirer of Thomas Jefferson and when he found that Jefferson's home, Monticello, was in ruins and decay, he bought it on May 20, 1836. He worked hard to restore and preserve it for future generations.

Levy, a religious man, was the first president of Washington, D.C., Hebrew Congregation and was a member of the Shearith Congregation in New York. In World War II, a destroyer was named the U.S.S. *Levy* in his memory and it served in the war with distinction. The first permanent Jewish chapel ever built by the U.S. Armed Forces also honors him.The Commodore Uriah Levy Jewish Chapel is located near the main gate at the historic naval station in Norfolk, Virginia, and the public is invited to visit it.

9

John Ordroneaux
Fought the British During The War of 1812

One of the most heroic men who fought for the United States during the War of 1812 was the French privateer, Commodore John Ordroneaux. The War of 1812 was fought mainly between ships on the Atlantic Ocean. William Maclay, a historian of the American Navy, describing Ordroneaux's remarkable feats at sea, said of him that "he commanded respect by his ability and bravery during the battle."

Ordroneaux was a short man and it was hard to believe that he could command and convince a weather-beaten, hardy and experienced crew to accept his authority. It is told that he once halted a retreat by his men in the face of a British boarding party by running to the powder magazine with a lighted match, and threatening to blow up the whole ship if his crew retreated further.

Ordroneaux commanded an armed ship named Prince De Neufchantel, which was fitted out with private funds. One of the most remarkable actions of the War of 1812 took place when the Prince De Neufchantel encountered the 40-gun British frigate, Endymion. A battle ensued between the two ships with many cannon shots being exchanged. The much more heavily armed British Endymion kept pounding Ordroneaux's ship and it couldn't get the upper hand.

The commander of the Endymion became frustrated as he lost as many men as if he had fought a man-of-war of equal force. He privately acknowledged the heroism that the crew members of the privateer displayed in their fierce and skillful defense. It is said that Commodore Ordroneaux himself fired some 80 shots at the enemy.

The British tried many times to have their men board the Prince De Neufchatel, but they were repulsed with every attempt. The casualties were high for the British and, after 20 minutes, they cried out for quarter. The Americans ceased firing and captured the ship with its crew.

Commodore John Ordroneaux proved himself to be a brave and adroit leader. He continued to roam the seas looking for the British ships until the war came to an end.

10

Judah Touro

A Philanthropist and Soldier

When Judah Touro died in 1854, his famous will left bequests to Jewish and non-Jewish institutions. The monies left were the largest ever given by anybody at that time.

He was born in 1775 in Newport, Rhode Island. He was the son of Isaac Touro, the hazzan of the Yeshuat Israel Synagogue, and his wife Reyna nee Hays. Judah had an unhappy and troubled childhood because the Revolutionary War had shattered the prosperity and security of the Jewish community of Newport.

His father, Isaac, was a Tory and he went with the British to New York where he lived on a military dole. In 1782, the family moved to Jamaica, British West Indies, where after a brief time, Isaac Touro died. Judah and his mother and the other four children moved to New York City where they lived with his uncle, Moses Michael Hays, a wealthy businessman.

After training and experience in his uncle's business, Judah went to New Orleans which was still ruled by Spain. He apparently made the right choice in moving there and going into business. The city was soon transferred to the French, who in turn sold it to the United States. Soon after, the population and industry grew rapidly and his fortunes rose.

Touro served as a civilian volunteer in the American Army during the War of 1812. The final action of the war was at the Battle of New Orleans on January 8, 1815, after the British had signed a peace treaty. General Jackson defeated the British forces in this battle.

Judah Touro was severely wounded and his life was saved by his good friend, Rezin Shepard, a Virginia merchant. His recovery was slow and Touro was left with a limp. He dropped out of the social life in New Orleans as he became more engrossed in developing his business. Touro invested in steamships and in real estate.

He once told Rabbi Isaac Leeser that he "made a fortune by strict economy while others had spent one by their liberal expenditures." Touro was not a speculator and he was able to weather the severe periods of panics and depressions.

Touro had no sense of Jewish responsibility until Gershom Kursheedt, a recent newcomer to New Orleans, instilled in him a feeling of Jewish loyalty. Rezin Shepard and Kursheedt had persuaded Touro to buy an Episcopalian church which was converted into a synagogue called Nefutzoth Yehuda. Gershom Kursheedt was a tremendous influence on Judah Touro. He was largely responsible for Touro's large bequests to institutions and organizations which were made when he died.

He left $108,000 to Jewish congregations and societies and to the Touro Hospital; $10,000 for the upkeep of the synagogue and the Jewish cemetery; $60,000 to be used for the poor in Eretz Israel; another total of $140,000 to Jewish institutions in seventeen cities.

He was also very generous to non-Jewish institutions. His gifts to them totaled $153,000. When he died in 1854, his bequests were made to all recipients. Judah Touro was the first American Jew to ever give so much to Jewish and Non-Jewish organizations and institutions. He will always be remembered as a philanthropist and soldier.

11

Rebecca Gratz

Dedicated Her Life to the Less Fortunate

Rebecca Gratz was a devout Jew who dedicated her life to the service of the less fortunate in America. She was born in Philadelphia in 1781 into a wealthy and highly esteemed family that supported the American Revolution. As a young lady, she was one of the most beautiful and gracious women of her time. The attributes didn't deter her from devoting her life to needy and charitable causes.

When she was 20, she organized the Female Association for the Relief of Women and Children of Reduced Circumstances in Philadelphia. She served as its first secretary and was a motivating force in its administration and in raising much needed funds. Gratz was also one of the founders of the nonsectarian Philadelphia Orphan Asylum, chartered in 1815 and served as its secretary for more than 40 years.

Sensing that there was a further need to service the needy and the unfortunate in the Jewish community, she organized and founded the Female Hebrew Benevolent Society in 1819. She created the Jewish Foster Home and Orphan Asylum in 1855 and led in the establishment of the Fuel Society and the Sewing Society.

While she was involved with these charitable organizations, she also managed to raise the nine children of her sister, Rachel, who died in 1823.

Rebecca Gratz was always concerned about the religious education of Jewish children. In 1818, she conducted a religious school for 11 Jewish children in her home with the help of an itinerant young rabbinical scholar from Richmond. Unfortunately, the school didn't last long.

Using the Christian Sunday school as a model, she tried again. In 1818, she organized a counterpart. Under the sponsorship of the Female Hebrew Benevolent Society, the Hebrew Sunday School Society of Philadelphia was created on March 4, her birthday, with about 60 students. She served as its president until 1864. The school was opened to children from all parts of the Philadelphia Jewish community without a fee.

Many Americans called Rebecca Gratz "the foremost American Jewess of her day." Her fame was widespread as many people believed that she was the prototype for Sir Walter Scotts's Rebecca, a Jew, in his novel, Ivanhoe.

Rebecca Gratz, in her time, was one of the most noble women in the world, who can be compared in modern times, for her work, devotion, and dedication to the needy, to a Mother Teresa of the Catholic faith. She died in 1869 at the age of 88 and was buried in the Mikveh Israel Cemetery in Philadelphia.

Mordecai Manuel Noah

An Ardent Patriot and Zionist

Mordecai Manuel Noah was the most influential Jew in the United States in the early 19th Century. He was an editor, journalist, playwright, politician, lawyer, court of appeals judge, New York Port surveyor, a major in the New York military and, foremost, an ardent utopian Zionist.

Noah was born July 19, 1785, in Philadelphia of Portuguese Jewish ancestry. His father, Manuel M. Noah, served with General Marion in the Revolutionary War and contributed a considerable sum of money to the cause.

When Noah was 10, his mother died and he went to live with his maternal grandfather. He stayed with that family until he became old enough to go to Charleston, South Carolina, where he studied law and he became involved in politics.

He was an ardent patriot and, at the age of 26, he wrote forceful editorials in a Charleston newspaper advocating war (of 1812) with England. As a result of his editorials, he was appointed the U.S. Consul to Tunis. In 1815, he returned and settled in New York to engage in journalism and politics. He published the National Advocate and edited several other newspapers.

Noah broke off his relationship with the powerful political machine of the Tammany Society and opposed them by publishing the New York Enquirer from 1826 to 1829. He was a prolific playwright, which reflected his patriotic fervor. He wrote Fortress of Sorrento (1808), She Would Be A Soldier (1819), and Siege of Tripoli (1820), which was produced many times under different titles.

Noah supported education and medical care. He was a founder of New York University and he projected the idea of a Jewish hospital—Mt. Sinai—which was to come into being after his death.

In 1825, Noah helped purchase a tract of land on Grand Island in the Niagara River near Buffalo, where he envisioned a Jewish colony to be called Ararat. This project elicited interest and discussion, but it turned into a failure. After this disappointment, he realized that Palestine was the only answer for a homeland for Jews. He lectured and wrote on the need for such a homeland, expressing ideas that preceded those of Leo Pensker and Theodor Herzl.

Noah was very active and supportive of the congregations of Mikveh Israel in Philadelphia and Shearith Israel in New York. He was the best-known Jew in America when he died of a stroke in 1851.

13

Penina Moise

Poetess of Judaism

P enina Moise was one of the most prolific and creative writers of poetry on Jewish themes in America. Her dedication and devotion to Judaism was the driving force in her life and writing.

Her father was a Sephardic Jew who immigrated to the West Indies from Alsace, France. He was a successful businessman who had to flee with wife to Charleston, South Carolina, when a slave insurrection began in 1791. Penina was born on April 23, 1791, in Charleston, and her siblings were also born in the United States.

Penina was twelve years old when her father died leaving her with the major responsibility of managing the household as her mother was very sick. Despite dropping out of school to take care of her mother and family, she managed to find time to study and write.

When she was 12 years old, Penina had many of her poems printed in Jewish and non-Jewish publications. She was the first Jew to publish a book of poetry in the United States. Her reputation as a writer became widely known. She was a favorite among the cultured Jews of Charleston.

Penina became the superintendent of the first Jewish religious school in Charleston. She wrote many poems for the children to recite and composed songs for them to sing. All of her creations were of the glories of Jewish history to help them be proud of their Jewish heritage. Though her love of Judaism was profound, Penina recognized the good in all religions. When a prominent Christian minister died, she was asked to write a poem in his honor which was read at the funeral service.

Penina's sister and her daughter returned to Charleston after a 30 year separation. Their joyous reunion was disrupted by the Civil War. Her loyalty was with the South and she wrote poems to encourage the soldiers as they went to battle.

It was at this time that she began to experience problems with her sight and recurrent headaches. It was during this period that she wrote some of her best hymns, rejoicing in God's mercy and thanking him for his goodness. Many of these hymns are still sung in many Jewish Sabbath Sunday Schools.

She was confined in her home for the last fifteen years of her life where she and her sister conducted a Sunday school to support themselves. When the children's classes were over, they would go to her room to read to her and she in turn would tell them stories. Her courage remained high after her sister died and she passed away when she was eighty-four.

Penina's later works were written in the form of hymns on Jewish themes. Many of them are included in the collection of the Union Hymnal used by many congregations including Temple Emanu-El in New York City.

Penina Moise was the first Jewish woman in America to share her love of God with others through her poetry and hymns. She has left a legacy to the people of America and she is a role model for our children to emulate.

14

Captain Mordecai Myers
A Military Hero and Politician

After not faring well as a storekeeper in Richmond, Virginia, Captain Mordecai Myers, who was self-educated, achieved success as a military hero and a politician. He was born in Newport, Rhode Island, in 1776, the same year that the American Revolution began. One of the great thrills of his life happened while watching General George Washington take the oath of office as the first President of the United States of America.

He joined the military company under the command of Colonel John Marshall, who was to become the Chief Justice of the U.S. Supreme Court. After his tour of duty in the army, he went to New York to try again operating a retail store, which also turned out to be a failure. He then turned to politics, where he achieved success.

He became a member of Tammany, which was a political group fighting the old conservative Federalist Party in New York. This political machine managed to break the strangle-hold of the Federalists and Myers started politically moving up the ladder.

While he was engaged with his newfound political life, Myers studied military tactics for two years. He joined an artillery company under the command of Captain John Swarthout and, later, he was commissioned as an officer in the infantry. When the War of 1812 started, Mordecai Myers was commissioned a captain in the 13th Pennsylvania Infantry. Captain Myers became a hero when he saved more than two hundred men and their military supplies.

General John Parker Boyd sent Captain Myers to Sacketts Harbor, where two boats loaded with more than 250 men and military supplies were wrecked. When he arrived to rescue them, he found the two boats were fast filling up with water, the sails were flapping aimlessly in the wind, many of them were drunk from partaking freely of the liquor from the hospital stores and there was complete chaos among the crew.

Exercising great energy and skill and risking his life, Myers and his men rescued more than 200 men and saved what was left of the military supplies. However, fifty men lost their lives by drowning.

Myers distinguished himself in a number of engagements during the Canadian campaign. During one of these engagements at Chrysler's Farm, he was seriously wounded. He recovered from his wounds and became involved in politics in New York City. He was elected to the New York State Assembly and then decided to move to Schenectady, where he became the city's first Jewish mayor.

Myers died at the age of 95 in 1871, remaining active to the end in politics and Jewish circles.

15

Captain Levy Myers Harby
Began HIs Naval Career at age 14

aptain Levi Myers Harby was born in 1793 in Charleston, South Carolina, which had the largest and most active community in American Jewry. He had his heart set on a naval career and, as a young man, he enlisted as a midshipman in 1807. He was 19 when the War of 1812 began.

His ship was involved in many battles and he was finally captured by the British. He was interned in the notorious prisoner of war stockade in Dartmoor, England.

An interesting story is told regarding his imprisonment. It seems that a Jewish baker sold his bread daily among the prisoners. One day Myers was offered a loaf of bread, which at first he refused to buy. The baker insisted on the sale and Harby reluctantly gave in. Breaking open the bread, he found a newspaper telling of the great American victory at the Battle of New Orleans.

Harby didn't wait to be formally released; he escaped to return to the United States. He then joined Commodore Decatur's fleet as a captain of a ship. The fleet was dispatched to the Mediterranean to crush the Barbary Pirates that were roaming the waters and pillaging commercial vessels.

After a number of naval and land engagements, the Barbary Pirates were defeated. Tunis, Algiers and Tripoli, who were abetting the pirates, were made to compensate the victims.

Captain Harby came back to the United States and left the Navy. He became militarily involved in the Seminole Indian War in Florida in 1828, after which he joined in the struggle for Bolivia's independence. In 1835, Texas sought help in its battles with Mexico to gain independence. Harby responded to the call for volunteers and once again was militarily involved.

Harby was 68 years old when the Civil War erupted. Despite his age, the Confederacy needed his half-century of naval experience and gave him command of the fighting ship **Neptune**. His naval skills proved a factor in the South's victory in the Battle of Galveston. The Union had blockaded the Gulf Coast and had captured Galveston Island in the bay. The Confederacy waited for the right time, then struck back with more than one thousand men and ships in a daring counterattack. After much land and sea fighting, in which Captain Harby played an important role, the Confederacy recaptured the island and the coast.

Captain Harby was decorated for his leadership and bravery.

16

Major Alfred Mordecai
A Man Torn Between Two Loyalties

Major Alfred Mordecai entered West Point at age 15 and he graduated first in his class in 1823. He was born in Warrentown, North Carolina, in 1804 and he died in 1887.

Upon graduation, Mordecai became an assistant professor at the United States Military Academy in New York. Later, he was commissioned in the engineers and was involved in the construction of two forts in Virginia. Eventually, he became commander of the Washington Arsenal.

Mordecai was recognized for his meritorious service in the line of duty during the Mexican War (1845-1847) with his promotion to major. When the war was over, he was sent to Mexico to adjust claims for losses suffered by Mexicans during the conflict.

The military sent him and Captain George B. McClellan, who became one of the top generals in the Civil War, to observe the Crimean War in 1854. They were granted a private conference with Czar Nicholas I and Mordecai's observations were published by Congress.

Mordecai made important contributions to the military technology with his introduction of scientific research and development to the military art. He wrote several notable books on the military, which included Second Report of Experiments in Gun Powder (1849) and Ordinance Manual for the Use of Officers of the United States Army (1841, revised in 1950).

When the Civil War between the states broke out in 1861, it created a dilemma for him. He was torn with his love for the South, his distaste for secession and his loyalty to the army and country. Mordecai made a decision to retire from the U.S. Army at age 57, so he wouldn't have to fight against either side.

His devotion to his conscience probably cost him a higher place in American history. When he resigned, he was one of the best military professionals in the country. He was on a par with all the well-known generals of the Civil War.

His son, Alfred Mordecai, Jr., whose feelings were less sensitive to his Southern heritage, joined the North in the Civil War in 1861. He died with the rank of General in 1920.

17

The Cardoza Family's Legacy
War Heroes and Jurists

The Cardozo family distinguished itself in American history with war heroes and jurists. David Nunez Cardozo was a patriot and a hero of the American Revolution. He was born in New York in 1752 and settled in Charleston, South Carolina, in 1775.

David enlisted in the South Carolina Grenadiers and fought many times against the British. He led an assault on British-held Savannah, Georgia, in which Count Pulaski was killed. Cardozo was taken prisoner by the British while defending Savannah, but was released at the end of the British stay in that area.

David had three brothers. Isaac Nunez Cardoza was one of the many Jews to help defend Charleston Harbor against the British during the American Revolution. His other two brothers, Moses and Abraham, were also involved in the American Revolution.

Jacob Newton Cardoza, the son of David Nunez, was born in 1786 in Savannah, Georgia. He was self-educated and was an outstanding economist. Jacob was one of the editors of the Southern Patriot in Charleston, and later became its publisher.

He published **Notes On Political Economy and The Economic Mind in American History**. Jacob was a strong advocate of free trade and wrote many papers on the subject.

Other famous Cardozos were Albert Jacob Cardozo (1828-1885), who was elected to the New York Supreme Court. His son, Benjamin Nathan (1870-1938), became a member of the United States Supreme Court. As soldiers, jurists and writers, the Cardozo family left its imprint on American history.

18

Dr. David Camden DeLeon
Hero of the War with Mexico

David Camden DeLeon acquired the nickname of the "Fighting Doctor" because of his exploits in the Mexican War in 1845. When the hostilities erupted between Mexico and the United States, DeLeon served as a doctor under General Zachary Taylor.

In a bitter and furious battle with Mexico's General Santa Anna's troops at Chapultepec, all of the American officers were either killed or wounded. He kept the American troops from panicking and fleeing by taking command.Dr. DeLeon, without any military training, turned defeat into victory by rallying his soldiers and leading them into a successful counter-attack. His actions in this battle earned him the nickname of the "Fighting Doctor."He was twice cited for his gallantry, including a Congressional Citation.

David Camden DeLeon was born in 1816 in Camden, South Carolina, into a prominent Sephardic Jewish family. He followed in his father's profession when he graduated from the University of Pennsylvania Medical School as a doctor in 1836.

Dr. DeLeon enlisted in the United States Army as a surgeon in 1838. He was involved in the Seminole War in Florida and was active in the frontier outposts from the West. When the Civil War broke out, Dr. DeLeon wrestled with his conscience. He finally decided to fight with the South and resigned from the United States Army.

Confederate President Jefferson Davis appointed Dr. DeLeon as the first Surgeon General of the Confederacy in 1861.He served in that position for a short time, preferring instead to be active on the battlefields.

When the Civil War ended, Dr. DeLeon was an unhappy and frustrated man, and went to Mexico. At the personal invitation of his former colleague in the Mexican War, General Ulysses S. Grant, Dr. DeLeon returned to the United States and settled in New Mexico, where he owned property.Dr. DeLeo practiced medicine and planted crops. Dr. DeLeon died in 1872. He will always be remembered as the "Fighting Doctor."

19

Hannah Solomon

Founder of The National Council
of Jewish Women

Hannah Greenebaum Solomon founded the National Council of Jewish Women in 1893, the oldest active Jewish women's volunteer organization in America. She was also active in philanthropy and the civic life of Chicago.

She was born on January 14, 1858, the fourth of ten children of Sarah and Michael Greenebaum. Her parents emigrated from Germany and her father soon became a very successful hardware merchant in Chicago. Hannah's parents were important figures in Chicago's growing Jewish community and belonged to the reformed temple. She went to their religious school where German and Hebrew were taught.

On May 14, 1879, she married Henry Solomon, a young merchant who shared her interest in classical music and the arts. They had three children Herbert, who died in 1899, Helen and Frank, who replaced his father as the head of the business when he died in 1913.

Hannah Solomon and her sister, Henriette Frank, were always active in many social clubs and organizations. They became the first Jewish members of the Chicago Women's Club. Henriette became its president in 1884 and the club became more involved in the problems of children and women.

In 1890, Hannah Solomon was asked to organize a national Jewish Women's Congress for the World Columbian Exposition Parliament of Religions to be held three years later. She managed to get together many

Jewish leaders and their organizations for the first such assembly in America. This Congress made this assembly a permanent organization called the National Council of Jewish Women. Their goals were to teach all Jewish women their obligations to their religion and community.

Hannah Solomon was elected as the Council's first president and served until 1905 when she was made honorary president for life. During her tenure, local chapters sprung up throughout the country and they became active with the social issues confronting women.

Solomon was active in many other organizations in the Chicago area. She and Susan B. Anthony represented the Council of Women of the United States at a convention of the International Council of Women in Berlin in 1904.

She was involved in helping the Russian-Jewish immigrants who were crowding into Chicago in the 1890s. With funds received from the Chicago section of the National Council of Jewish Women, she formed the Bureau of Personal Service, an organization designed to give guidance and legal advice to these new Jewish immigrants.

Her interests were wide when it came to working for the betterment of life for women. Solomon worked with the Illinois Industrial School for Girls in 1905 and had the school rehabilitated and moved to a more desirable area. In 1907, she became president of the school and instituted many positive changes. She was an active member of the Women's City Club and was responsible for many civic reforms.

Solomon was involved in the founding of the Chicago Juvenile Court and was on the board of the Chicago Civic Federation. She was instrumental in helping to improve the laws and city ordinances affecting juvenile delinquents and the underprivileged.

Hannah Greenebaum Solomon died on December 7, 1942. Her legacy to the United States and Judaism was the establishment and the development of the National Council of Jewish Women, an outstanding Jewish women's volunteer organization.

Colonel Leon Dyer

Served His Country in Three Wars

olonel Leon Dyer was an Orthodox Jew who fought in three wars for his country to secure freedom and justice. He was born in Baltimore, the son of Philip Maximillian Dyer. His father arrived in America from Germany in 1812, and changed his name to Dyer from Heim out of gratitude to a New Englander who had befriended him.

Dyer and his father were very active in the Jewish community. He was in the leadership of a group that started and built Baltimore's first synagogue. He later became president of the Baltimore Hebrew Congregation. Dyer always worked closely with his father in fulfilling their religious responsibilities and duties. The two helped organize and start the United Hebrew Society of Baltimore.

Dyer was also involved in the family meat-packing business and, in 1835, he went to New Orleans for the firm, a trip that altered the course of his life. While Dyer was there, the Governor of Louisiana talked him into taking the job of quartermaster general of the State

Militia. For Dyer to accept that offer seemed strange, as this trip was going to be a short one and he had recently been elected to serve as a trustee of the Baltimore Hebrew Congregation.

About this time, Stephen Austin, a leader of the American settlers living in Texas, announced that they had declared their independence from Mexico and that they were in need of volunteers to help repulse the attack of the Mexican Army. After Mexican General Santa Anna led his army into Texas and slaughtered the defenders of the Alamo, Dyer and several hundred from New Orleans joined volunteers from the rest of the country to help the Texans.

Arriving in San Jacinto as the battle was ending, Dyer and his men helped in the final defeat of the Mexican Army. Dyer was part of the honor guard to escort General Santa Anna to Washington, D.C., after he was captured. He later received a letter of appreciation from the Mexican general.

After the war, Dyer joined the American Army, serving as a major on the staff of General Winfield Scott. One of Dyer's junior officers was Lt. George B. McClellan, who became a famous Civil War general. Dyer was with General Scott in Florida when they engaged the Seminole Indians, who massacred 100 American soldiers.

Dyer returned to Baltimore and, from 1840 to 1845, he devoted himself to business and his religious duties. He was very active in the building of a double tower granite synagogue on the corner of Lloyd and Walter Streets.

Once again, Dyer responded to his country's call when he fought in the Mexican War (1845-47) as a colonel under the command of General Scott. In 1852 President Millard Fillmore enlisted Dyer to deliver confidential dispatches to the Prussian government in Berlin. Dyer was commended for this mission.

Dyer died in Louisville, Kentucky, at the age of 76.

21

Ernestine Rose

A Key Leader in the Women's Rights Struggle

E rnestine Rose was a leader in the struggle for full rights for women and, as a result of her activities, is considered one of America's great women of the 19th Century. She was born January 13, 1810, in Piotrkow, Poland, the daughter of an Orthodox rabbi.Ernestine, whose mother died when she was 16, rebelled against her strict environment by leaving home at the age 17, when her father remarried.

She traveled throughout Europe and England, where she met the social reformer, Robert Owen, and became one of his disciples. In 1832, she met William Rose, a jeweler and a silversmith, who was a non-Jewish Owenite. They married the same year and lived in England until 1836, when they moved to New York City.

Ernestine Rose became involved with the struggle for human rights, especially those of women. She traveled throughout the Eastern United States, pushing for reform in laws that discriminated against women.

For 30 years, she took an active role in the National Women's Suffrage Association. If Susan B. Anthony was the "soul," then Ernestine L. Rose was the "brain" of the suffrage movement. She petitioned the New York State Legislature to give married women equal rights with their husbands in property ownership and in the guardianship of children. Her initial effort failed, but she kept up the struggle until, in 1848, these reforms became law.

In 1850, Rose helped to organize the first National Woman's Rights Convention, which met in Massachusetts. As a result, she became acquainted with such feminists and abolitionists as Ralph Waldo Emerson, William Lloyd Garrison, Lucretia Mott, Susan B. Anthony and others. When the Territory of Wyoming's legislature became the first to grant women the right to vote, it was a great personal victory for her.

Rose, who was considered to be one of the more radical leaders of the feminist movement, attacked the 14th and 15th Amendments which emancipated blacks but did not include women's rights. However, she never seemed to attach any importance to her Jewish background until 1863, when she had a published debate with Horace Seaver, the abolitionist editor of the Boston Investigator, whom she accused of being anti-Semitic.

Eventually Ernestine Rose's health started to fail and she returned with her husband to England, where she died in Brighton in 1892.

22

Levi Strauss
The Originator of "Levi's"

hen the cry was heard, "There's gold in them thar hills," in 1849, thousands of people throughout the country left what they were doing to rush to California to dig for their fortune. Levi Strauss also went to California, but not with a shovel. Instead, he went there with bundles of cloth to sell to tailors.

He didn't arrive in California in 1850 because the ship from New York had to travel around Cape Horn to reach San Francisco. While traveling on the ship, he sold practically all of his bundles of cloth to his shipmates. When he landed, he had only a roll of canvas cloth left, which he hoped to sell to a tentmaker.

When Strauss landed, a miner approached him and asked if he had any pants to sell. Levi asked him, "Why pants?" It seems that the miners in digging for gold found that the rough terrain quickly wore out their pants, which created a shortage in stores. Being an experienced merchant and not a miner, a thought flashed in Levi's mind: He would take the tough canvas cloth and make this man a pair of pants. He went immediately to a tailor, who made the pants for the man to wear.

It didn't take long before Levi was overrun with orders for the new trousers. It seems that the miner had been bragging to his friends about the durability and virtues of Levi's canvas pants.

The above story is one of many versions as to why and how Levi's were first made. The true history was burned up when the 1906 San Francisco earthquake destroyed the records and history of the Levi Strauss Company.

Meanwhile, Levi wrote to his brothers in New York asking them to ship him more canvas cloth. The demand for canvas-cloth pants was growing daily. Everybody wanted Levi's. Strauss gradually started making pants from a durable material called "denim," which consisted of cotton threads woven in a twill pattern. Levi was the first to start coloring them dark blue, using an indigo dye.

One of the problems that many miners had was that their pocket seams burst because they would stuff ore in them. Jacob Davis, a tailor, was buying material from Levi and making pants for the miners. To try to solve the problems of the pockets, Davis riveted them to the denim material. Davis patented the copper riveting process in 1870.

Davis had turned out many pairs of pants with riveted pockets before Levi and he formed a partnership in 1873. Their business grew as word spread throughout the country about the durability of their pants. Cowboys used them because they endured the roughness of the saddle and long rides on horseback. Factory workers used them to protect themselves from the grit and grime. Soon the fashion world made them the "in" thing to wear.

Levi Strauss was born in Bavaria in 1829. His father, Hirsch Levi, was a drygoods salesman who had four children by his first wife and two, Fanny and Levi, by his second wife, Rebecca Haas. After his father died in 1845, they immigrated to the United States in 1847.

Strauss never married; he died on September 26, 1902, in San Francisco, leaving millions of dollars to Jewish and non-Jewish organizations. The University of California still has the trust fund that he donated, which awards 28 scholarships annually.

Levi Strauss was a philanthropist who will always be remembered for his charity, as well as for his fashion-world "jeans."

23

Adah Isaacs Menken
Noted Actress and Poet

Adah Isaacs Menken's extraordinary beauty, her flamboyant style of acting and her daring display of her shapely figure made her the sensation of the Victorian Age.

She was born on June 15, 1835, near New Orleans, Louisiana, to Adah Bertha Theodore and was raised in the Jewish faith. Her father died when she was two years old. Her mother married a man named Joseph and had two children by him before he died in 1853. That was the same year that Adah and her sister, Josephine, made their stage debut at the French Opera House in New Orleans.

After a successful tour with her sister, Adah decided to go to a private school to learn to speak, French, German, Spanish and Hebrew. She claimed that she published her first book of poems, "Memories," in 1856, under the *nom de plume* "Indigena."

She married Alexander Isaacs Menken, an orchestra leader and the son of a prominent Jewish family in Cincinnati. She loved the stage and returned to it, making her husband her manager. She went to New York in 1859 and starred in "The Soldier's Daughter." Her marriage to Menken fell apart and she divorced him. She married John Heenan, a famous boxer, in 1859, and they had an infant son that died. This marriage also fell apart and they were divorced.

Menken went back to the stage and appeared in the play "Mazeppa," based on a poem by Lord Byron. In this play, she wore flesh colored tights with a wispy loincloth that gave the impression that she was naked and in one scene, she was tied to a horse that ran wildly around the stage. The audiences responded with thunderous applause and the press called her the "naked lady" and the "most perfectly developed woman in the world." Her role as a sex symbol was with her the rest of her life.

She married Robert Henry Newell, a journalist, in 1862. Two years later, she went on a stage tour of England with him. He remained with her a short time and then returned to United States. Menken's nudity illusions in "Mazeppa" caused contradictory comments that brought her much publicity. This resulted in her receiving the record sum of $500 a performance.

She returned to the United States in 1865, after her divorce to Newell. She married James Barkley, a wealthy man, and after three days, she left him to return to Europe. In Paris, she gave birth to a son and named him Louis Dudevant Victor Emanuel Barley in honor of George Sands, his godmother.

All of her life, Menken was proud of her Jewish heritage. She never performed on Yom Kippur and she slept with a Hebrew Bible under pillow. She was sometimes militant against anti-Semitism and in 1857, she protested against the exclusion of Jews from the British House of Commons. She died on August 10, 1868 from tuberculosis and is buried in the Jewish part of the Montparnasse Cemetery in Paris.

Adah Isaacs Menken introduced a new form of acting style on the stage which pierced the Victorian Age armor of rigid propriety. Her poetry was an artistic expression that gave her another dimension as a person. Her contributions were invaluable to the arts.

24

Isaac Mayer Wise

A Leader in Reform Judaism

I saac Mayer Wise was America's outstanding Jew and leading rabbi during the 19th Century.mHis major achievements were the establishment of the Union of American Hebrew Congregations in 1873, the Hebrew Union College in 1875, and the Central Conference of American Rabbis in 1889.

Wise was the oldest son of Regina and Leo Weiss, and was born on March 29, 1819, in Steingrub, Bohemia (currently a part of Czechoslovakia). He was a brilliant student, and at the age of nine, his father, a teacher, had taught him all he knew about the Bible and the Talmud. He then went to study with his grandfather, a physician, who died three years later. Weiss continued his studies in the Talmud and the Bible at various schools. He completed his formal education by attending the University of Prague and the University of Vienna for three years.

At the age of 23, in 1842, he appeared before a Beth Din—or a rabbinical court—of three well-known rabbis: Solomon JudahRappaport, Samuel Freund, and Ephraim Loeb Teweles, who together conferred on him the title of rabbi. Two years later, he married Therese Bloch, who gave birth to ten children by him.

Wise found that being a rabbi in Bohemia brought him problems with the government, because of the restrictions still in force against the Jews. He decided to come to America because of its religious freedom, arriving in New York on July 23, 1846. At this time, he decided to change his name to Wise from its original German spelling, Weiss.

Wise became the rabbi of Congregation Beth El in Albany, N.Y. He was there four years, initiating new reforms in the religious services. He introduced choral singing, confirmation to replace Bar Mitzvah, and the seating of men and women together in pews for services.

His changes resulted in much disapproval. In 1850, on the morning of the beginning of Rosh Hashanah that evening, Wise was dismissed at a rump meeting of the board of directors. The next day havoc broke loose between his followers and those who opposed him. Soon after, a group broke away from Beth El and, with Rabbi Wise, established a new Reform synagogue called Anshe Emet —"men of truth."

In 1854, Wise went to Cincinnati, Ohio, to become rabbi of Beth Eichim, a Reform congregation. He stayed there the rest of his life. It was from there that he tried creating a national organization of congregations. He found this a difficult task, as the Orthodox rabbis were at odds with the Reform movement. Nevertheless, despite his setbacks, Wise continued to advocate a union of congregations, a common prayer book, and a college to educate and train American rabbis.

Parts of his dreams came true when, in 1873, delegates from 34 Reform congregations met in Cincinnati and organized the Union of American Hebrew Congregations. Two years later, in July 1875, the Union established the Hebrew Union College, the first Jewish seminary in the United States. Wise became its president and teacher.

Wise was also an organizer and mover in the establishment of the Central Conference of American Rabbis, in 1889. Elected its president, he served until he died. This conference adopted the Union Prayer Book that would be used by all Reform congregations.

Isaac Mayer Wise died on March 26, 1900. He was a pioneer Reform rabbi who tried to unite American Jewry, as well as a mover in establishing the Union of American Hebrew Congregations, Hebrew Union College, and the Central Conference of American Rabbis.

25

Maud Nathan

Social Worker and Suffragist

Maud Nathan was an outspoken advocate for better working conditions for women and for the right of women to vote. She is perhaps known best for her leadership and work as the president of the Consumers' League of New York.

She was born on October 20, 1862, in New York City, the first daughter of Annie Augusta and Robert Weeks Nathan. Her parents were descendants from one of the most distinguished Sephardic Jewish families in the United States. She was a first cousin of Emma Lazarus and Supreme Court Justice Benjamin Cardozo. Her sister, Annie Nathan Meyer, was an author and the founder of Barnard College.

When Maud was seventeen, she married her first cousin, Frederick Nathan, who was a successful broker in his mid-thirties. They had a daughter, who died when she was eight years old. She became involved in charitable activities. She joined the board of directors of the Hebrew Free School Association, where she taught English to the Jewish immigrants.

Her many activities brought her in contact with Josephine Shaw Lowell, who interested her in helping to improve the working conditions of the New York shop-girls. In 1890 with other women, they formed the

Consumers' League of New York. The league's goal was to better the working conditions of women retail clerks.

Nathan investigated the working conditions of women in retail stores and discovered that they worked sixty hours a week for two to three dollars. She was appalled by the filth in the stores, hidden from the customers, and found that there was sexual harassment on the job.

In 1897, she became the league's president, a position that she held for 21 years. Under her leadership, the league publicized the deplorable working conditions in the retail stores and factories. They created a "white list" which named the stores and factories that met the league standards for wages and conditions and urged the public to patronize them.

Nathan realized that lobbying in Albany was fruitless as women did not vote and they did not have any clout over the legislatures. She started to devote more time for the right for women to vote. She joined the Equal Suffrage League of New York. Her brothers and sister were against women's suffrage and even her cousin, Benjamin Nathan Cardozo, the supreme court justice had second thoughts about it. She was almost sixty when the Nineteenth Amendment was ratified giving women the right to vote.

She and her husband attended Shearith Israel Synagogue and she was active in the National Council of Jewish Women. She believed in liberal religion and loved Judaism for its universal truths.

In 1897, she was invited by Temple Beth-El to read a paper on "The Heart of Judaism" in place of the sermon. This was the first time that a woman had played such an active role in an American Jewish service of worship.

Maud Nathan 84 when she died on December 15, 1946. She dedicated her life to help women work under decent conditions for a fair wage and to help women obtain the right to vote. Her philanthropy in helping others was in keeping with her character. She has contributed to the legacy and contributions of her American Jewish ancestors.

26

Judah P. Benjamin

A Noted Lawyer and Politician

Judah Philip Benjamin is regarded by many as one of the most outstanding Jews of the 19th Century in America. He was born in St. Thomas, the West Indies, in 1811 and died in Paris in 1884 from injuries sustained in an accident. His father, Philip, was an English Jew, and his mother, Rebecca de Mendes, came from a Portuguese-Jewish family. They brought him to America when he was a young boy.

Benjamin attended Yale for two years without getting a degree. He prepared himself to become a lawyer by working as a clerk for a notary. In 1834, he attained wide recognition as a lawyer, which was enhanced by his legal writings.

Politically, Benjamin was a conservative who had joined the Whig Party. In 1842, he was elected to the Louisiana Legislature, the beginning of a long elected and appointed political career. Ten years later, he was the first Jew to be elected to the U.S. Senate.

Benjamin was a leading voice to advocate the Southern view while Lincoln was campaigning for the presidency of the United States. When Lincoln was elected President, Benjamin advocated that the South secede from the Union.

On February 4, 1861, after Louisiana had seceded, Benjamin made a brilliant last speech to the Senate and resigned his seat. Three weeks later, President Jefferson Davis appointed him to be the Attorney General of the Confederacy. Benjamin didn't last long in this position. President Davis changed his appointment to Secretary of War, where Benjamin was confronted with all kinds of problems. There were shortages of ammunition and weapons for the Confederate Army. Some people held Benjamin responsible for the Confederate losses at Roanoke Island and Forts Henry and Donelson because of the shortage of ammunition.

At this time, Secretary of State Hunter resigned and President Davis asked Benjamin to be his replacement. As Secretary of State, he knew that the South needed more soldiers. The only way to recruit was to enlist the slaves with a promise of freedom.

While a debate was being held by political leaders on the question of using slaves as soldiers, the Northern Armies picked up momentum and swept through the South. President Davis withdrew his cabinet into seclusion and sent out emissaries to negotiate a peace with the North. Benjamin went with his family down the coast and managed to escape to the West Indies, where he boarded a ship for England.

In London, he started his career again and became famous for his legal work and writings. He regained his wealth, becoming a famous personality at the same time.

Judah Philip Benjamin didn't practice his religion, nor did he get involved with Jewish organizations. However, he always acknowledged that he was a Jew and never backed away when confronted with it. As a politician and a lawyer, he was second to none in America.

27

The Civil War

Creates Jewish Soldiers and Heroes

When the Civil War erupted in 1861, it divided the nation and the Jewish population. Jews enlisted in the armies of the North and the South, giving them the opportunity to become good soldiers and heroes.

There were approximately 150,000 Jews in the country, with about 8,500 of them fighting for the North and South. In the North, the record shows that there were many Jewish officers: 8 were generals, 21 colonels, 9 lieutenant colonels, 40 majors, 205 captains, 325 lieutenants, 48 adjutants and 25 surgeons.

General Oliver O. Howard wrote "that there were no braver and patriotic men to be found then those of Hebrew descent..." General Stahel also acclaimed the bravery and heroism of the Jewish soldiers in the North.

It is reported that New York had 2,000 volunteers and Illinois had 1,000. Six Jews received the nation's highest award, the Congressional Medal of Honor, while many received other medals for heroism.

The Jewish casualties were high, for example Marcus M. Spiegel, who was killed in Louisiana when he was about to be promoted to brigadier general, or Leopold C. Newman, who was fatally wounded at Chancellorsville, where President Abraham Lincoln visited him on his deathbed.

In the South, Jewish volunteers flocked to the Confederate cause. Captain J. Roessler and Private Leon Blum were widely recognized for their role in the Southern resistance. In Charlotte, North Carolina, Jewish women raised $150 for the Confederate cause. The role of the Confederate Jewish soldiers in the Civil War can best be described by the words of T.N. Waul, who commanded a Southern Legion:

In the Civil War, Jews responded to the call of duty whether it be for the North or the South and they proved that they could be good soldiers as well as heroes in fighting for their country.

"Two of the infantry companies had a large number of Jews in their ranks and the largest company in command—120 men— were officered by Jews and three-fourths of the rank and file were of that faith. There were also a number of Jews scattered throughout the command in other companies. They were all volunteers; there was not a Jew conscript in the Legion. As soldiers they were brave, orderly, well-disciplined and in no respect inferior to the gallant body of which they formed a prominent part. Their behavior in camp, as in the field, was exemplary. No Jew in the command was arraigned before a court-martial and in proportion to their numbers, there were few applications for leaves of absence, and their regular habits caused very few of their names to appear on the hospital roles. In battle, without distinction of race or religion, all were apparently willing and eager for the contest. I will say, however, I never saw or heard of any Jew shrinking or failing to answer any call of duty or danger."

61

The First Jewish Chaplains
Are Approved During The Civil War

The right to have Jewish chaplains in the United States Army was finally achieved in the second year of the Civil War when Congress was prodded and persuaded to change the law to make this possible.

This action came about after Congressman Clement Vallandigham's bill to allow ordained rabbis to be commissioned as chaplains was defeated in July 1861. While this bill was being debated, the 5th Pennsylvania Cavalry, either in defiance or ignorance of the law, elected one of their men, Michael Allen, to be the regimental chaplain.

Allen was a Philadelphia Hebrew teacher who wanted to study to become a rabbi, but instead changed his mind and became a liquor dealer. He was well liked by the Christian and Jewish soldiers in his regiment and his services and sermons reflected his mixed congregation.

While the 5th Regiment was encamped outside of Washington, D.C., a YMCA worker visited them and discovered that the regimental chaplain wasn't an ordained minister or a Christian. The YMCA worker saw the appointment of Allen as a violation of the law and of the laxity that existed in the army. Allen resigned and the regiment, under the command of Colonel Max Friedman, decided to test this law with the nomination of Rabbi Arnold Fischel, an ordained rabbi and an experienced lobbyist.

The Secretary of War was compelled by law to deny the nomination and Rabbi Fischel began a year of lobbying until Congress passed another law allowing rabbis to be commissioned as army chaplains. On July 17, 1862, Congress changed the wording in the law to include the words "religious denomination" instead of "Christian denomination," and legal discrimination against Jews ended in the military. Rabbi Fischel was finally commissioned to replace Allen as the chaplain of the 5th Pennsylvania Cavalry.

Rabbi Jacob Frankel, a well known cantor of Congregation Shalom of Philadelphia, was commissioned on September 18, 1862, as the first official Jewish chaplain. He attended to the military hospitals in the Philadelphia area.

The first regimental chaplain was Ferdinand Leopold Sarner, a native of Germany, who was elected by the 54th New York Volunteer Regiment. Most of the soldiers in the regiment were German-speaking. Rabbi Sarner was commissioned on April 10, 1863. He was the first Jewish chaplain to be wounded and the first Jewish chaplain to go AWOL (absent without leave). He was severely wounded in Gettysburg and was hospitalized awaiting his formal discharge papers. Feeling better, however, he didn't wait for his discharge papers to arrive and left on his own to go home.

The Jewish military chaplain was created in the Civil War. It started a long tradition and legacy of brave and dedicated Jewish chaplains serving God and country.

29

Edward S. Salomon

A Hero of Gettysburg

Colonel Edward S. Salomon was the commander of the 82nd Illinois Volunteer Infantry which included more than 100 Jews, when the Confederate and Union armies collided and fiercely battled at Gettysburg, Pennsylvania, on July 13, 1863.

Salomon calmly commanded and led his men in this bloody and intense battle, disregarding the Confederate cannon balls fired at them. His experience in the Battle of Atlanta had taught him to keep his cool in battle and his constant cigar smoking seemed to help him stay calm.

Confederate General George E. Pickett decided to send 15,000 men charging across an open field in a suicidal attack. Colonel Salomon and his 82nd Regiment were in the middle of the heat of the battle to repulse them. He received a commendation for bravery and leadership and he was honorably promoted to brigadier general.

Salomon was born in Schleswig-Holstein and came to America when he was in his teens. He held down various jobs and then he decided to go to Chicago to study law. When the Civil War erupted, he helped form the 82nd Illinois Infantry Regiment. His ability to lead men was quickly recognized and he rapidly rose through the ranks.

After the Battle of Atlanta, Colonel John Cleveland Robinson recognized the feats of Colonel Salomon when he wrote: "I consider Colonel Salomon one of the most deserving officers. His regiment is deserving of high praise. In point of discipline it is second to none in the corps. Its record will bear safe comparison with any other of the same age in the army."

At the end of the Civil War, General Salomon led his men in a six-hour parade on Pennsylvania Avenue in Washington, D.C., where General Sherman bade them farewell.

Salomon returned to Chicago and he was chosen to be Clerk of Cook County. In 1869, he was given a "birthday present" by President Grant when he appointed him to be the Governor of the Territory of Washington.

After his tenure as Governor, Salomon moved to California and he was elected to the legislature. He was also elected the Department Commander for California of the Grand Army of the Republic. General Salomon demonstrated through his feats and leadership in battle that Jews in America can and do serve and fight for their country when the need occurs.

30

Edward Rosewater

Telegrapher for President Lincoln

E dward Rosewater will always be remembered as the young Jewish member of the Telegraphers Corps of the Union Army, who transmitted President Abraham Lincoln's Gettysburg Address. The son of Rosalia and Herman Rosenwasser, he was born in Bukoven, Bohemia. In 1854, the Rosenwassers and their eight children came to the United States and settled in Cleveland. They changed their name to Rosewater and were quickly integrated into the main currents of American life.

Edward Rosewater worked as a bookkeeper and was fascinated by the Morse telegraph, which was a new way of communication. In 1858, he became a telegrapher and was stationed in the South. When the Civil War broke out, he left there for the North. In 1862, he enlisted in the U.S. Military Telegraphers Corps and served with Femont in West Virginia and with Pope during his disastrous campaign in Virginia.

Rosewater was then transferred to the War Department in Washington. President Lincoln was a frequent visitor to his office and would read the field dispatches to keep abreast the latest movements of the army.

Rosewater, in his writings, tells of an embarrassing encounter with Lincoln. He and his friends were on duty refreshing themselves with a pail of beer, which was against army regulations, when Lincoln walked in on them.

The President didn't admonish them but instead gave one of them a quarter to get a fresh pail of beer. When the pail of beer was passed around, Lincoln drank from the bucket the same as the others.

When the war was over, Rosewater went to Omaha, Nebraska, to work as a telegrapher and as a newspaper correspondent. He founded the Omaha Daily Bee and was elected to the State Legislature in 1871. Rosewater became a member of the Republican National Committee and served as a member of many federal government committees. He died in 1906.

31

Sergeant Leopold Karpeles

Received The Congressional
Medal of Honor

Sergeant Leopold Karpeles was one of six Jewish soldiers who received the Congressional Medal of Honor for bravery and heroism in the Civil War.

He joined the 57th Massachusetts Infantry as a sergeant. On April 17, 1864, the regiment left New England to go south to meet the enemy. They went through Washington, where President Abraham Lincoln watched them pass in review. By the end of April they arrived at the Wilderness, Virginia, where General Grant hoped to take the first step in taking Richmond.

Sergeant Karpeles and his regiment were soon under fire as they fought a bloody three-day battle. It was in the early evening of the last day with the woods full of smoke and fire when the Confederate forces charged the regiment's lines. The colors entrusted to Karpeles were the only ones visible on the field.

He stood upright holding the colors for all to see and General Wadsworth, seeing them, rode up and down the lines calling on every man in Blue to rally around the flag to check the Confederate attack. The men responded and rallied around the flag lining up and firing back at the enemy. They stopped the charge and Sergeant Leopold Karpeles received the Congressional Medal of Honor for his bravery.

Karpeles was in many more battles after this engagement.He saw the action at White Hall, Kingston, Goldsborough, Gum Swamp, Gettysburg, etc. He was wounded several times and once so severely that he was permanently lamed. He was in Mount Pleasant General Hospital in Washington, D.C., with his badly wounded leg when his romance developed. Rabbi Simon Mundheim of the Washington Hebrew Congregation was a chaplain for the Union Army. His wife, Hannah, and his two daughters, Henrietta and Sarah, went with him on visitations to the hospitalized soldiers where they would read to them or write their letters.

It was on one of these visits that Sarah and Leopold met and fell in love. The doctors wanted to amputate his leg but they felt that if he received care at a home, the leg might be saved. The Mundheim family took Leopold home with them and he was able to save his leg.

Five years after he was married to Sarah, she and her third baby died in childbirth. His sister-in-law, Henrietta, came to take care of the remaining children. He married her and they were blessed with six children. The oldest boy was Herman Leopold Karpeles, who served as the first president of the Brotherhood of Congregation B'nai Jeshurun when it was in Newark, New Jersey.

Dr. Simon Karpeles, another son, and his wife, Dr. Kate Karpeles, served with honor in World War I and they are buried in Arlington Cemetery.

Little did Leopold Karpeles think that when he came here as a teenager from Austria, in 1849, that he would be a hero and leave a legacy and family to enrich our country.

32

Five Additional Jewish Civil War Medal of Honor Recipients

The Medal of Honor is the highest military award for bravery that can be given to any individual in the United States of America. This medal is presented to the recipients in the "name of the Congress of the United States." The first medal presented was during the Civil War in 1863.

Sergeant Leopold Karpeles was only one of the six Jews who received the Congressional Medal of Honor in the Civil War for bravery.

Benjamin B. Levy was a drummer boy and a private in Company B, 40th New York Infantry, stationed in Newport News, Virginia. He was aboard a steamboat carrying dispatches from General John Mansfield when it was attacked by a Confederate gunboat.

Levy's boat was being held up because it was towing a water schooner and the Confederate gunboat was gaining the advantage. He had the presence of mind to use his pocketknife to cut the tow to allow his steamboat to pick up speed and escape.

In the Battle of Charles City Crossroads, he rescued two standards (flags) dropped by their wounded color bearers. He unfurled them because his outfit was covered with dirt and the men couldn't be distinguished from the Confederates, and he wanted to stop the other Union regiment from firing at them.

Levy was severely wounded at the Battle of the Wilderness in January 1864. He recovered in time to be present at General Robert E. Lee's surrender at Appomattox. Before he returned to his regiment, he received the Congressional Medal of Honor.

Henry Heller was a sergeant in Company A, 66th Ohio Infantry, and he received his Congressional Medal of Honor for his daring in the battle of Chancellorsville. He was in a party of four and they were under heavy fire from the enemy. They came across a wounded Confederate officer and they volunteered to go through heavy gunfire to return him to their lines. The Union Army obtained much needed information from this officer which saved many lives.

Abraham Cohn was the sergeant major of Company K, 4th Vermont Infantry. He received his Congressional Medal of Honor for two different acts of bravery. At the Battle of the Wilderness, he rallied and reformed the disorganized fleeing troops from several regiments and established a new line of defense that held. At the battle of Petersburg, Virginia, on July 30, 1864, he bravely and coolly carried orders to the advanced Union line under severe fire from the Confederate troops.

David Orbansky was a private in Company B, 58th Ohio Infantry. He received the Congressional Medal of Honor for gallantry in many actions, which included the battle of Shiloh and Vicksburg.

Isaac Gause was a corporal in Company E, 2nd Ohio Cavalry. He received the Congressional Medal of Honor for capturing the colors of the 8th South Carolina Infantry in hand-to-hand combat while on a reconnaissance along the Berryville and Winchester Pike in 1864.

There were six Jewish recipients of the Congressional Medal of Honor in the Civil War. They were the forerunners of the many Jewish military heroes who were to receive this prestigious medal in the future wars of our country.

33

The Seligman Family

In The Civil War and After

Jewish financial contributions to the Civil War were overshadowed by the more dramatic and significant battles. Yet, the Seligman family's role in obtaining financial aid for the North is compared to the victories of the Union forces at Gettysburg and the contributions of Haym Salomon to the American Revolution by the Dictionary of National Biography.

When the Civil War began, the South had no problems in getting European credit while the North had trouble. Union bonds could not be sold abroad and the North was hurting financially.

The Seligman brothers, through their international banking firm, J.&W. Seligman and Company, were able to break this "no credit" wall when their Frankfurt, Germany, branch sold over $200 million worth of bonds. This was the opening that enabled the North to be financially sound in the continuation of the Civil War. As a result of being able to sell the United States bonds in Frankfurt, the government appointed all of their European branches as their fiscal agents in selling U.S. bonds.

At this time, the North owed the Seligman family over a million dollars for clothing purchased from them in their dry goods business. Fanny and David Seligman had eight sons and three daughters and their eldest son, Joseph, immigrated to the United States from Germany in 1837. Joseph worked hard and he sent for his seven brothers as he accumulated enough fare. Jesse and Henry opened up a dry goods store in Watertown, New York, in 1848.

It was here that Jesse became friendly with a young lieutenant named Ulysses S. Grant, who was stationed there, and who was to become a great general in the Civil War. Jesse Seligman recalls in his writings that he was learning the English language and smoking penny cigars when he and Grant were having long conversations.

In 1850, Jesse and Leopold Seligman went to San Francisco with merchandise and established a lucrative business taking care of the needs of those involved in the gold rush. They returned to New York, where they had a large import and clothing firm. It was this firm that sold merchandise to the North during the Civil War and gave them over a million dollars of credit.

Jesse Seligman was a vice-president of the Union League Club of New York, but he resigned in 1893 when his son was blackballed because of his religion. He was for over 20 years the president of the Hebrew Benevolent and Orphan Asylum of New York and he was selected by Baron de Hirsch in 1891 as an original member of the board of trustees of the Baron de Hirsch Fund.

Jesse Seligman enjoyed the confidence and esteem of President Grant and some of his successors. Joseph Seligman was active in finance and he submitted a plan to the government on how to fund their operations. His plan was selected and he joined with the House of Rothschild in this undertaking.

Joseph Seligman was offered the position of Secretary of the Treasury by President Grant, but he refused the prestigious offer. He was very active in charity and Jewish affairs. Prior to his death in 1880, he was considered to be one of the leading Jews in the country.

34

Three Unknown Jewish Military Heroes

For personal and other reasons, many Jews fought and died for the United States in combat using other than their birth names. Many of them received the nation's highest award, the Congressional Medal of Honor. At the present time, research has revealed that seventeen Jews have received this prestigious award and that there are others that could be uncovered.

Simon Suhler was one of those heroes who used other names in the Army. In fact, he enlisted in the Army many times, always using another name. He used his mother's maiden name, Newstattel, when he enlisted in the New York Heavy Artillery on June 9, 1863. When the Civil War ended, he was discharged on September 26, 1865.

He used the name Charles Gardner when he went to San Francisco, California, to enlist in the 8th Cavalry on October 15, 1866. He was sent to fight the Apaches with the 8th U.S. Calvary in Arizona where his bravery earned him the Congressional Medal of Honor. Suhler's citation commends him "...for his bravery in scouts and actions." He was recommended promotion to second lieutenant, but never joined the officer rank.

Simon Suhler was born in Bavaria in 1884. He emigrated to the United States around 1860. His military career ended on September 6, 1878. His brother, Aaron, was the first Reformed Rabbi of Dallas, Fort Worth and Waco, Texas.

Another veteran of the Indian Campaigns and a Congressional Medal of Honor recipient was George Geiger. He was a sergeant in Company H, 7th United States Cavalry. There is very little known of him except for his bravery as recorded in the records of the military and that he was Jewish.

It was on June 25, 1876, at the Little Big Horn River, Montana, that a very fierce battle took place between the Indians and his cavalry unit. His citation reads: "George Geiger with his three comrades during the entire engagement courageously held a position that secured the water for the command." The medal was issued on October 5, 1878.

Samuel Marguiles enlisted in the United States Marine Corps using the name of Samuel Gross. He was serving with a detachment of Marines aboard the U.S.S. CONNECTICUT. They were sent to Haiti because of the turmoil that was taking place there.

There had been a revolution in January 1915, in Haiti. General Vilbrun Guillaume Sam became the new leader. His regime was brutal. He executed 167 political prisoners in July 1915. The people rose in revolt and overthrew the government, executing General Sam, on July 28. On that same day, President Wilson ordered the Marines to land to restore order and to protect American lives and property.

The problem of the Caco Bandits still existed with the new government. It was on November 17, 1915, Gross and other Marines attacked Fort Riviere, an old French fort, to cut off the avenues of retreat for the Caco bandits. There was a breach in the wall, which was the only entrance into the fort. Gross was the second man to pass through the breach in face of constant fire from the bandits.

The casualties were high; the Marines engaged the enemy in hand-to-hand combat. After ten minutes of fierce fighting, the Caco bandits were defeated. Samuel Marguiles (Samuel Gross) was awarded the Congressional Medal of Honor for his bravery. Born on May 9, 1891, he died on September 13, 1934. He is buried in the Har Nebo Cemetery in Philadelphia.

These three Jewish heroes proved that even in small campaigns one can still be courageous and brave when fighting for our country.

75

35

Julia Richman

Educator

J ulia Richman was the first woman district superintendent of schools in the City of New York. Her innovations, leadership and curriculum brought an entire new dimension to public school education at the beginning of the twentieth century.

She was born on October 12, 1855, in New York City, the third of five children of Theresa and Moses Richman. Her father was a painter and glazier and they lived in Huntington, Long Island, New York, from 1861 to 1865. They then moved to New York City where Julia finished her education. The idea of her becoming a teacher caused heated discussions in the family. In those days, the idea of a Jewish girl going to work was unthinkable. Despite the objections, Julia stood firm and became a teacher in New York City.

At age 17, she began to teach in the Grammar Department of one of the largest schools in New York. Her father coaxed her into teaching part time at the temple sabbath school. Richman was very active in the Council of Jewish Women. She worked with them all her life to improve the sabbath school system. When she was 29, she became the principal of the Girls' Department of Public School 77 and held it for 19 years. She was the first Jewess and the first Normal College graduate to acquire such a position.

Julia Richman was deeply interested in Jewish religious affairs. She had come from a long line of rabbis in Prague, Czechoslovakia, that dated back to the fifteenth century. She was the director of the Hebrew Free School Association, first president of the Young Women's Hebrew Association (1896-98) and a member of the Jewish Chautauqua Society's education council.

She frequently traveled abroad. In 1903, while traveling in Europe, a vacancy occurred in the Board of Superintendents. She was unanimously selected to fill the vacancy. When she returned from Europe, Richman was given the choice of districts by the other four male superintendents. Much to their surprise, she chose the Lower East Side instead of an easy uptown district. She was now responsible for 23,000 students and 600 teachers.

She wrote books on curriculum and she started school optical programs, special schools for delinquents, chronic absentees and above average pupils. In 1906, she converted her house into a social center for the teachers of her district. Richman was actively involved in the community by fighting prostitution around 1910. She also was very active in aiding children and established many types of clubs for them to join.

In 1912, she resigned her position so as to give a younger woman an opportunity to take her place. She had plans for many projects and activities during her retirement. She sailed to Europe and the day before the steamer was to land in Cherbourg, France, she was taken ill. Four days later complications set in and she died on June 24, 1912.

She was 56 years old when she died and forty years of her life was dedicated to the education of children. In New York City, there stands "The Julia Richman High School" as a tribute to her dedication.

The Talmud says: "It is not our knowledge that God requires; it is our best that He requires." Julia Richman gave her best and she will long be remembered.

36

ℋannah Bachman Einstein
Leader in Social Welfare and
Jewish Philanthropy

H annah Bachman Einstein was a leader in helping widowed and deserted mothers and their children and Jewish philanthropies. Being a deeply religious individual, she dedicated her life to these noble causes.

She was born on January 28, 1862, in New York City, to Fanny and Herman S. Bachman, who had recently emigrated from Germany. She married William Einstein, a woolens manufacturer, on June 23, 1881. They had two children, William and Marian.

They lived in New York City where she became involved with the Temple Emanu-El Sisterhood, which was engaged in helping the sick, the needy and any other charity that was necessary.

In 1897, Hannah Bachman Einstein became the president of the Sisterhood and two years later, she became the president of the New York Federation of Sisterhoods. She managed to find time to be active in the United Hebrew Charities of New York. Her need for a better understanding of the social problems led her to take courses in sociology and criminology at various colleges.

Her dedication, energy and leadership resulted in her becoming the chairperson of the relief committee of the United Hebrew Charities. Her experience in working with dependent children and widowed and deserted mothers convinced her that institutions were not the answer for these children. Einstein felt very strongly that the problems of these dependent children were in the breakup of the family unit. The single mother was needed at home to raise the children and when that didn't happen, the children would soon be a problem for society.

After a few attempts at having private philanthropy keep the family as a unit, she realized that public funding was needed. She and Sophie Irene Loeb were major players in fighting for the passage of "mothers' pension" legislation. This was opposed by the orphanages and children's institutions. Finally, it was approved by the state legislature and in 1915, she helped pave the way for the Child Welfare Law. Einstein became chairperson of the "strategic families' committee of New York City's child welfare board and served from 1915 until her death.

She became president of the New York State Child Welfare Boards and was a founder of the National Union of Public Child Welfare Officers. Her influence and drive for aid to widowed and deserted mothers was felt throughout the nation and by 1920, most of the states had passed "mothers' pension" legislation.

Her career was not confined to widowed and deserted mothers and their children. She was very active in Jewish charitable organizations. She was the secretary of the Mount Sinai Hospital Training School for Nurses, a director of the National Jewish Hospital for Consumptives in Denver, a vice president of the New York Conference of Charities and Correction and she was a founder of the Federation of Jewish Women's Organizations.

Hannah Einstein was not a professional in Jewish philanthropies or child welfare. She became proficient in her work through experience, volunteering and her concern with those needing help. She freely gave her services because of her dedication and love of God and humanity.

She died on November 28, 1929. She left behind a legacy that made it possible for single women to be with their children to raise them to become better citizens and leaders in America.

37

"Lip" Pike
Baseball's First Pro

Lipman E. "Lip" Pike became baseball's first professional player when the Philadelphia Athletics recognized his talent in 1866. The team gave him $20 a week to play third base. Pike was soon followed by others. The baseball players of the time were professional and amateurs.

Pike was born in New York City on May 26, 1845. He was one of five children of Jane and Emanuel Pike, emigres from Holland. His older brother, Boaz, was the first in the family to play baseball on an organized team. The first time that Pike's name appeared in a box score was a week after his bar mitzvah. He had played for the Nationals at first base and his brother had played shortstop. The two brothers played for many teams from 1864 through 1865.

Pike established himself as a home run hitter for the year that he was with Philadelphia Athletics as a professional. Hitting home runs was a rarity in those days. Pike hit them in clusters. He hit six home runs in a game against the Alerts in 1886. Five were hit in a row.

Pike left the Athletics and became the playing manager of the Irvington team in 1867. However, he didn't finish the season with the team. Boss Tweed of New York City made him an offer to play for the Mutuals and he accepted it.

He stayed with the Mutes for one year and left the team to join the Brooklyn Atlantics.The Cincinnati Red Stockings came East and beat every team they played, including the Atlantics, in 1869. The following year, the team returned to Brooklyn and was undefeated in 130 games. They played the Atlantics in a game that went into extra innings. The Atlantics took the lead 8 to 7. Pike played second base and was the key figure in retiring the Reds for Atlantics victory.

The first baseball league composed of only professional players began in 1871. Pike went to Troy, New York, to become the manager of the team there. During this period, teams quickly came into being and then quickly disappeared. There wasn't a reserve clause. Many players were drifters, drunkards, and gamblers. Pike was an exception.

Pike moved to Baltimore for the 1872-73 season and played in the outfield. He was a very fast runner. It is told that Pike won $200 when he defeated a horse in a race.

Pike played and managed many teams after his stay in Baltimore. He moved around the East Coast, going from one team to another. He finished the year with the Worcester, Massachusetts, team in 1881. The team had a bad season and Pike was made the scapegoat. Pike was the first to be put on baseball's blacklist.

He opened up a haberdashery store and announced his retirement from baseball. The store was a gathering place for baseball enthusiasts. Pike made an attempt to play again when he was 42 years old. He joined the original New York Mets, later announcing his retirement.

Pike became an umpire in the National League and the American Association while still operating his haberdashery. He died of a heart attack at the age of 48.

"He was eulogized in many newspapers," the Sporting News said. "He was one of the baseball players in those days, who was always gentlemanly on and off the field-a species which is becoming rarer as the game grows older..." Pike will always be remembered as the first professional player in baseball.

38

Florence Prag Kahn

Congresswoman

F lorence Prag Kahn was the first Jewish woman to sit in the United States Congress as a representative. She served from 1925 to 1937.

She was born on November 9, 1866 in Salt Lake City, Utah, to Mary and Conrad Prag. Her parents were Polish Jews, who were early settlers of California. Her father was a merchant who sold supplies to the miners during the Gold Rush.

In the mid-sixties, her parents moved to Salt Lake City. He became a friend of Brigham Young, the Mormon leader. Her mother wrote a book entitled *My Life Among the Mormons*. The family returned to San Francisco when their business failed. Her mother taught history at the San Francisco Girls' High School for over fifty years. She was also an advocate of state pensions and was later elected to the San Francisco Board of Education.

Florence Prag graduated from her mother's school in 1883 and went on to receive a degree from the University of California. She married Julius Kahn on March 19, 1899. He was the newly elected congressman from California. He served for twenty-six years until he died on December 18, 1924.

When she and Julius Kahn were invited to the Executive Mansion to have dinner with President McKinley, they walked there as a carriage cost one dollar to hire. "In what country," asked Julius Kahn, "could two poor Jews be on their way to dine with the head of state?" He was not a wealthy man and when he died he left $4,430. Florence Prag Kahn was elected to Congress to replace her husband in a special election.

The Kahns were Republicans who were dedicated to Judaism.Their sons were bar mitzvahed at Temple Emanuel. Most of the influential San Francisco Jews were among her friends and fans.

She was a brilliant woman and the San Francisco Chronicle in August, 1926, described her as "a Republican who knows how to get things done." She had a keen sense of humor. Once when asked "Would you favor a birth control law?" "I will if you make it retroactive," she replied. On another occasion, she heard that the Democratic Party leaders planned to buy an island in the San Francisco bay for a weekend retreat. She quickly sent a note to the Attorney General suggesting Alcatraz for the place.

She worked hard for the re-election of Herbert Hoover as president, but he lost to Franklin Delano Roosevelt. Mrs. Roosevelt praised Mrs. Kahn and sent her an open invitation to the White House.

When she lost her bid for re-election in the Roosevelt landslide, in 1936, she returned to private life. She participated in the American Association of University Women, Hadassah and the Council of Jewish Women.She traveled throughout California trying to get women interested in national politics. She died on November 16, 1948, of a heart disease.

When Florence Prag Kahn became the first Jewess elected to Congress, she started a long chain of other Jewish women following in her foot steps. Recently there were two Jewish women elected to the United States Senate from Mrs. Kahn's home state of California, which was a tribute to her efforts in having women in national politics and the legacy that she left for all women.

39

Zigmund Schlesinger

A Defender of the West

After the Civil War, many former soldiers and others went out West to start a new life. They found that there was plenty of land available and that the buffalo, bison and other wildlife could sustain them while they farmed and built settlements. However, there was one problem that confronted them—the Indians.

The Indians had been living off the land for countless years. They saw the white men come and destroy the forests. Herds of buffalo and bison were being slaughtered and the newly built railroads were cutting up their territories. The Indians soon realized that in order to save their lives and their livelihood, they had to fight back. They burned houses and stockades of white settlers and murdered any travelers.

The situation became very serious for the white settlers. Action had to be taken. General George Forsyth was delegated by General Philip Sheridan to hire 50 first class frontiersmen to fight the attacking Indians. One of the first to apply was a young Hungarian-Jew, Zigmund Schlesinger, who had immigrated to America in 1864.

Schlesinger came to New York City and worked at many jobs. He heard about the opportunities that existed in the West and left New York to go to Kansas. In Kansas, he tried his hand at business by baking bread and cake and selling the foods under a canvas tent. The bakery failed as did some other business ventures.

When Schlesinger applied for the frontiersman with Forsyth, they were not anxious to have him. He was small with a high-pitched voice and had very little experience or knowledge of firearms and horsemanship. He was told if they couldn't get 50 men, he would be hired. Schlesinger was lucky. He was hired since a 50th man was not found.

In his diary, Schlesinger wrote of his first day as a member of the scouts in August 1868. After riding all day, Schlesinger recalled how stiff and tired he was when it was over. His riding abilities bore the brunt of ridicule from others. He was also reminded that he was a Jew.

Schlesinger had been involved in many minor encounters with the Indians. The encounter that earned him the respect of the others took place at the Arikaree Fork of the Republican River in 1868. His scouting expedition was set upon by Chief Roman Nose with his band of Cheyenne and Sioux Indians. The scouts were pinned down for 9 days.

Their horses had been killed and they suffered 19 casualties. Schlesinger had been wounded in both legs and the head. Yet, he managed to shoot down any Indian who exposed himself. They held off the Indians until a U.S. Army relief column came to their rescue.

Forsyth wrote a letter to Rabbi Henry Cohen of Texas, lauding the heroism of Schlesinger: "...He was the equal in manly courage, steady and persistent devotion to duty, and unswerving and tenacious pluck of any man in my command."

Schlesinger took leave of his frontier life on October 21, 1868. He left the company and returned to New York. Eventually, he settled in Cleveland, where he established a successful cigar store business. Active in Jewish organizations, Schlesinger was one of the organizers of the Hebrew Free Loan Association, vice-president of his temple, and president of the Hebrew Relief Association.

He died in 1928, leaving behind a legacy as a Jewish Indian fighter and as a philanthropist.

40

Annie Nathan Meyer

Writer & Founder of Barnard College

Annie Nathan Meyer was one of the founders of Barnard College despite the opposition of the establishment. Her personal experiences at Columbia College gave her the reasons why there should be a college for women.

She was born on February 19, 1867, in New York City, to Annie August and Robert Weeks Nathan. Her descendants were one of America's oldest and distinguished families of Sephardic Jews, who were prominently involved in the commercial and cultural life in New York since the Revolutionary War.

Her father's speculation on Wall Street brought him to the brink of bankruptcy. He took a job on a small railroad in the Middle West. The five children saw their parents fall apart as her their mother turned to drugs and died in Chicago in 1878 and the children went to live with their grandmother in New York.

Annie prepared herself for college with special tutoring and she was finally enrolled in Columbia College. After a year, she dropped out of college to marry Alfred Meyer, a prominent physician, who was her cousin and thirteen years older.

A few weeks after their wedding, she began organizing a committee to work for the development of a women's college at Columbia. She reasoned that if Columbia didn't have to pay for it, they might be receptive to the idea. She persuaded fifty well know New Yorkers to support the concept of a college for women.

Meyer was an astute politician when she named the college after F.A.P. Barnard, Columbia's recently deceased president. While his widow and many members of Columbia's board of trustees were against erecting another add-on college, this move defused them. They could not oppose naming the college after one of their presidents.

Large donations started coming in with her husband being the first to contribute. In September, 1889, the college became a reality when it opened its doors for women to start the first semester. Annie Meyer became a trustee and was active until 1942.

Meyer was a prolific writer. She had written a play, *"Black Souls"*, in 1935, which was one of 26 plays that she had written. She also wrote articles against women suffrage, not because she didn't want them to have the vote, but she was against the notion that women would purify politics. She wrote three novels, an autobiography and two books of non-fiction. Most of her themes were on the conflicts that women experienced in having a career and marriage.

Meyer was very proud of her Jewish-American ancestry. She was active in the Daughters of the American Revolution. She raised money to purchase a portrait of Issac Moses for the Museum of the City of New York, in 1933, and she also raised enough money for a performance of Ernest Bloch's "Sacred Music', in 1944. She was an early critic of Nazi Germany and she was an ardent Zionist.

Meyer died of a heart attack on September 23, 1951, in New York City. Her major contributions were in her role as a founder of Barnard College for women and for her advocacy for the full developments of women's talents.

41

ℋelena Rubinstein

Businesswoman & Philanthropist

Aladdin had his lamp, and Helena Rubinstein had her 12 pots of face cream to help her become a multimillionaire and a moving force in the cosmetic industry.

She was born in Cracow, Poland, on December 25, 1870, the oldest of eight children of Augusta and Horace Rubinstein. She briefly studied medicine in Switzerland and immigrated to Australia in 1902. She noticed that the Australian women had rough reddish faces that required cosmetic attention. Rubinstein opened a modest shop in Melbourne where she dispensed her "Creme Valaze" and instructed women individually on how to care for their skin.

She worked long hours and her shop prospered. In 1908, her sister Ceska joined her and took over the management of the shop as she went to London with a $100,000 to start what would become an international organization.

She met Edward Titus, an American journalist in London, and they were married in 1908. They had two sons, Roy, in 1908, and Horace in 1912. They lived in Paris and when World War I started, they moved back to the United States. She opened beauty salons throughout the country where her skin care and her creams were in demand. The department stores were clamoring to sell her products.

Rubinstein was a brilliant innovator in developing her business so that it required routines and women. She trained sales people to teach women skin care and devised a diet plan for beauty. She inaugurated a "Day of Beauty" in her salons which became an instant success. She understood and appreciated the value of advertising and she made full use of it in developing her business.

She divorced her husband in 1937 after a shaky marriage for the past ten years. She married Prince Artchil Gourielli-Tchkonia, a Russian prince twenty years her junior, in 1938. She developed a line of male cosmetics which bore his name. He died in 1956 and her son, Horace, died two years later.

Rubinstein was very much concerned and interested in the welfare of Israel. She was very generous with monetary contributions. She founded the Helena Rubinstein Pavilion of Contemporary Art in Tel Aviv where her collection of miniature rooms is housed.The Helena Rubinstein Foundation, created in 1953, provided the necessary funds to organizations concerned with health, medical research and rehabilitation.The Foundation also supported the American Israel Cultural Foundation and awarded scholarships to Israelis.

Rubinstein hated small talk and was very frugal. She carried a bag lunch to work with her although she was a very wealthy woman with over millions of dollars worth of the masters in art and sculpture. Despite her frugality, she bought her clothes from the top fashion designers in the industry. Her top executives in the business were relatives as she was very family oriented.

In 1959, she went to Moscow where she officially represented the cosmetic industry in the United States at the American National Exhibition. Helena Rubinstein was always involved with her organization and even when her health was failing, she carried on from her sick bed. She died in New York City on April 1, 1965. Her philanthropy, material support for Israel and her enhancement of women looking and feeling more beautiful will long be remembered.

$\mathcal{A}dolphus$ $\mathcal{S}imeon$ $\mathcal{S}olomons$

Helped Organize The Red Cross

Adolphus Simeon Solomons was a moving force in helping to establish the American Red Cross. He held many meetings in his District of Columbia home to plan and prepare for the day when the United States would join the International Red Cross. It was at his home that a proposal was approved to form the Association of the American Red Cross and incorporate it in Washington, D.C.

In 1882, the United States finally ratified the Red Cross treaty. President Chester A. Arthur appointed Solomons as one of three delegates to represent the country at the Geneva Congress, where he was elected vice-president. During the Spanish-American War, he was still a member of the executive board of the American Red Cross, which rendered important service to our troops in combat.

Solomons, a publisher, was held in such high esteem in Washington, D.C., that when Vice President Schuyler Colfax couldn't appear at the dedication of the Young Men's Christian Association building in the capital, he was asked to substitute for him.

Solomons was active in Jewish life and was very outspoken. In 1862, General Grant issued an order expelling "Jews as a class" from his lines on the grounds that their mercantile activity interrupted the movement of his troops, but Solomons got General Henry W. Halleck to rescind it. In 1873, President Grant offered Solomons the governorship of Washington D.C. While feeling honored, Solomons had to decline because he was a Sabbath observer and it would interfere with his duties of the office.

Solomons was born in New York City in 1826. At the age of 14 he enlisted in the New York State Militia and served for seven years. On June 25, 1851, he married Raachel Seixas Phillips, a descendant of colonial patriot families. They had eight daughters and a son.

Solomons moved his printing business to Washington, where he did government printing. He added to his plant a book department, which became the literary headquarters of General Grant, Supreme Court Justice Salmon Portland Chase and other dignitaries. He then added a photographic gallery in which many prominent people of the day were featured, including the last photograph of Abraham Lincoln.

Solomons was very active in helping people. He organized the first training school for nurses in Washington and the Washington Night Lodging-House Association, which supplied homeless men with lodging. He was an officer of the Provident Aid Society, the Emergency Hospital of the Society for the Prevention of Cruelty to Animals and many other worthwhile causes.

In New York, he helped to organize Mount Sinai Hospital and the Montefiore Home for Chronic Invalids. He was a founder of the Jewish Protectory and Aid Society, and of the Russian Jews Immigration Aid Society.

Adolphus Simeon Solomons died in 1910, leaving behind a legacy of charity, helping the sick and needy, and working and organizing Jewish organizations that helped people. His greatest feat was his contribution in helping to create the American Red Cross.

43

Hetty Goldman

Archaeologist

Hetty Goldman was a well know archaeologist who unearthed many new excavations that gave historians a better insight of the past in Greece. She was very active in sponsoring Jewish refugees fleeing Nazi Germany.

She was born on December 19, 1881, in New York City, to Sarah and Julius Goldman. Her parents were of German-Jewish descent and her father was an established lawyer.Her grandfather, Marcus Goldman, was a co-founder of the Goldman, Sachs and Co., a well know banking and investment firm.

When attending her Uncle Julius Sachs' School for Girls, she became interested in archaeology. Hetty graduated Bryn Mawr College with a B.A. degree in 1903. Her interest in archaeology became her major. She enrolled in Radcliffe College, in 1909, where she took courses in archaeology and classical language. She earned an A.M. in 1910 which was the same year that she had her first article published, The Orestia of Aeschylus as Illustrated by Greek Vase-Painting. This article was the major reason for her being the first woman to be awarded the Charles Eliot Norton Fellowship to attend the American School of Classical Studies at Athens, Greece. She worked and studied here from 1910 to 1912.

Goldman received her Ph.D. from Radcliffe in 1916. She pursued her interest in archaeological field work and she was interrupted twice. The first was the Balkan Wars, 1912-13, and World War I. She returned to New York City to work for the American Red Cross. She was asked by the American Joint Jewish Joint Distribution Committee to return to Greece for a report on the Jewish communities.

In 1922, she directed a project for the Fogg Museum of Harvard University in excavating at the site of Colophon in ancient Ionia. She became one of the early pioneers in the investigations of the pre-Greek and earliest Greek people. In 1924, Goldman went to central Greece as director of excavations for the Fogg Museum. She spent three years on this project and documented her findings in "Eutresis in Boetia," 1931.

Goldman was sponsored jointly by Bryn Mawr College, Harvard and the Archaeological Institute of America (AIA) for her 4th major excavation at Tarsus near the southeast coast of Turkey. The excavation was to search for possible links between Greece and Anatolia.

She carefully studied her historical facts and the Trojan War. She led a young team of apprentices who unearthed seals, inscribed tablets, seal impressions and other important artifacts. Her evidence indicated that there was a relationship between Tarsus and the Hittite kings.

Goldman became the first woman to be appointed professor at the Institute of Advanced Study in 1936, in Princeton, New Jersey. She spent most of her time in research and writing. Goldman was very active in sponsoring German-Jewish refugees, who had fled the Nazis. She saved many lives in her sponsoring project.

She retired in 1938 and spent the next fifteen years publishing the results of the Tarsus excavations. In conjunction with her associates, they wrote three volumes of "Excavations at Gozlu, Tarsus," 1950, 1956 and 1963.

Hetty Goldman was recognized for her outstanding contributions to archaeology when she was awarded a gold medal by the AIA in 1966. She died on May 4, 1972, in Princeton, leaving behind a legacy of information for historians and scholars.

44

Minnie Guggenheimer
Fund Raiser of Lewisohn Stadium

Minnie Guggenheimer was a director of New York City's Lewisohn Stadium, where she organized summer concerts for over forty years. Her flair for showmanship made her the joy of the stadium-goers, the idol of the newspapermen and a scandal of the grammarians.

Minnie Guggenheimer was born on October 22, 1882, in New York City. Her father, Samuel Shafer, was a member of Shafer Brothers, a banking firm that was founded in 1860. Her grandfather made a fortune in the California gold rush which made it possible to set up his sons in business.

Her parents sent her to most fashionable private schools and she was taught to play the piano. In 1903, she was married to Charles S. Guggenheimer, an attorney, whose father was at one time the president of the N.Y.C. Board of Alderman and acting mayor.

It was during World War I that Minnie Guggenheimer was approached to join a committee to support good music at Lewisohn Stadium. Her participation grew until she was ruling the concerts singlehandedly. Every year she raised money for the concert season because the tickets were moderately priced so that working people could afford to attend.

She hired the artists, handled negotiations with the various unions and worried about all operations, including the weather. Lewisohn Stadium was an open arena and exposed to the elements. She once called the weather bureau about the prediction for the night of a concert about two months later. The forecaster said to her, "Lady, you want to talk to God."

Minnie Guggenheimer always made intermission speeches about the current and coming events. She prefaced her remarks with "Hello everybody!" and the audience of 3,000 to 15,000 people would answer back, "Hello, Minnie!" If for some reason she was absent or late for the intermission speech, the audience would set up a rhythmic chant of "We want Minnie!"

Despite her mannerisms and speeches, she made it possible for many people to hear good music at very low prices. She also made it possible for young performers to be introduced to the public. Marian Anderson, winner of a city-wide talent search, was one of these young artists who was given an opportunity to perform. George Gershwin played his "Rhapsody in Blue" for the first time at the stadium in 1925. Van Cliburn repeated two concerti that he played to win the first prize in Moscow's International Tchaikovsky Competition in 1958.

Minnie Guggenheimer was always having trouble with the reading and pronunciation of words and names. This delighted the audiences. At one time she confessed, "I have a beau in the wings. He is from Junkoslavia." She then proceeded to call upon Lawrence Steinhardt, the U. S. Ambassador to Czechoslovakia, to take a bow.

Guggenheimer died on May 23, 1966. Her life was dedicated to making it possible for people to hear good music and for young artist to have the opportunity to perform. She unselfishly gave of herself to make these goals a reality.

95

Aline Bernstein

Noted Costume Designer for the Stage

Aline Bernstein was the first woman designer to achieve professional recognition in the American theater. She was an artist of many talents, who didn't start her stage and costume designing career until she was in her early forties.

She was born on December 22, 1880, in New York City, the oldest of two daughters of Rebecca and Joseph Frankau. Her father was an actor of German-Jewish ancestry and she travelled the acting circuit with her parents. By the time she 17, both of her parents had died and her aunt, Rachel Goldsmith, became her guardian. She lived with her aunt, who had a theatrical boarding house on West 44th Street in New York City.

She was a talented artist and Tom Watson, a close friend of the family, arranged for her to receive a scholarship at the New York School of Applied Design. Here she met and studied with Robert Henri, one of the most important painters at the time.

She met and married Theodore Bernstein, a Wall Street broker, on November 19, 1902. They had two children: Theodore, in 1904, and Edna, in 1906.

Aline Bernstein found time to volunteer as a backstage worker at the Henry Street Settlement. It was here that she met the Lewisohn sisters, Alice and Irene, who were producing plays and pageants. She designed and created costumes for fifteen plays from 1915 to 1924. She emerged as a major developer of sets and costumes when in 1924, she designed The Little Clay Cart. She received national acclaim for her design concepts which were based on Rajput style of miniature painting.

She created expressionistic settings for the Jewish classic, The Dybbuk, for the Neighborhood Theater in 1925. Her grotesque settings matched the mysticism of the play. She also made the settings for the annual Grand Street Follies through 1925.

In 1934, she designed Herman Schulmin's production of Lillian Hellman's first play, The Children's Hour. This combination of Schulmin, Hellman and Bernstein stayed together for four more Hellman plays, from 1934 to 1949.

Bernstein went to Hollywood in 1935 to do two RKO spectaculars, She and The Last Days of Pompeii. She returned to New York and became active in creating sets and costumes. At age 70, Bernstein was the recipient of the Antoinette Perry (Tony) Award for her costume creations for the opera, Regina. Her last show that she designed costumes for was for the Off-Broadway production of The World of Sholom Aleichem, in 1953.

She was the first woman admitted into membership of the Brotherhood of Painters, Decorators and Paperhangers of the American Federation of Labor in 1926. She was also involved in establishing the famous Costume Institute at the Metropolitan Museum of Art and she was the president for the last nine years of her life.

Aline Bernstein died in New York City on September 7, 1955. She left the theater many new ideas and creations that would help the new costume and scenic designers with their work. Aline Bernstein didn't just leave a spiritual legacy but also a materialistic legacy which can be seen at the Metropolitan Museum of Art.

46

Jennie Maas Flexner

Reader's Adviser, Librarian & Author

For the last 20 years of her life, Jennie Maas Flexner was the readers' adviser at the New York City Public Library and author of many books on the library and librarians.

She was born on November 6, 1882, in Louisville, Kentucky, to Rosa and Jacob Aaron Flexner. The Flexners were a distinguished family in many areas of life in America. Her uncles were Simon Flexner, the eminent bacteriologist, Abraham Flexner, known for his studies and surveys of medical colleges and higher education in the United States, and Bernard Flexner, a noted attorney.

Her sisters were Hortense Flexner King, a poet and a teacher at Bryn Mawr and Sara Lawrence Colleges, and Caroline Flexner who was with UNRRA in Washington, D.C. Her father was a pharmacist and then a physician.

Jennie Flexner never finished college. She joined the staff of the Free Public Library of Louisville as a secretary, 1903-04, and then became a member of the library professional staff. She served as head of the circulation department from 1912 to 1928.

Flexner was a strong advocate of the newly developing library concept of a reader-centered philosophy as against the older book-centered one.

She was soon in the forefront of writing and talking about this new concept. In Louisville, she was an advocate of service to the black community and the training of black and white librarians.

In 1926, she took a leave of absence to serve on the curriculum staff of the American Library Association. Flexner worked on developing criteria and materials for the professional education of librarians. As a result of her involvement, she wrote a book, "Circulation Work in Public Libraries," 1927, which was a standard text in library schools.

In 1928, The New York Public Library added her to the staff to initiate a special counseling service for adult readers. They opened the Readers' Advisers Service Office, in 1929, which gave her the opportunity to develop the most productive period of her life.

She worked closely with the book selection department to build up a collection of materials to meet the needs of individuals of all ages and varied educational, racial, social and ethnic backgrounds. Flexner developed a staff from the main library to service the branch libraries.

Flexner believed that the library should go beyond its physical borders to bring it closer to the people. Her innovations were supplying reading lists to the radio program Town Meeting of the Air, the Great Books Program, concerts of recorded music in the library and the library's involvement in the adult education program.

In the thirties, she became involved with the education and training of the refugees coming to America. In World War II, she was an adviser to the Council on Books in Wartime in helping them prepare lists for the war effort at home and abroad.

On November 17, 1944, she died in New York City. She was buried in Adath Israel Cemetery in Louisville. She left behind a strong functioning Readers' Adviser's Office in the New York Public Library. She was a catalyst in raising the criteria, standards and ideals in the library profession. Jennie Maas Flexner will always be remembered for her many contributions in helping libraries serve all of the people.

47

Jewish War Veterans

Born Out of Anti-Semitism

hen the prestigious magazines Harper's Weekly and North American Review, as well as Mark Twain, wrote that American Jews didn't serve and fight in the Civil War, 78 Jewish veterans of the Union Army met in New York City's Lexington Opera House on March 15, 1896, to refute these lies by organizing the Hebrew Union Veterans, the precursor group to the Jewish War Veterans of the USA.

These Veterans had a right to be mad and angry: there were more than 6,000 Jews who served in the Grand Army of the Republic, with many of them being killed or wounded. Six Jews were awarded the Congressional Medal of Honor and many others received various decorations and medals. After a year, Mark Twain apologized to the veterans for his anti-Semitic remarks.

These 78 Civil War veterans made the following the basis for their existence: They pledged to maintain a true allegiance to the United States; to combat anti-Semitism and to combat bigotry wherever it originated and whatever the target; to uphold the fair name of the Jew

and fight his battles wherever unjustly assailed; to assist such comrades and their families as might stand in need of help; to gather and
preserve the records of patriotic service performed by men of Jewish
faith; and to honor the memories and shield from neglect the graves of
heroic Jewish veterans.

Today, these principles have been expanded to include support for
Israel, Jewish Boy Scouts and Eagles, college scholarships and Soviet
Jewry, and working with the community for common goals and causes.

Some of the major accomplishments of the JWV have been when it
organized a boycott of German goods (1933), effectively campaigned
for the G.I. Bill (1944), had a successful drive to supply blood for our
soldiers during the Korean War (1951), was the only national veterans'
organization that joined Reverend Martin Luther King, Jr.'s historic
march on Washington (1963), and spearheaded a drive in response
to President Reagan's visit to Bitburg (1985).

The Jewish War Veterans of the USA sponsor the National Museum
of American Jewish Military History in Washington, D.C. It is the only
accredited veterans museum in the country. It houses the artifacts,
memorabilia and many records of Jewish men and women who served
and fought in the wars of the United states of America from Colonial
times to present.

The Jewish War Veterans of the USA is the oldest active veterans
organization in the country, and the only active Jewish organization
that has a Congressional charter. JWV interacts with other Jewish veterans
throughout the world when they meet each year in Israel.

The Jewish War Veterans of the USA today has continued with the
purposes set forth by those 78 Jewish Civil War Veterans in 1896. It is a
major force on the national and local veterans scene, and it continues
to be visible and vocal so that nobody will ever again question whether
Jews fought for our country.

Beatrice Fox Auerbach

Philanthropist & Business Executive

Beatrice Fox as a young lady never had to worry about finances as her parents were well-to-do. She went to local and private boarding schools and she traveled very often with her family.

She was the daughter of Theresa and Moses Fox and was born on July 17, 1887, in Hartford, Connecticut. Her two sets of grandparents were of the German-Jewish migration of the mid-1,8000's and they each established dry goods stores. Gerson Fox established his store in Hartford about 1845, and Ferdinand Stern established his store in Newburgh, New York, about 1857.

After the death of his father, Moses Fox became the president of the Hartford store which was firmly established and growing. When he went to Europe on buying trips, he often traveled with his family. It was on one of these trips that Beatrice Fox met and married George Auerbach. He was involved in his family business in Salt Lake City, Utah,, a non-Mormon department store. They lived there and had two children Georgette Fox, in 1916, and Dorothy Brooks, in 1919.

In 1917, a devastating fire destroyed G. Fox and Company in Hartford. Beatrice and George Auerbach was persuaded to return to Hartford when the store was rebuilt. He became the secretary-treasurer and he played a major role in the new and expanded store.

Beatrice Auerbach's life turned around when her husband died in 1927. She became involved in G. Fox and Company; first on a part-time basis and then becoming more involved in the management of the business as her father's health was slowly curtailing his activity. She became president of the store when her father died in 1938.

Under her leadership, the business grew tenfold. Fox was the largest privately owned store in the country. Beatrice Fox Auerbach was one of the first to institute labor reforms for her staff. She had a five-day week, retirement plans, medical and non-profit lunch facilities and interest free loans for her employees when they had a crisis.

Fox was one of the first stores to hire black employees for positions that gave them the opportunity to advance. She also started free delivery service, toll-free telephone order department and fully automated billing. She remained president until 1965 when she sold her privately owned stock for 40 million dollars of publicly held shares of May Department Stores Company.

After the sale of G. Fox and Company, her attention and activities turned to philanthropy and civic leadership. She served on many hospital, school and cultural organization committees and board of directors. She established the Beatrice Fox Auerbach Foundation to help finance educational and civic activities.

She was very involved in The Service Bureau for Women's Organizations and she supported it financially. The bureau trained and helped women's groups in techniques of community organization. It later served as the host organization for the State Department's foreign visitor program. She was very active in her organizations until she died on November 29, 1968, in Hartford.

Beatrice Fox Auerbach was nationally recognized as an innovative merchandiser and civic-minded philanthropist. Her leadership role as a woman in the business world will always be an inspiration and model for all women.

103

49

Jews Who Served with Honor in The Spanish-American War

When the battleship Maine was sunk on February 15, 1898, there were 15 Jewish sailors who went down with the ship. The executive officer of the Maine, and later a vice admiral in the United States Navy, was Adolph Marix, a Jew.

Marix was the chairman of a board of inquiry to investigate the mysterious sinking of the MAINE. It is interesting to note that his father was an interpreter in the Lincoln Administration and that Abraham Lincoln appointed Adolph Marix to the United States Naval Academy.

When the United States declared war against Spain on April 21, 1898, the first volunteer was Colonel Joseph M. Heller, who left a thriving medical practice to become an acting assistant surgeon in the Army. About 5,000 Jews served in this war. When the Jewish High Holy Days were approaching in 1898, there were 4,000 requests for furloughs to attend services.

There were indeed 30 Jewish Army officers and 20 more in the Navy in the Spanish-American War. Jewish casualties ran high for the percentage of Jews in the service. Twenty-nine were killed, 47 wounded, and 28 died from disease—for a total of 104.

Corporal Ben Prager received the Silver Star Medal for his bravery in the Philippines in 19 skirmishes and engagements. The official citation describes his accomplishments: "When the engagement was fully opened up, Corporal Benjamin Prager and seven other soldiers from Companies A and L,19th United States Infantry, moved out and charged the enemy...and after twice charging in the face of heavy fire, succeeded in dislodging the enemy and putting the entire force to rout. With true soldierly spirit, the success was followed up and the enemy was driven out of the city across the river and mountains."

Colonel Teddy Roosevelt commanded the Rough Riders, which included a large number of Jews. The first Rough Rider killed was a 16-year-old Jewish boy, Jacob Wilbusky. Colonel Roosevelt promoted five men in his command for their bravery in the field without knowledge of their religion. One of them was a Jew.

Sergeant Maurice Joost of the First California Volunteers, a regiment that had more than 100 Jewish soldiers, was the first man to fall in the attack on Manila. There were 280,000 American soldiers in this war, which was four-tenths of 1 percent of the population. Jewish soldiers were one-half of 1 percent of the American Jewish population; therefore, Jews served in greater proportion than did the remainder of the nation's citizens.

In the Spanish-American War, Jews once again demonstrated that they are willing and ready to fight and serve in defense of our country.

50

Blanche Wolf Knopf
Publisher

Blanche Wolf Knopf was the president of Alfred A. Knopf Inc., one of the most prestigious publishing houses in the country. Her publishing business acumen established her as one of the leaders in the industry.

She was born on July 30, 1894, in New York City, and she was the youngest of two children of Bertha and Julius W. Wolf. Her father was a wealthy jeweler, who was born in Vienna.

Her family spent the summers at Lawrence, Long Island, and in 1911, she met Alfred Knopf, Jr., whose family were neighbors. They were married on April 14, 1916.

She encouraged Alfred to follow through with his ambitions to be a publisher. In 1915, he launched his publishing company with Blanche as his all-around assistant. Knopf started to gain stature when they published Gogol's "Tara Bulba," Kropotkin's "Ideals and Realities in Russian Literature," and a book of short stories by Guy de Maupassant. They were also financially successful when they published W.M. Hudson's "Green Mansions."

Blanche Knopf acquired the technical knowledge of the mechanics of printing. By hiring a nurse to care for her son, she was able to work full-time. She was responsible for the famous Borsoi imprint on Knopf books. By 1921, she became vice president.

She made many trips to Europe to look for good authors. Her knowledge of French and German helped her meet and talk to many authors and European publishers. She arranged to publish in the United States the works of Andre Gide, Ilya Ehrenberg, Mikhail Sholokhov and Thomas Mann. She persuaded Sigmund Freud to have Knopf publish his latest book, "Moses and Monotheism."

In 1936, she visited Germany and was appalled at what she had seen. In an interview with the New York Times (July 14, 1936) she said "There is not a German writer left in Germany who is worth thinking about. The gifted writers and enterprising publishers who had any independence had left Germany. Only the Nazi writers and publishers remain so as to please the Nazi government."

She made several trips to Latin America during World War II looking for authors. She signed Brazilian sociologist Gilberto Freyre and other writers. After WW II, she returned to Europe to look for authors. She became president of the publishing house when her husband became the chairman. They had a home in Purchase, New York, but she had an apartment on fifty-fifth street in New York City for her social life. Most of her friends were from the publishing world.

She was responsible for shaping and advancing the careers of many authors. She was their mentor and advisor in their time of crisis. She helped many of them financially.

Blanche Knopf was an enthusiastic concert-goer whose friends in the music world were Mr. and Mrs. Artur Rubinstein and Mr. and Mrs. Jascha Heifetz. Her clothing was high fashioned and one of her favorite designers was Christian Dior.

In her later years, she was plagued by illness. She died in her sleep on June 4, 1966. Blanche Wolf Knopf was one of the few women to reach her position in publishing. Her achievements in the industry paved the way for other women to follow her to help dismantle an exclusive male world in publishing.

51

Dankmar Adler

An Architectural Pioneer

Dankmar Adler was a pioneer and a leader in developing and building steel-framed skyscrapers in the 1880s. Adler was also an expert in acoustics for building auditoriums and theaters. Adler was born in Eisenach, Germany, on July 3, 1844. His mother died when delivering him. For this reason, his father, Liebman Adler, named him Dankmar. The name is a compound of the German words dank (thanks) and mar (bitter). Adler was a public school teacher and a cantor in the local synagogue.

In 1854, Liebman Adler decided that he and his son would immigrate to Detroit. There, he became the rabbi and cantor of Congregation Beth El. Dankmar received his education in the public schools. He failed to get into college and received private instruction in drawing. After he expressed an interest in architecture, his father placed him as an apprentice with Mr. Shaeffer, a well known architect.

He was taught the conventional five orders and drew many sketches of the Byzantine and Romanesque ornaments that were so popular in that period. Mr. Shaeffer taught him to erect houses of worship.

After Liebman Adler was named rabbi of Kehilath Anshe Ma'ariv Synagogue in Chicago in May 1861, the Adlers moved there. Dankmar Adler started to look for an architect's job but this was cut short in July 1862, when he enlisted in Company M, First Regiment, of the Illinois Light Artillery to fight in the Civil War. He was involved in many battles from 1862 through 1864 and was also wounded.

In between the battles, he was constantly reading scientific publications. In the last nine months of service, he was assigned to be a draftsman in the Typographical Engineer's office of the Military Division of Tennessee. When he was discharged, he returned to Chicago.

He had many jobs as an architect from 1865 to 1871, when he formed a partnership with Edward Burling. Eight months after the partnership began, they were inundated with work as a result of the great Chicago fire in October of 1871. Adler married Dila Kohn in 1872. Kohn was the daughter of Abraham Kohn, who was a pioneer settler in Chicago and a founder of the Kehilath Anshe Ma'ariv Synagogue.

Adler decided to be independent and opened his own firm in 1879. Soon after he went into business, he hired Louis Sullivan, who was later to become his partner. (The two of them would later build more than 100 buildings, including steel-framed skyscrapers.) Adler's father had the satisfaction of having his son build a new synagogue for his congregation before he died in 1891.

American architect Frank Lloyd Wright went to work for Adler and Sullivan and received his training from them. In 1895, Adler and Sullivan dissolved their partnership. Adler was involved in all of the architects' organizations and wrote articles on architecture.

Adler was a hero in the Civil War, an expert in acoustics and a pioneer in the development of steel-framed buildings and skyscrapers. His work and legacy is a valuable contribution to the development of America. He died at the age of 56, on April 16, 1900.

52

Amy Loveman

Editor and Author

Amy Loveman was one of the founding editors of the Saturday Review of Literature and an associate editor of the Book-of-the-Month Club for many years from its inception.

She was born on May 16, 1881, in New York City to Adassa and Adolph P. Loveman. Her interest and love for literature came from her parents. Her mother was a descendant of a long line of Jewish writers and scholars. Her father was well educated and a linguist. In 1842, her grandfather, Michael, left Piotrkow, a part of Russian-held Poland, to join Louis Kossuth's short lived Hungarian revolution. His family migrated to the United States in 1856.

Her grandfather was a regular contributor to the nation, a noted encyclopedist and an outspoken foe of slavery. Her mother contributed many unsigned political columns to many weekly magazines during the seventies. Amy's father came to the United States in 1850 and he was a successful cotton broker who spoke six languages and loved to read books.

Amy was one of six children, graduated Horace Mann School in New York, and received a degree from Barnard College in 1897. Her first job was with her uncle, Louis Heilprin, helping him revise the New International Encyclopedia and Lippincott's Pronouncing Gazetteer of the World. She did the editing, checking proof and writing some articles.

She became a book reviewer with the ***New York Evening Post***, where she joined Henry Seidel Canby, Christopher Morley and William Rose Benet to establish the newspaper's literary section. This literary section was dropped by the Post even though it had gained wide popularity. On August 2, 1924, The Saturday Review of Literature appeared with Canby as editor, Benet and Loveman as associate editors, and Morley as a contributing editor. The magazine's success is a matter of history and Loveman was an editor for thirty-five years.

Loveman wrote a column called "Clearing House" where she answered questions from the readers. Her column led her to write her book, "I'm *Looking for a Book*," in 1936. When Benet died in 1950, she took over his position of poetry editor.

She began to work for the Book-of-the-Month Club when it started in 1926. She was chairperson of the reading department and in 1951, she replaced Dorothy Canfield Fisher as editor.

Amy Loveman received recognition for her contributions to the literary world. In 1942, a group of friends gave her a surprise party and presented her with a gold medal. She received the Columbia University Medal of Excellence in 1945 and the Constance Lindsay Skinner Award in 1946.

Amy Loveman lived a solitary life in New York City. Her life was literature and her close relationship with her brothers. She worked until she died on December 11, 1955. She was unassuming, optimistic, rationalistic and unfailingly modest. She will always be remembered for helping and bringing out the best in people.

53

Nathan Strauss

Cared for People and Palestine

Nathan Strauss served his country without a uniform. When the American expeditionary forces were fighting the Spaniards in Cuba in 1898, Straus presented them with refrigerating plants that helped to check the mortality rate from disease. He was recognized for this donation by Admiral Schley, who expressed his appreciation and thanks for his assistance.

He was born in Otterberg Rhenish Bavaria on January 31, 1848, the son of Sara and Lazarus Straus, and brother of Isadore and Oscar. He came to this country when he was a child and was educated in a log cabin school in Talbotton, Georgia. After the Civil War, the family moved to New York, where, in 1866, he joined his father's firm.

In 1888, he became one of the owners of R.H. Macy and Co. He started many innovations in the store, such as rest rooms, a depositors' account system, medical care, and a cost-price lunchroom for the Macy employees.

On April 28, 1875, he married Lina Gutherz, an educated and cultured woman who was equally enthusiastic about his philanthropies.

Straus became park commissioner in New York City (1889-93) and president of the board of health in 1898. He turned down the nomination for mayor from the Democratic Party in 1894.

Straus was always helping people. In the terrible winter of 1892-93, he distributed food for the poor and sold a million and half buckets of coal for only five cents each. In the following winter, he gave away more than two million five-cent tickets good for coal, food or lodging. He also established lodging houses that provided bed and breakfast for five cents.

He was a great believer in the pasteurization of milk and started a campaign to educate the public. This ultimately led to compulsory pasteurization of milk in most cities. Prior to this treatment of milk, 241 babies out of a thousand died before their first birthday. After pasteurization of milk, during four years, only four babies died.

In 1911, President William Howard Taft appointed Straus as the only United States delegate to the Third International Congress for the Protection of Infants, which was held in Germany.

Philanthropy became his ruling passion as the years rolled by. He never acquired great wealth because he was always supporting organizations and causes. His greatest devotion was to Israel. He gave more than two-thirds of his fortune to Palestine and he devoted the last 15 years of his life to this cause.

In Palestine, Straus established a domestic science school for girls in 1912, a health bureau to fight malaria and trachoma, and a free public kitchen. He also opened a Pasteur Institute, child-health welfare stations, and the monumental Nathan and Lina Straus Health Centers in Jerusalem and Tel Aviv.

Straus' wife, Lina, died in 1929 and he died a year later. Straus was hailed as the greatest Jew in the last quarter of a century by President Taft. He will always be remembered as a philanthropist and as "a man who care and loved people and Palestine."

54

Edna Ferber

Writer of Short Stories, Novels and Plays

Edna Ferber was a very successful and well known writer of short stories, novels and plays. Her novels reflected the growth of many regions of the United States. In all of her writings, Ferber portrayed the heroine as being aggressive, assertive and successful.

She was born on August 15, 1885, in Kalamazoo, Michigan, the second of two daughters of Julia and Jacob Charles Ferber. Her father was a Hungarian immigrant who had a family store. His sight and health caused the family to move a number of times to different cities until he died.

In her autobiography, Ferber describes some of the anti-Semitism she experienced when she was a young girl. Her father wouldn't come home for lunch from the store on Saturdays. She would bring him a full hot lunch and she had to be careful so as to not spill the soup. As she walked down the street, the other children would taunt her with remarks like "Here comes the sheeny!" or "The sheeny wets her bed!" On the next street, she encountered men in their twenties who would make anti-Semitic remarks as she nervously walked by them.

She was proud that she was Jewish. She recalls being one of eight to attend a dinner party of a society woman in New York. The woman didn't know that Ferber and two other guests were Jewish. She told them that she threw away a book when she learned that the author was Jewish. It was at this point that all three Jewish guests, including Ferber, told her that they were Jewish and walked out.

She worked on a number of newspapers, going from one to another to enhance her position and gain experience. It was during this time that she became sick and while convalescing she started to write fiction. After selling her first story, her work was in demand. In 1912, her short stories were collected in volumes. Many reviewers thought that a man had written them but was using a woman's name as a coverup. Ferber was proud of that charge because she believed that every writer should be judged by their writing and not their sex.

Ferber's career as a playwright wasn't successful until she collaborated with George S. Kaufman.Their plays resulted in hits: Minick in 1924; The Royal Family in 1927; Dinner at Eight in 1932; Stage Door in 1936; and Show Boat in 1937, which was based on her novel.

Ferber was awarded the Pulitzer Prize in 1924 for her first big seller, So Big, which sold over 300,000 copies. Her published works included two autobiographies, thirteen novels, eight plays, and many collections of short stories. Eight of her novels and two collections of short stories were made into films.

Edna Ferber lost her battle with cancer and died on April 16, 1968. Ferber was never married because she didn't see it as part of her game plan for life. While she left her estate to her sister and nieces, Edna Ferber gave the United States her writings which encouraged women to become aggressive and assertive so that they enjoy success in their lives.

55

Jennie Loitman Barron
Judge, Lawyer and Suffragist

J ennie Loitman Barron's stamina and zeal helped her achieve success in most of her undertakings: mother, judge, lawyer, suffragist and community leader.

She was born October 13, 1891, in Boston's West End to Fannie and Morris Loitman, who were Russian-Jewish immigrants. Jennie's mother was an outstanding woman. She knew five languages and soon her home became a meeting place for new immigrants who needed an interpreter.

Her father was very active in the Jewish community and became a charter member of the Hebrew Progressive Lodge. Jennie's father was very proud of her and would take her to meetings to recite poetry to his friends.

Jennie was the third of four daughters of the Loitmans. She earned at Boston University her A.B., 1911; LL.B., 1913; and her LL.M., 1914. She was able to work her way through school by teaching Americanization classes and working in the Women's Educational and Industrial Union's Department of Law. She was also involved in Boston University's League for Equal Suffrage. She spoke and lectured for equal rights for women at many meetings sponsored by this group.

She married Samuel Barron, Jr., a distant relative who had graduated Harvard Law School on June 23, 1918. They organized a husband and wife law firm, Barron and Barron. They had three daughters: Erma in 1919, Deborah in 1923, and Joy in 1931.

The family was a very important part of her life throughout her career. Friday night dinner at her home to begin the Sabbath was an ongoing ritual for her and her children. This was part of their Jewish tradition and culture.

She became president of the Massachusetts Association of Women Lawyers and organized a successful campaign for women to become notaries in 1918. She became involved in many campaigns relating to women. She organized women to exercise their newly won right to vote, to have uniform laws on marriage and divorce and the right to serve on juries.

In 1934, she was appointed by the governor as a special justice of the Western Norfolk District Court. This was to be the beginning of a 30-year career as a judge. In 1937, she was named to be an associate of the Boston Municipal Court and she remained until 1959. She then became an associate of the Massachusetts Superior Court and the first woman to hold this position.

During her 30 years as a judge, Barron found time to be active in the Jewish and non-Jewish communities. She was the first president of the Women's Auxiliary of Beth Israel Hospital, 1926-29; she served on the first board of Brandeis University National Women's Committee, 1945-55; first president of the New England Women's Division of the American Jewish Congress; and she was on the national boards of Hadassah and the National Conference of Christians and Jews.

A week after their fiftieth wedding anniversary in June, 1968, Samuel Barron died and Jennie died within a year from a heart attack on March 28, 1969.

Jennie Loitman Barron was one of the early pioneer to struggle for women's rights in society. Perhaps, if you had asked her what was her greatest achievement? She would have replied, "Mother of the Year Award, in 1959."

56

Emile Berliner

His Legacy of Innovation and Invention

E mile Berliner's introduction of the flat disk to replace the cylinder in Thomas Edison's phonograph was the basis for the modern gramophone in 1887. The Victor Talking Machine Co. acquired his patent and began to mass produce this new form of entertainment.

Berliner was born in Wolfenbuttel, Germany, in 1851. He immigrated to the United States in 1870, and worked as a salesman in New York and then in Washington D.C. He became interested in electricity and, in 1876, began experimenting with Bell's newly invented telephone. He invented the loose-contact telephone transmitter and the use of an induction coil. This invention made it practical, for the first time, to use the telephone for long distance calls.

The Bell Telephone Company bought his invention and appointed him chief electrical instruments inspector of the company. He was with the company for a number of years and continued his experiments with electricity.

Berliner became interested in aviation and engaged in many experiments, which led to his introduction of the use of a revolving light engine. He focused his attention on the helicopter. Between 1919 and 1926, he built three helicopters, which he tested in flight.

Berliner was also involved in the fields of hygiene and health. In 1890, he organized and founded the Society for the Prevention of Sickness. He also organized, in 1907, the first milk conference in Washington, D.C., for the pasteurization of milk and the improvement of its quality. He was very active in the fight against the spread of tuberculosis, and he wrote many articles on hygiene and preventive medicine.

In 1899, Berliner wrote a book, Conclusions, that speaks of his agnostic ideas on religion and philosophy. At the end of his life, he supported the rebuilding of Palestine and was very active on behalf of the Hebrew University of Jerusalem. He died in 1929.

His son, Henry Adler Berliner, was an engineer who worked with his father on the pioneering experiments with the helicopter. He was president of Berliner Aircraft, Inc., in Washington, D.C., from 1930 to 1954. In World War II, Henry was chief of war plans for the Eighth Air Force and lost an arm in combat.

Emile Berliner, through his innovations and inventions, left a legacy to America, which his son continued with distinction and honor.

119

57

Ida Rosenthal

Co-founder of "Maidenform Brassieres"

Ida Rosenthal and her husband, William, exemplify the "rags to riches" success of many Americans. Two Russian immigrants coming to America penniless and becoming multi-millionaires

Ida Rosenthal, nee Cohen, was born on January 9, 1886, near Minsk, Russia. Her father was a Hebrew scholar and her mother worked hard in running a small general store. When she was nineteen, she immigrated to America to follow her boyfriend, William Rosenthal, who had left a few months earlier. After arriving, they were married in 1907.

She was a dressmaker and they decided to form their own business. She handled sales and financial matters and he oversaw the design and tailoring. They were never satisfied the way a dress fitted around the bosom. In the twenties, women wore a towel like brassiere with hooks in the back which didn't flatter their appearance. The Rosenthals felt that a woman paying a minimum of a $125 for a custom dress should have it fit well around the bosom.

They designed a little bra with two pockets which produced a better fit. They developed the cups by rounding them and having them come to a point. Women were better fitted and their clothing became more stylish. Maidenform Brassieres became a success with Ida playing a very active role in its production and development. In 1928, they gave up the

120

dressmaking business and concentrated only on brassieres. Later, they introduced women's lingerie and swimsuits.

They aggressively advertised their products in the newspapers, magazines, radio and television. It was in 1949 that a New York advertising agency came up with the slogan, "I dreamed that I went shopping in my Maidenform bra." This slogan was an instant success and lasted for over twenty years.

During World War II they had no problem receiving all the material they needed for their products. Studies showed that working women wearing bras were less fatigued than those who didn't.

The Maidenform Company started with 10 employees and now has over 5,000. Ida Rosenthal was part of an industrial team that visited the Soviet Union in 1963. She saw a potential market in the Soviet women.

"The Soviet woman," she said, "is badly in need help when it comes to foundations. I believe we'll eventually have them for customers."

When her husband died in 1958, Ida Rosenthal became the chief executive officer of the company. She moved from her large estate on Long Island to a small apartment in the lower part of Fifth Avenue. She went to her office every day until she died on March 29, 1973, at the age of 87.

She served on the board of directors of the Bronx Lebanon Medical Center for many years. She and her husband established the Ida and William Rosenthal Fellowship in Judaica and Hebraic at New York University. They also gave them many of the materials on display.

They donated Camp Lewis in Sussex County, New Jersey, to the Boy Scouts of America in memory of their son, Lewis, who died while a student at Columbia University. Ida Rosenthal left material and monetary donations to many Jewish institutions.

Ida Rosenthal will always be an inspiration and model for Jewish women wanting to be owners or executives in business. Ida Rosenthal showed them that it can be done if you work hard at it.

58

Emma Lazarus

A Poetess and Helper of Immigrants

ive me your tired, your poor, your huddled masses..." is part of "The New Colossus," a sonnet written by Emma Lazarus that expresses her belief in the United States as the haven of Europe's masses yearning to breathe the fresh air of democracy. The sonnet, written in 1883, is engraved on a memorial plaque that was affixed to the pedestal of the Statue of Liberty in 1903.

Emma Lazarus was born on July 22, 1849, in New York City. She was the daughter of Esther and Nathan Lazarus, Sephardic Jews, who were wealthy and devoted to the family. Emma Lazarus was educated by private tutors. In her early life she was very precocious. She composed many poems and, in 1867, in her teen years, she had a volume of poems, titled Poems and Translations, published.

She continued to write poems and essays that attracted the attention of Ralph Waldo Emerson, a leading American poet and essayist. He invited her to spend a week at his home in Concord,

Massachusetts. They had a life-long correspondence. She also corresponded with Henry Wadsworth Longfellow.

Lazarus had a thorough knowledge of Jewish history and literature. She kept herself apart from writing about Jewish themes. Even when her Poems and Ballads of Heinrich Heine appeared, she considered him, in her introduction, as being more of a German than a Jew. She stopped being a pleasing litterateur when she read George Eliot's novel Daniel Deronda, which called for a national Jewish rival. Her interest in what was happening to the Jews of the world was further reinforced with the Russian pogroms of 188-82.

Lazarus started to translate the works of Jewish poets. She wrote essays and commentaries attacking and responding to the anti-Semites of the day. The precociousness of her youth was gone and her maturity as an adult woman came to the fore with her concern for the plight of the immigrants and Jews.

She became especially interested in the plight of the Russian-Jews as she encountered them on Wards Island, where they landed from overseas, and where she did volunteer work. In her writings, Lazarus set forth her ideas and plans for the rebirth of Jewish life by a national and cultural revival in the United States and in the Holy Land.

In 1883, Lazarus went to Europe, where she was acclaimed for her poems and writings. She was at the prime of her life and at the peak of her writing career when she was stricken with cancer. Lazarus was only 38 years old when she died. She will always be remembered for her work and concern for the "huddled masses" who came to this country to be free, the interests of Jews, and her poems and essays.

59

Jacob Henry Schiff

Hero of Finance and Philanthropy

Jacob Henry Schiff was an important participant in actively accelerating the rapid industrialization of the United States economy during the late 19th and early 20th century. Through his firm, Kuhn, Loeb and Company, he was able to help finance the development and growth of such corporations as Westinghouse Electric, U.S. Rubber, Armour, and American Telephone and Telegraph.

He also served as a director and advisor of numerous insurance companies, banks and other corporations. Schiff was a prime mover in helping to consolidate and expand the American railroad networks.

Schiff was prominent in floating loans for the U.S. government and for foreign nations. He took great delight in floating a spectacular bond issue of $200 million for Japan to help them in their war with Czarist Russia, 1904-1905. Schiff was angered and infuriated with the anti-Semitic pogroms and policies of the czar. Helping Japan fight Russia was one of his methods of striking back at anti-Semitism.

Jacob Henry Schiff was born on January 10, 1847, in Frankfurt-am-Main, Germany. The son of Moses and Clara (Niederhofheim) Schiff, he was a descendant of a distinguished rabbinical family that could trace its lineage back to 1370. He received a secular and religious education at the Israelitische Religionsgesellschaft (a local school).

At age 18, Schiff emigrated to the United States and became a citizen.

He went to work in a brokerage firm in New York and he later became a partner in Budge, Schiff and Company. He met and fell in love with Theresa Loeb, the daughter of Solomon Loeb, head of the banking firm, Kuhn, Loeb and Company. They were married on May 6, 1875, and he entered her father's firm.

In 1885, he was named head of the firm because of his financial abilities. Schiff was a strong advocate for the gold standard and he opposed the Silver Purchase Act of 1890. Despite his success in the financial world, he always felt he had a special obligation to the Jewish people. He fulfilled this commitment through his philanthropies.

Schiff was a Reform Jew, but he still retained many of the Orthodox habits of his youth. He was especially active in the establishment and development of the Jewish Theological Seminary and the Hebrew Union College. He was a large contributor to the relief programs for the Jewish victims of the Russian Czar's anti-Semitic programs.

There was hardly a Jewish organization which was not the recipient of his contributions. His interest and love for Jewish literature found him contributing generously to the Jewish Publication Society. He funded a program for a new English translation of the Bible. He helped to establish the Jewish Division in the New York Public Library.

Schiff was always concerned about humanity and sickness. He contributed heavily to Montefiore Hospital in New York where he served as president for 35 years. During those years, he visited the hospital weekly. He contributed generously to many Jewish and non-Jewish organizations, including the Semitic Museum at Harvard University; he gave one million dollars to Barnard College; contributed to the American Red Cross, Tuskegee Institute, the Henry Street Settlement, etc.

He was one of the founders of the American Jewish Committee and was active in the Jewish Welfare Board.

Jacob Henry Schiff died on September 25, 1920, in his beloved New York City.

60

Samuel Gompers

Leader of The American Federation of Labor

I n 1886, the American Federation of Labor was organized. Samuel Gompers, a former cigarmaker, was elected to be its president. With the exception of one year, he remained in this position until he died in 1924. Gompers was the son of Solomon and Sarah, nee Rood, Gompers. He was born in a London tenement on January 27, 1850. Both of his parents were originally from Holland.

When Gompers was six years old, he attended a tuition-free Jewish school. At the age of 10, he was taken out of school to become an apprentice shoemaker since his family was struggling to make a living.

The family immigrated to New York during the Civil War. Gompers' cigarmaker father taught him the trade. At the age of 17, after he became a cigarmaker in his own right, he met and married Sophia Julian. He joined the Cigarmakers' Union and became very active. In 1877, his union's strike collapsed because of no money or member discipline.

Following the strike, Gompers reorganized the cigarmakers and remained as president of their union. Lessons were to be learned from the strike. The international officers became supreme over the local unions. The dues were raised to build up a strike fund. Benefits were established for sickness, accident or unemployment.

In 1881, after other unions had emulated the Cigarmakers' Union program, the Federation of Organized Trades and Labor Unions of the United States and Canada was formed. Gompers was chairman of the Constitutional Committee. The federation was reorganized in 1886. It was renamed the American Federation of Labor. Gompers was its first elected president.What made this federation unique was that there could only be one affiliated craft union.

Gompers felt that labor could not displace capitalists in the man agement of business. He was criticized for being vice-president of the National Civic Federation, which sought to promote stable labor relations through collective bargaining and personal contact between labor leaders, industrialists and bankers.

In World War I, he supported President Woodrow Wilson's policies and organized the War Committee on Labor. The committee included representatives of labor and business. After the war, Wilson appointed him as a member of the International Labor Legislation. He fought those who would erode the gains that labor had made during World War I.

In 1894, Gompers became the editor of the official journal of the federation. He maintained the journal until he died. He wrote many articles on labor for the publication. During all of his years as president of the federation, Gompers had time for his family. He was family-oriented and believed in family loyalty. He had five children: three sons and two daughters. His wife died in 1920. A year later, he married Grace Gleaves Neuscheler.

Gompers was elected president for the last time at the 1924 convention. He had come to the convention knowing that he didn't have much time to live.He died on December 13, 1924. For almost four decades, Gompers had been the dominant figure in the American labor movement. He had broadened the horizons of the working man and his trade union. He was a pioneer in making the American labor movement free and strong.

61

Fania Mary Cohn

Labor Leader and Educator

Fania Mary Cohn was demanding, domineering and self-centered in her quest that women have a major role in the organized labor movement. She wrote in the February, 1934 issue of the American Federalist, "While organization gives the workers power, purposeful dynamic education gives them the ability to use that power intelligently and effectively."

Fania was the daughter of Anna and Hyman Cohn, who was the manager of the family owned flour mill. She was born on April 5, 1885, in Kletzk, Russia. In 1904, the family emigrated to New York City and she worked for a short while with the American Jewish Women's Committee on Ellis Island.

In 1905, she decided to get involved with the trade union movement so she took a job as a sleeve-maker in a garment factory. Fania felt that she needed the experience of life as a worker in a shop if she was to understand their minds and aspiration.

It didn't take long for her to be elected to the executive board of the Wrapper, Kimono and House Dress Makers' Local 41 of the International Ladies Garment Workers Union (ILGWU), in 1909. She became chairlady of the board for two years, 1913-14, when she left to attend the National Women's Trade Union League Training School for Women Organizers in Chicago.

She became an organizer for the ILGWU and she reached a high point when she led the first successful strike of Chicago's dress and white goods workers in 1915. Her fame spread throughout the union and she returned to New York in 1916. Fania was aware of the male dominance in the labor movement and she constantly fought for the greater organization of women.

In 1917, she was appointed to the ILGWU's General Education Committee. The following year, she became the executive secretary of the Education Department. Under her leadership, she expanded the program giving the ILGWU the largest union educational department in the country.

She believed that the education of workers was important for them to become labor leaders, to create a union loyalty and to instill in workers a "social conscience" which would lead to a world with social justice. She felt that the trade union movement was the only force to give the workers this education.

In 1925, she was defeated for her bid for the fifth term as vice-president. She attributed her loss to her non-involvement in an inner political struggle that was going on within the union. She continued as head of the Education Department of the ILGWU. David Dubinsky, president of the ILGWU felt that union needed younger people to present a favorable image to the younger American born workers. He considered the foreign born organizers and leaders, like Fania Cohn, a thing of the past. In 1935, he hired Mark Starr to be the education director. Fania retained her title as executive secretary. For the next twenty years, her duties and responsibilities were whittled away.

In December 1962, she died of a stroke, four months after she retired. In her life, Fania demonstrated through her activities the importance of educating workers socially, economically and culturally. Her tenacity and perseverance succeeded in having more women achieve leadership positions within the trade union movement. In her death, the trade union and women's movements lost a great ally and leader.

62

World War I

Jews Answer The Country's Call to Action

When the United States declared war against Germany in April 1917, a call went out for men to enlist in the military. Jews represented only 3.27 percent of the total population, yet they made up 5.73 percent of the country's armed forces.

Congressman Julius Kahn of California, a Jew who was chairman of the House Military Affairs Committee, drew the first draft number from a glass bowl. At that time, he made a pledge that was picked up by the Jewish community:

> *I desire to congratulate my co-religionists on the splendid showing they are making in the matter of serving our country in this war. Many of the boys who go down to the front will be wounded. Many of them will be killed. But Jews at all periods in the world's history have been ready to make the supreme sacrifice whenever the land that gives them shelter demands it. I know that I voice the sentiment of the over-whelming majority of the Jews in the United States when I say that we will do our share toward keeping Old Glory floating proudly in the skies so that it may continue to shelter under its folds the downtrodden and the oppressed of every land.*

Typical of the Jewish family's commitment to the war effort was the one of Mrs. Gustave Jacobson of New York City. After the declaration of war, her oldest son, Gustave, enlisted in the army. Two more sons, Harry and Samuel, joined the Signal Corps. Another son, Simon, signed up with a gas contingent. Her fifth son, Benjamin, joined the 305th Artillery, and her sixth son, Jacob, enlisted in the aviation branch of the service. Her seventh son, Daniel, remained at home because he was only 15.

Within the year, Mrs. Jacobson received word that Harry had been killed, Simon had been wounded and that Jacob had been injured in an airplane crash.

One day, the youngest son, Daniel, disappeared. A search for him proved futile. He was nowhere to be found. When armistice was declared, five of her six sons had returned home, two wounded and one killed. On a Sabbath eve, Daniel also returned home. He had changed his name and falsified his age so that he could enlist and serve in the Marine Corps.

The Jacobsons served their country without any hesitation and the mother, Mrs. Jacobson, never complained. To offer seven sons to the service of our country was a tremendous sacrifice.

More than 250,000 Jews served in the armed forces in World War I. They received 1,135 decorations, including three Congressional Medals of Honor. There were more than 9,000 commissioned officers, including two generals and an admiral. Approximately 3,500 were killed and more than 12,000 wounded. The Jewish Welfare Board was organized in 1917 to help meet the war needs. It established 200 centers with more than 500 workers in the training camps and 57 overseas behind the trenches. It also helped with enlistment and with raising funds for the war.

Once again, Jews responded to our country's call to help it repel its enemies so that we could remain free.

63

Sergeant Benjamin Kaufman
Decorated for Heroism
in World War I

S ergeant Benjamin Kaufman was an unassuming young man who grew up in Brooklyn, rooted for the Dodgers and found himself going to Syracuse University when the United States became a participant in World War I in 1917.

Kaufman responded to the call to arms and joined the Army, where he was assigned to Company K, 308th Infantry. He excelled in camp sports and the company respected him as being a tough soldier and a good sport. He quickly rose to the rank of sergeant and he twice refused the honor of becoming an officer.

Kaufman proved to be a hero almost as soon as he was in combat in France. He became blinded by a gas shell while aiding in the rescue of several of his men. Despite his refusal of medical help, doctors forced him to go to the hospital. For fighting men like Kaufman, the hospital was no place to be. He borrowed a uniform and made his way back to his outfit. Kaufman was quickly faced with a court martial for leaving the hospital. However, Army officers saw it Kaufman's way and dropped the charges so that he could rejoin his outfit.

While serving in an advance detail in the Argonne on October 4, 1918, Kaufman and his men came under heavy fire from a German machine gun.Two of his men were wounded. Kaufman realized that he had to silence the machine gun before help could reach the wounded men.

Before he could use his own weapon, Kaufman was struck in the arm by an enemy bullet. With his shattered, bleeding right arm hanging limp at his side, Kaufman advanced on the enemy, lobbing hand grenades with his left arm. He eventually reached the German position and captured a surviving German soldier.

Kaufman returned to the American lines with his prisoner. He fainted from the loss of blood after revealing the position of the German lines, which made it possible for the Americans to move forward.

Kaufman received awards for bravery from nine foreign governments. The United States awarded him the Congressional Medal of Honor. After the war, he became active in the Jewish War Veterans of the United States of America, serving as national commander in 1941-1942. The Ben Kaufman Post 156 of the JWV in Trenton, New Jersey, is a living memorial to a man who always had a smile on his face even when the going was rough.

64

Sergeant Sam Dreben

The Subject of Runyon's "The Fughting Jew"

World War I hero Sergeant Sam Dreben was not only acclaimed by the men he fought with, but also by the American people at home. His heroics touched many people, including the writer and poet, Damon Runyon, who expressed his feelings in a now-famous poem, "The Fighting Jew."

In this poem, Runyon wrote that whenever he read about prejudices against the Jews and of racial hatred, he was reminded of the heroic fighting Jew, Sam Dreben. He was also reminded of the Distinguished Service Cross, the Croix de Guerre, the Militare and other medals that were awarded to Sergeant Dreben. Runyon ended his poem with:

> ...THANK GOD ALMIGHTY, WE WILL ALWAYS
> HAVE A FEW, LIKE DREBEN A JEW

Sam Dreben was a refugee from Czarist Russia, where the pogroms taught him how to face his enemies and how to fight back. He had a hard task of adjusting to life in America and worked at many jobs. He finally found a career that he liked when he enlisted in the Army.He saw action in the Spanish-American War, the Philippine insurrection, and later in the Boxer Rebellion in China.

Dreben fought under General "Black Jack" Pershing when President Wilson sent them across the Mexican border to capture Pancho Villa. In later years, General Pershing had a high regard for Dreben because of his service in this campaign.

Dreben returned to civilian life after the Mexican campaign, but it didn't last long as America became involved in World War I. He enlisted once again and was one of the first of the Yankee troops to land in France and to go into battle against the Germans.

It was at St. Etienne that Dreben distinguished himself. A German machine gun had been keeping the American troops from getting out of the trenches and advancing. The American artillery was unsuccessful in trying to destroy this machine gun nest. Dreben observed the situation for a few days and then decided to make his move to destroy the machine gun nest. He zig-zagged his way alone to the enemy post, where he killed 23 of the 40 Germans there. He received the Distinguished Service Cross for his heroism.

Sam Dreben was one of the many Jewish immigrants who served in the American Army and fought overseas against the Germans. He was one of the many Jews who received recognition for their heroism in World War I. He and the other Jewish soldiers were part of the legacy that Jews serve and fight for their country in a crisis.

65

Captain Elkan Voorsanger

The "Fighting Rabbi of World War I"

The NewYork Times, San Francisco Chronicle, and other newspapers, when writing about Captain Elkan Voorsanger, referred to him as the "Fighting Rabbi" of World War I. He got this title as a result of serving as the senior chaplain of the 77th Division, a melting pot of religions and nationalities. Whenever the 77th went out of the trenches to attack the German soldiers, Captain Voorsanger always went over the top with his men. He was the division burial officer, school and entertainment officer, and the Jewish Welfare Board adviser to the 77th Division.

Captain Voorsanger had the highest praise for the men in the 77th. He was quoted as saying in an interview that the "Jewish men in this division were good soldiers, brave, fearless, and resourceful. They fought, knew how to fight and were glad to do it."

Voorsanger came in contact with the JWB as a soldier-recipient when the organization supplied him with an automobile, making it possible for him to visit Jewish fighting men. JWB also supplied him with material and money to help him serve the soldiers.

He resigned his position as the assistant rabbi of Congregation Shaare Emeth, St. Louis, to enlist in the Army as a buck private in May, 1917. He was with the first 750 American soldiers to go overseas to France to fight the German Army. He quickly rose up the ranks to sergeant, lieutenant, chaplain, captain and senior chaplain of the 77th Division.

Captain Voorsanger found himself the chaplain of not only Jewish soldiers but non-Jewish soldiers as well. He gave prayer and counseling to all who needed it as they lay wounded or dying. He often said in speeches "that each chaplain was responsible for the religion of ever man and it didn't matter to us how a man prayed but that he prayed."

He related how a Catholic chaplain organized Yom Kippur services for Jewish servicemen in a ruined cathedral. Captain Voorsanger arrived late because he was organizing Yom Kippur for other Jewish soldiers at the front.

As the JWB adviser, he organized many activities and services not only for the Jewish soldiers but also for the others. He found that if there were 200 Jewish soldiers in a detachment, 200 would come to services—not because they had to, but because they wanted to be there to pray.

It was during the Argonne engagement that Captain Voorsanger was wounded and received the Purple Heart. He also received the French Croix de Guerre and was recommended for the Distinguished Service Medal.

After the war, he worked with the JWB, became field director for the American Relief Committee and he was active in many Jewish organizations. Captain Elkan Voorsanger died on April 3, 1967. He will always be remembered as the "Fighting Rabbi" of World War I.

66

Other Jewish Soldiers Recognized for Bravery in World War I

ar brings out the best or the worst in a fighting man. In World War I, Jewish soldiers displayed bravery and courage, which was recognized by the awards they received.

One such hero was Sergeant William Sawelson, who received the Congressional Medal of Honor for his bravery. Born in Newark, New Jersey, he entered the Army in Harrison, serving as a member of Company M, 312th Infantry, 78th Division.

It was in France at Grand Prix, on October 26, 1918, that Sawelson heard a wounded man in a shell hole some distance away cry out for water. Acting on his own initiative, Sawelson left his protective shelter to crawl through heavy machine gun fire to bring the wounded man a canteen of water. He returned safely to his shell hole, obtained more water, and was returning to the wounded man when he was killed by machine gun bullets.

Three Jewish soldiers received the Congressional Medal of Honor in World War I: Sergeants Sidney Gumpertz, Ben Kaufman, and William Sawelson.

First Sergeant Sidney G. Gumpertz was in Company E, 132nd Infantry, 33rd U.S. Army Division. It was on September 29, 1918, at Bois de Forges that he displayed his heroism. His outfit was advancing against the Germans when it was held up by an enemy machine gun. An American heavy artillery barrage failed to destroy the machine gun nest. Using that barrage as cover, Gumpertz and two of his men went out to try and silence the enemy position.

The artillery shells killed the two men with Gumpertz. Alone, he zig-zagged to dodge the machine gun bullets, continuing his advance until he was able to jump into the machine gun nest and take the nine German soldiers prisoner.

Corporal Barney Satler was responsible for rescuing an entire battalion in the Battle of the Marne in France. Salter escaped from an Army hospital after being wounded because he was determined to rejoin his outfit. He hitchhiked rides and made his way across the country until he found his outfit in St. Mihiel. He reported for duty, filthy, ragged and starved, with a festering wound on his stomach as big as his hand. He pleaded not to be sent back to the hospital. His commanding officer acquiesced, and gave him light duty until his wound healed.

In a fierce battle, the Second Battalion had been practically destroyed and its right flank was in trouble. Acting on his own, in the absence of any officers alive, Salter took command.He ordered a bayonet charge that saved the battalion and destroyed the enemy. He received many awards for his bravery.

67

Yet More Jewish Servicemen Who Became World War I Heroes

Corporal Louis Abend was one of the youngest seasoned soldiers in the United States Army when America became involved in World War I. He was 15 when he enlisted in the Army and gained experience on the Mexican border against the banditos. He was 18 years old when America entered World War I and he was shipped to France to fight.

He was a member of Company M, 28th Infantry, when it attacked the Germans at Cantigny on May 28, 1918. There were heavy casualties on both sides. With all of the officers in his outfit killed or badly wounded, Corporal Abend took command and his men repulsed three counter-attacks. His battalion captured the town, taking 800 German prisoners. Corporal Abend received the Distinguished Service Cross for his bravery and leadership.

In another engagement at Somme, he received the Croix de Guerre from General Petain for saving the life of a French officer despite a wound to his left hand. Corporal Abend was transferred to General Pershing's regiment, and later served with the Army of Occupation.

Sergeant Benjamin Shapiro, a member of Company A, 104th Infantry, 26th Division, was involved in many heroic episodes. His exploits earned him the Croix de Guerre and other decorations. It was during an engagement with the Germans that Shapiro was wounded and sent to a base hospital. He was discharged in time to rejoin his company, where he played an important role in getting his outfit to advance.

In another engagement in the Argonne Forest, his company was ordered to clear an area of machine gun nests, a task that proved more difficult then the men had figured. Spotting a machine gun nest, Sergeant Shapiro jumped into the shell-hole, capturing one German soldier and killing the rest.

The citation for Shapiro's act of bravery read: "A brave and daring non-commissioned officer, who, on October 16, 1918, in the Bois de Beaumont, attacked a machine gun nest alone and captured the piece after having killed the gunners."

One of the great stories in World War I was that of the "Lost Battalion" of the 77th Division and how Private Abraham Krotoshinsky saved the day. It was November 2, 1918, in the Argonne Forest, that his battalion found itself in trouble. His commander, Colonel Whittlesey, had led the battalion into the forest to clear out the German machine guns. The enemy backed up, leading the Americans to believe that the Germans were on the run. However, the Germans led the Americans into their own territory and encircled them.

Private Krotoshinsky and another soldier were sent out to make contact with their division. As soon as the two started out, the other man was killed. Private Krotoshinsky slowly made his way through the German lines to his division, which moved forward to save the "Lost Batallion."

68

Jewish Officers Who Led the Way with Acts of Bravery in World War I

Major General Milton J. Foreman of the Illinois National Guard received the Distinguished Service Cross for bravery while serving as a colonel in France. When his unit came under heavy artillery and machine gun fire, he crept through the German gunfire, laying out telephone wire so that he could tell his artillery where the enemy had its gun positions. Foreman found the enemy gun positions and directed his artillery to lay down a barrage of shells to destroy them.

General Foreman was one of the organizers of the American Legion and he was elected chairman of its executive committee at the Paris Caucus, at which he represented Illinois. During the Legion's third national convention in 1921, he was designated a past national commander by resolution.

Brigadier General Abel Davis was recognized for his valor and leadership when he was a colonel in the 132nd Illinois Infantry in France. He left a very successful career as a banker when he enlisted to fight in

World War I. His initial military experiences started when he enlisted to fight in the Spanish-American War as a private. When he was mustered out after the war, he returned to Chicago and started his career in banking.

General Davis was the leader of the 132nd Illinois Infantry Regiment that was involved in many battles. They encountered and fought the Germans at Amiens, Meuse-Argonne and at St. Hilaire. It was at St. Hilaire that Davis displayed his leadership and courage. Davis repulsed the enemy again and again, exposing himself to enemy gunfire while directing his regiment. He received the Distinguished Service Cross and the ribbon of an officer of the French Legion of Honor for his bravery.

Lieutenant Benjamin B. Prager was recognized for his heroism when he was a first sergeant in Company E, 111th Infantry Regiment, 28th Division. It was at Le Chateau Diable near Fismes on August 11, 1918, that his outfit became pinned down by a German machine gun nest.

Prager took a squad of his men and they started to work their way to a house on the hill. The German machine gun kept firing at them and Prager ordered his men to remain behind as he and another soldier advanced toward the house. When they reached the house, Prager exposed himself to enemy fire to locate the position of the German machine gun. He and his men were able to capture the German soldiers and destroy the machine gun. Prager was recognized for his heroism and was promoted to lieutenant.

The finest tribute paid to the Jewish fighting men in World War I was given by General John J. Pershing: "When the time came to serve their country under arms, no class of people served with more patriotism or with higher motives than the young Jews who volunteered or were drafted and went overseas with our other young Americans to fight an enemy."

69

Julius Stieglitz

A Pioneering Chemist who Aided the War

Julius Stieglitz was very active in World War I developing war gases, dyes, and chemicals for the American military forces. He served as chairman of the committee on synthetic drugs of the National Research Council.

Stieglitz was born in Hoboken, New Jersey, on May 26, 1867, the son of Hedwig and Edward Stieglitz, German immigrants who were successful in the woolen business in New York City. He and his identical twin brother, Leopold, attended private and public schools in their early years. They received higher education in Germany, with Julius going in for chemistry and his brother electing to go into medicine. Julius Stieglitz and his brother looked so much alike that many had trouble telling them apart. Even when it came to marriage, their likes were similar: they both fell in love with sisters and married them.

Julius became a full professor at the University of Chicago in 1905 and served as chairman of the chemistry department from 1915 until he retired in 1933. He also served on committees for the guidance of doctoral candidates. He had a great influence in the field of chemistry through his writings and lectures, and did a great deal of research in organic chemistry. Stieglitz developed a self-taught understanding of the principles of physical chemistry, which created a new branch of science. His book The Elements of Qualitative Analysis, written in 1911, opened up new avenues for scientists to investigate in chemistry.

Stieglitz was recognized for his many contributions to chemistry when he was elected president of the American Chemical Society in 1917. He also received the prestigious Willard Gibbs Medal. He received many other honors, including honorary degrees from Clark University and the University of Pittsburgh, and membership in the National Academy of Sciences, the American Philosophical Society and the American Academy of Arts and Sciences.

His wife, Anna, died in 1932. Two years later, he married Mary Rising, a former graduate student who became a member of the chemistry department at the University of Chicago. They had two children, who later became successful physicians.

Stieglitz had many interests in life, including photography, music, sports and a love for the cello. He had a photographic mind that could reveal all kinds of statistics and data relating to sports and trivia.

Stieglitz, who died of pneumonia at the age of 69, will always be remembered for his scientific contributions to World War I and to the field of chemistry.

70

Julius Rosenwald

A Prominent Philanthropist
in both War & Peace

Julius Rosenwald served his country in war and peace. President Woodrow Wilson appointed him as a member of the Advisory Commission of the Council of National Defense in 1916. He was sent on many missions at home and abroad by the secretary of war.

Rosenwald was born on August 12, 1862, in Springfield, Illinois, the son of Augusta and Samuel Rosenwald. Born in a house across the street from where Abraham Lincoln had lived, Rosenwald was greatly influenced by Lincoln.

In 1879, Rosenwald went to New York to start his business career with Hammerslough Brothers.In 1885, he left the firm to go to Chicago, where he became the president of Rosenwald and Weil. He later became involved with Sears, Roebuck and Company, serving as president from 1910 to 1925 and then as chairman until his death in 1932.

Rosenwald married Augusta Nusbaum of Chicago, and they had five children. His wife died in 1929, and a year later he married Adelaide Goodkin. Rosenwald was a philanthropist and humanitarian. A religious man, he attended services regularly at the Chicago Sinai Congregation, where he was also an officer. He was very active in Jewish charities and activities, and was one of the pioneers who organized the Federation of Jewish Charities in Chicago in 1923. He was also very active as a member of the American Jewish Committee, and helped to develop a good financial base for the Hebrew Union College of Cincinnati and the Jewish Theological Seminary of America in New York City.

Rosenwald equated Judaism with service to humanity and he believed that Jews were a people, not a nation. Although he wasn't a Zionist, he gave generously to the Jews in Palestine and to the Hebrew University of Jerusalem.

Rosenwald didn't confine his philanthropy to Jews. He helped feed the hungry children in Germany after World War I. He helped establish colleges in Syria and Constantinople.He contributed almost $4 million to help build black YMCA-YWCA buildings throughout the country. He believed, like Booker T. Washington, that the salvation of the black people lay in education, and he contributed heavily to that cause. Rosenwald established the Julius Rosenwald Fund in 1917 to help serve humanity. By 1929, the fund had grown to $30 million.

In Chicago, Rosenwald was active in doing away with the "red light district."He was also involved with the Chicago Planning Commission and served as president of the Federation of Jewish Charities. He built the Museum of Science and Industry and gave it to the city.

Julius Rosenwald will be remembered as a philanthropist who served his country in war and peace.

Fannie Hurst

Writer

Fannie Hurst had a very active career that spanned over fifty years. She had written 17 novels, nine volumes of short stories, three plays, many articles, speaking engagements, a television talk show and collaborated on a number of films.

She was born on October 18, 1889, in Hamilton, Ohio. She was the only child of Rose and Samuel Hurst, who was a successful manufacturer of shoes. Her parents were Bavarian-Jews, who immigrated to the United States in 1860. Fannie Hurst was raised in St. Louis, Missouri, in a "middle-western world of assimilated Jews."

After receiving her A.B. degree from Washington University in St. Louis, in 1909, she went to Columbia University for graduate courses. Despite the objections of her parents, she left for New York in 1910.

She wanted to be a writer and for that she had to study people. She worked as a waitress and as a salesgirl. She also did bit acting roles in the theater, attended night court and studied people on the street.

Hurst was neither a radical or intellectual, but she was preoccupied with many social issues: equal pay for equal work, the right of a woman to retain her name after marriage, relief of the oppressed Jews in Eastern Europe, the social and medical problems of homosexuals, etc.

Her first story, "Ain't Life Wonderful," had been published in Reedy's Weekly, a St. Louis newspaper, while she was attending college.

There followed a string of rejections until 1912, when a second story was accepted and she received $30. Her writing talent was quickly recognized and the Saturday Evening Post wanted all of her future stories. Her novels and stories were eagerly greeted by the publishing world so that by 1925, she and Booth Tarkington were the highest paid writers in the United States.

She became a long-time friend of Eleanor Roosevelt and supported the New Deal and labor. She chaired a national housing commission, 1936-37; the committee on workmen's compensation in 1940, a member of the national advisory committee to the Works Progress Administration, 1940-41; and she was a member of the board of directors of New York Urban League.

Hurst was very active in raising funds for the refugees from Nazi Germany in the 1940s, a staunch supporter of Israel in the 50s, and donated $50,000 to the support of writers. When she died, she left one million dollars to Brandeis and Washington Universities to establish professorships in creative writing.

In 1915, she had secretly married pianist Jacques Danielson and they each had their own residence. When their marriage was revealed in 1920, a New York Times editorial took them to task for having separate residences when there was a housing shortage.

Hurst retaliated by stating that a married woman had the right to retain her own name, her own special life and her own personal liberty. They remained happily married until his death in 1952.

She was very sharp and to the point in vocalizing her views on the rights of women. When Justice Arthur Goldberg declared in 1962, "that it is time that we evaluated women on merit and fitness for a job," she snapped back, "Time sir! You are a half century too late."

Fannie Hurst died in New York City, on February 23, 1968, at the age of 78. She left behind her writings to stimulate the mind to the social issues that she had raised.

Fanny Brice

Star in Vaudeville, Radio, Theater & Movies

Fanny Brice was in a class by herself when it came to mimicry, comedy, comedy dialogue and the ability to put over a song. She was able to establish a close rapport with audiences which sky-rocketed her to stardom and fame.

Fanny was born as Fanny Borach on October 29, 1891, in New York City, to Rose, nee Stern, and Charles Borach, both immigrant parents. Her father's gambling and drinking caused her mother to leave him with Fanny and her other three children, Philip, Caroline and Lew.

Her career started when she began singing on the neighborhood streets for pennies. When she was thirteen, she wanted to avoid paying the admission charge at Kenney's Theater in Brooklyn, so she entered the "Amateur Contest" to get in free. Her singing touched the hearts of the audience and she won the five-dollar first prize.

She changed her name to Fanny Brice as she started her career in the theater. In 1914, George M. Cohan and Sam Harris had a review, Talk of the Town, and she managed to get herself cast as a chorus girl. Her inability to dance cost her the job and she decided to take dancing lessons.

She joined the Traveling Burlesque Company and when the leading lady took sick, she was asked to sing her songs. Not having the strength and fullness of an adult voice, she decided to sing them comically. This launched her career as a comedienne.

In 1910, Florenz Ziegfeld offered Fanny a contract to appear in his fourth Follies.The audiences loved her comic routines and Brook Atkinson, of the New York Times, described her as "the burlesque comic of the rarest vintage."

Fanny was not only known for her humorous songs, but also for her tragic songs like My Man and Second-Hand Rose. In The Song of the Sewing Machine, she sang about the plight of women working in sweatshops. While her serious trademark was My Man, her comic trademark was Baby Snooks.

She met and married Jules "Nick" Arnstein, a gambler and confidence man. They had two children, William and Frances. Arnstein was in and out of jail for his scams and finally he disappeared from her life. She divorced him in 1927.

She met Billy Rose, a songwriter, and married him in 1928. She divorced him in 1938 because of his affair with Eleanor Holm Jarrell, a swimming champion.

Fanny Brice appeared in radio programs and movies. She starred in her own radio program as Baby Snooks, in 1934. Her first film appearance was for Warner Brothers in My Man, 1928. Her next film, in Be Yourself was released in 1930. She then did The Great Ziegfeld, 1936; Everybody Sing, 1938; and a repeat of The Great Ziegfeld, in 1946.

Fanny Brice suffered a mild heart attack in 1945. She died of a cerebral hemorrhage on May 29, 1951. Her daughter, Frances, was married to movie producer Ray Stark, who produced the movie, Funny Girl, in 1964, a fictionalized version of Fanny Brice's life. Barbara Streisand was the star and she brought back the realism and majesty of Fanny's comedy, burlesque routines and songs.

Fanny Brice never forgot, or let others forget, that she was Jewish. Her struggle as a poor, young kid who became a star is an inspiration and model for our youth.

73

Jennie Grossinger

Hotel Executive & Philanthropist

Jennie Grossinger turned a small rundown Catskill Mountain farm into a large hotel that became an American Institution. The catch slogan "Grossinger's Has Everything for the Kind of Person Who Likes to Come to Grossinger's," tells the story of its success.

Jennie Grossinger was born on June 16, 1892, in Baligrod, a small village in Galicia, Austria, to Malka and Asher Selig Grossinger. Her mother was the daughter of an innkeeper and her father was an estate overseer. Her parents saved enough money to immigrate to America in the hopes of a better life.

They lived on the lower East Side of New York City where Jennie went to public and Jewish schools. She left the schools to become a button hole maker, earning two dollars a week for an eleven hour day.

In 1912, she married her cousin, Harry Grossinger, and moved next door to her parents. She worked as a waitress in her father's dairy restaurant. In 1914, her father's health was failing and they decided to move to the Catskill Mountains where they bought a farm in Ferndale, N.Y. In order to make ends meet, they took in summer boarders. They gave their guests what they wanted: kosher food and a vacation away from the city heat.

They served plenty of food that her mother cooked and Jennie was the chambermaid, bookkeeper and hostess. Their reputation for plenty of good food at inexpensive rates attracted more people than they could handle. They sold the farm and bought a large piece of property with a hotel on it in Liberty, N.Y.

Jennie had two children: Paul, born in September, 1915, and Elaine Joy, born in December, 1927. Jennie continued to manage the hotel as she raised the two children.

Keeping abreast of the times and the competition, she built tennis courts, bridal paths, a children's camp, hired a social director and a residential theater group which graduated many stars in the entertainment field.

Many famous celebrities came through Grossinger's doors to visit and entertain. They included Bobby Fischer, Robert Merrill, Mrs. Franklin D. Roosevelt, Red Buttons, Vice President Alben W. Barkley, Chaim Weismann, Dore Schary and two Nobel Prize recipients: Dr. Selman A Waksman and Dr. Arthur Kronberg.

Grossinger's Hotel was also responsible in advancing the careers of many well known entertainers. Eddie Fisher was a young singer entertaining at the hotel when Eddie Cantor heard him. Cantor was so impressed that he started Fisher on his rise to national stardom.

Jennie Grossinger was always involved in charities and good causes. She raised millions of dollars in WW II war bonds at the hotel. An Army airplane was named "Grossinger's" in her honor. In Israel, there is a clinic and convalescent home that bear her name. She received many honorary degrees and awards for her philanthropy.

When Jennie gave up her management of the hotel, it contained 1,200 acres with 35 buildings and they served 150,000 people a year. On November 20, 1972, she died of a stroke in her cottage at Grossinger's.

Jennie Grossinger best personified America. She was poor when she started and rose to riches by her skill as an innkeeper. Jennie Grossinger will always be the symbol of what success is in the hotel industry of America.

153

74

Bernard Baruch

Adviser to President in both War & Peace

Bernard Mannes Baruch was often referred to as the "elder statesman" because through three wars the presidents of our country called upon him for his advice and expertise.

Baruch was born on August 19, 1870, the second of four sons of Belle and Simon Baruch. His father was a field surgeon for the Confederate Army during the Civil War. In 1881, the Baruchs moved to New York City, where his father continued his medical career as a general physician specializing in appendicitis and hydrotherapy.

Bernard and his brothers went to the public schools in New York City. He was quite active in sports at the College of the City of New York. It was during a collegiate baseball game that he injured an ear, which impaired his hearing. After graduating from college, he went through many jobs until he accumulated enough money to buy a seat on the New York Stock Exchange. His financial acumen made him a millionaire at the age of 30.

Baruch was a devoted member of the Democratic Party and contributed generously to it. When Woodrow Wilson became president, Baruch was a frequent visitor to the White House. During World War I, President Wilson appointed him to the Advisory Commission to the Council of National Defense. Accepting the appointment, Baruch resigned his positions with industry, liquidated his holdings and sold his seat on the Stock Exchange. He bought millions of dollars of Liberty Bonds.

Baruch played an active role on many government commissions. After the war, he went with President Wilson to the Versailles peace conference.He also played active roles in the administrations of Presidents Harding and Hoover, and was a member of the "Brain Trust" in President Roosevelt's "New Deal." In the early 1930s, Baruch urged the stockpiling of rubber and tin, which are necessary items for war. Baruch anticipated that the United States would be involved in World War II and constantly urged our government to build up the armed forces.

During World War II, Baruch was involved in many committees for the war effort. He did his best thinking sitting in the parks of Washington, D.C., and New York City. He could always be seen with other people discussing affairs of the government on a park bench, which became his trademark. During the Korean War, Baruch called for an expansion of the Voice of America to counteract the enemy propaganda.

Bernard Baruch contributed to charities and colleges, making a gift of a million dollars to Columbia University in memory of his father. He was married to Annie Griffen and they had three children.

75

Gerty Theresa Radnitz Cori

Nobel Price Recipient for
Medicine & Physiology

D r. Gerty Theresa Radnitz Cori was the first American woman to receive the Nobel Prize for Medicine and Physiology, in 1947, which was shared with her husband, Dr. Carl F. Cori, and Dr. B.A. Houssay of Argentina.

Dr. Cori was born on August 15, 1896, in Prague, which was part of the Austro-Hungarian Empire. She was the oldest of three daughters of Martha and Otto Radnitz, manager of a sugar refinery. The family was Jewish and she was educated by private tutors.

At age 16 and influenced by her uncle, who was a professor of pediatrics at the University of Prague, Cori decided to study medicine. She graduated with a medical doctor's degree in 1920.

When she was attending medical school, she met Carl Ferdinand Cori, a fellow student. They both shared many common outdoor activities and they both had a curious interest in laboratory research. They were married on August 5,1920, and accepted positions at the University of Vienna. They decided to pursue careers in medical research rather than medical practice.

In 1922, they both emigrated to the United States to join the staff of Buffalo's New York Institute of Malignant Diseases. He became an assistant pathologist and she was appointed as an assistant biochemist.

They both became United States citizens in 1928 and in 1936, they had their only child, Carl Thomas. While at Buffalo, they concentrated on studying the absorption of sugars from the intestines and the effects of insulin epinephrine on the fate on absorbed carbohydrates and on glycerin formation and degradation.

The Cori family accepted positions at Washington University School of Medicine in St. Louis. He was chairman of the Department of Pharmacology and she took a research position at a token salary. Gerty became a full professor in 1947, the same year she received the Nobel Prize in Medicine and Physiology with her husband and Dr. Houssay of Argentina.

She was the third woman to receive this prestigious award and became the first Jewish-American woman to receive such an honor. In 1952 President Harry S. Truman named her to the National Science Board of the National Science Foundation.

Dr. Gerty Cori received many honors and awards during her life and among them were The Midwest Award of the American Chemical Society, in 1946; the Squibb Award in endocrinology, in 1947; the Garvan Medal and the Women's National Press Award in 1948; the Sugar Research Prize of the National Academy of Sciences in 1950; the Borden Foundation Award for outstanding medical research in 1950. She shared with her husband, Carl, the Squibb and the American Chemical Awards. She received honorary degrees from Smith College, Yale University and Rochester University. She was also one of twelve women honored at Hobart and William Smith Colleges in Geneva, N.Y., in 1949, at ceremonies of the first medical degree bestowed on a woman.

In the summer of 1947, she started to feel the symptoms of myelofibrosis, a rare disease of the bone marrow. For ten years she continued her work, suffering with pain and refusing to stop her laboratory activities. On October 26, 1957, she died of kidney failure.

The famous newscaster, Edward R. Murrow, eulogized her dedication, intellectual integrity, courage and professionalism in her pursuit for answers in biochemistry.

76

Al Jolson

An Entertainer in both War & Peace

Al Jolson was never a soldier in the United States Army, but he did his best to support it in four wars. When he was fourteen years old, he tried to enlist during the Spanish-American War; during World War I, he sold Liberty Bonds; and he entertained the troops at home and abroad during World War II and the Korean War.

Born on May 26, 1886, in Srednike, Lithuania, he was the youngest of four children of Rabbi Moses Reuben Yoelson and his wife, Naomi (Cantor). Anti-Jewish pogroms were common and the family immigrated to Washington, D.C., in 1880, where Rabbi Yoelsin obtained a job as a cantor in a synagogue.

Jolson's mother died when he was 10. His formal education wasn't much but he learned much more from the streets, where he would sing and dance on the corner to earn spending money. In constant conflict with his father, who wanted him to follow a religious life, Al ran away to New York to join his older brother, Harry, who had left home and changed his name to Jolson. Al also changed his family name to Jolson and in 1899, he appeared as an extra in a Jewish play called Children of the Ghetto. At 15, he joined his brother in a three-man comedy act that toured the vaudeville circuits. They were known as Jolson, Palmer and Jolson. It was during this tour that he used burnt cork to darken his face, which became his trademark in show business.

After a few years with the group, he left them to be on his own. Jolson, who was not used to the pressures of delivering a set script, loved to improvise and to ad lib during his act. While he was in San Francisco playing the small night clubs, he decided to liven up his act. He came out in black face and sang a few songs with a southern style. The audience called him back for three encores and he was on his way to stardom.

He appeared in Hammerstein's shows in New York and then he went to work for the Schuberts in 1911. In the show Bombo, 1921, he introduced his famous song "My Mammy" and three other songs that were to be a part of his fame: "Toot, Toot, Tootsie," "California, Here I Come" and "April Showers." His records sold in the millions.

In 1927, Jolson was the first to star in a talking picture, The Jazz Singer, based on his own life. The talking picture put an end to the silent movies of the day and Jolson's career and success moved forward. He worked with Parkyakarkas and Martha Rae in a comedy radio series for the Columbia Broadcasting System.

His personal life was as turbulent as his career. He was married four times, the first being Ruby Keeler, star of the Ziegfeld Folliew and the stage. He had three adopted children.

During World War II, Joslon performed at the USOs at home and abroad.During the Korean War, he gave 42 shows in 16 days.Proud of the soldiers, he said, after returning home, "I am going to look over my income tax return to make sure that I paid enough. These guys are wonderful."

Shortly after returning from a strenuous entertainment trip to Korea, Jolson had a heart attack and died in San Francisco, on October 23, 1950.He was given a Jewish funeral and interred at the Hillside Memorial Park, in Los Angeles. He left millions to Jewish and other charities and received posthumously the Congressional Order of Merit.

Gertrude Berg

Star and Writer of Radio, Stage & Television

Gertrude Berg portrayed and was the personification of the "Jewish mother" on radio, television, the stage and the screen. Millions of radio listeners were tuned in to her daily fifteen minute program, The Rise of the Goldbergs, when it went on the air on November 20, 1929. This show elevated her to celebrity status and made her one of the most successful women writers in the history of American entertainment.

She was born in the Jewish Harlem section of New York City, on October 3, 1899. She was the only child of Dinah and Jacob Edelstein. She attributed her major source of humor and Jewish life to her grandfather, Mordecai Edelstein, who was an immigrant from the Russian occupied area of Poland.

Prior to World War I, her father took over the operation of a boarding house in Fleischmanns, New York. Her mother supervised the kitchen and bookkeeping and Gertrude entertained the guests by writing and performing skits, pantomimes and fortune telling acts.

It was here that she met Lewis Berg, a chemical engineer, who was regarded as an expert in his field as a sugar technologist. In 1918, they were married and for a while they lived on a sugar plantation in

Louisiana. Their stay was brief and they returned to New York City where they had two children: a son, Cherney Robert, 1922, and a daughter, Harriet, in 1926.

In 1929, she submitted her script for a daily radio show called The Rise of the Goldbergs, which was an instant hit. It was on the air six days a week and in 1931 it picked up a sponsor and it ran until 1934.

Sol Lessor called her to Hollywood, where she wrote screen plays for him and child star, Bobby Breen. In 1938, she received a five-year million dollar contract to write and star in the Goldberg series. It was on the air from 1938 to 1945. The problems of the Goldbergs became those of the listening audience.

Berg was concerned about the growth of fascism in the thirties and the welfare of European Jews. She became active in many Jewish groups and during World War II and participated in the larger war effort.

In her transition of The Goldbergs from radio to television, she achieved another success. Her opening television show line "Yoo hoo, Mrs. Bloom," became a national cliche. Gertrude Berg wrote and co-starred in the film, Molly, in 1951.

It was while in production of her starring role in The Play Girls that she had a heart attack and died on September 15, 1966. Brooks Atkinson, of The New York Times, in describing her writing and role of Molly said:

"In her code of values, Mrs. Berg is more nearly right than Noel Coward, who is an expert playwright; and her family makes better company than the over-civilized family J.B. Priestly introduced to us in The Linden Tree.

Gertrude Berg was a writer and actress who brought out the humanity, love and respect that people should have toward each other. Her contributions to American radio, television films and stage will always be remembered, especially by those who experienced hearing and seeing her perform.

161

78

Irving Berlin

The Nation's Great Composer of Patriotic Songs

I rving Berlin once said that, "a patriotic song is an emotion and you must not embarrass an audience with it, or they will hate your guts." This philosophy made him one of America's most outstanding writers of patriotic songs from World War I through World War II.

In World War I, he wrote the musical Yip, Yip, Yaphank, which was produced by the men of Camp Upton. In this musical, the big hit song was "Oh, How I Hate to Get Up in the Morning," which reflected Berlin's aversion to rising early. This musical raised more than $150,000 to build a service center at Camp Upton.

On Armistice Day, 1939, he introduced "God Bless America," which was sung by Kate Smith. This song threatened to replace the national anthem because of its patriotism and popularity.

In World War II, he wrote the musical This is the Army, which raised $10 million for the Army Emergency Relief. His hits in this musical were This is the Army, Mr. Jones and I Left My Heart at the Stage Door Canteen. He also wrote other patriotic songs such as Any Bonds Today?, Arms for the Love of America, and Angels of Mercy for the American Red Cross.

Berlin was prolific: He wrote more than 900 songs, 19 musicals and the scores 18 movies. Some of his songs that have become classics include There's No Business Like Show Business, Easter Parade, and White Christmas. He is the top money maker among songwriters in America.

Berlin was born Israel Baline in Eastern Russia on May 11, 1888. He was one of eight children born to Leah and Moses Baline. His father was a shochet (one who kills chickens as prescribed by Jewish religious laws) who was also the cantor in the synagogue. His family moved to New York in 1893 to escape the pogroms in Russia. At the age of eight, he took to the streets of the Lower East Side of New York City to help support his mother and family after his father had died. In the early 1900s he worked as a singing waiter in many restaurants and started writing songs. His first published hit was Marie From Sunny Italy. His successes continued through two years.

Berlin was married for only a year to Dorothy Goetz, who died from typhoid contracted while on their honeymoon in Cuba in 1913. He married Ellin Mckay in 1926. She was the daughter of Clarence Mckay, president of Postal Telegraph Company, a leading Catholic layman who opposed the wedding. The Berlins had three daughters.

Berlin supported Jewish charities and organizations and donated many dollars to worthwhile causes.On February 18, 1955, President Eisenhower presented him with a gold medal in recognition of his services in composing many patriotic songs for the country. Berlin's World War I doughboy uniform and many of his original patriotic scores are on display in the National Museum of American Jewish Military History in Washington, D.C.

Irving Berlin died on September 22, 1989, at the age of 101. His legacy of music and charity will always be an important part of American life.

79

Louise Nevelson
Sculptress

 Near the World Trade Center in New York City is an area that is named Louise Nevelson Plaza in honor of a great American Jewish Sculptress.

Louise Nevelson was born on September 23, 1899 in Kiev, Russia, to Mina Sadie and Isaac Berliawsky. Her father was a contractor and a lumber merchant. In 1902, he immigrated to the United States leaving his family in Russia. Louise felt deserted by her father's departure and was so traumatized that she stopped talking for six months. In 1904, they sold their home and with the money that her father sent, they left for the United States.

They settled in Rockland, Maine, where there were only thirty Jewish families. Her father became a successful builder, lumberyard owner and realtor. They had a beautiful home and quickly adjusted to their new life in America.

Louise had strong ties to the family, especially her father. He advocated equal rights for women. Her mother was a beautiful woman who was a freethinker. Louise knew at an early age that she wanted to be an artist. Being a Jew and wanting to be an artist, stigmatized her as she grew up. After she graduated from high school, in 1918, she met and married Charles Nevelson of New York.

For the first few years of her marriage, she studied drawing, painting, dramatics and dance. In 1922, she gave birth to her only child, Myron, who later became a famous sculptor. The expectations of her husband that she would fit into the mold of upper-middle class matrons playing mah jong and drinking tea was resented by Louise. In 1931, they separated and she never asked for alimony or support from her husband.

She took her son to her parents in Maine and she went to Munich, Germany, to continue her art studies. She was in Munich six months when the Nazis closed her art studies school.

She returned to the United States in 1937 and taught at the Educational Alliance Art School on the Lower East Side of New York City as part of a WPA-funded program.

Her first public showing of her sculpture was in 1933. Two years later, some of her work was part of an exhibit in the Brooklyn Museum. She managed to survive by selling some pieces of her works. Her reputation as a sculptress grew and as she exhibited she sold more of her works.

In 1967, she had a woman's show at the Whitney Museum which became the turning point of her life. She continued to create and exhibit her works during the seventies and the eighties.

In 1964, Nevelson created "Homage to 6,000,000"; a memorial to the Jews killed in the Holocaust. She was about to donate to the Centre Beauborug in Paris, a work worth about $125,000, when the French government released a Palestinian terrorist. She compared this action to the "Hitler era." In protest, she withdrew her donation of her work to the museum.

Louise Nevelson is a woman with an independent mind who threw off the shackles of restrictions and confinement of her life. Her works are a tribute and a testimonial to an outstanding sculptress, who wasn't intimated by new ideas and creativity in art.

80

George Gershwin
An Overnight Musical Sensation

George Gershwin and his older brother, Ira, elevated the Broadway musical to new and distinctive heights. George Gershwin also composed popular music and jazz for classical concert halls.

Gershwin was the son of Morris and Rosa, nee Bruskin, Gershwin. He was born on September 26, 1898, in Brooklyn, New York. When the Gershwins bought a piano for Ira, Geoge monopolized it. He took piano lessons and was introduced to classical music.

Gershwin wrote his first song in 1913. At the age of 15, he quit school to become a song plugger. In 1919, he completed his first score for the Broadway musical *La, La Lucille*. During the same year, he teamed up with Irving Caesar to write *Swanee*. Al Jolson heard Gershwin play *Swanee* at a party and put it into his Broadway show. It became an overnight hit and rocketed Gershwin to a new status in the musical world.

Gershwin worked with his brother to create the Broadway musical Lady be Good in 1924. In the same year, he composed the concerto Rhapsody in Blue for bandleader Paul Whiteman to use in a concert to demonstrate the versatility of contemporary popular music. Rhapsody in

Blue was a hit that remained most associated with the Gershwin name.

George and Ira Gershwin wrote many successful Broadway musicals, including Oh, Kay! (1926), Funny Face (1927), Strike Up the Band (1930), Girl Crazy (1930), and Of Thee I Sing (1931).

The Gershwin brothers wrote successful individual songs that are still popular today. Some of these hits are *Embraceable You, I'll Build a Stairway to Paradise, The Man I Love, Summertime, I Got Rhythm and A Foggy Day*. When not writing for the stage, George and Ira Gershwin were busy writing music for the movies. Some of their many hits were Shall We Dance and Damsel in Distress (both in 1937).

George Gershwin was always thinking about his serious compositions. One of his successes was Concerto in F (1925).After traveling through Europe, he wrote *An American in Paris* (1928). He was disappointed when his *Second Rhapsody* and *Cuban Overture* (both in 1932) were not well received.

Gershwin's ambition was to compose a jazz opera about black Americans. When he read DuBose Heyward's best-selling novel Porgy, he knew that the story was the ideal vehicle to use to write his opera. Gershwin felt that all modern jazz was built upon the rhythms and melodic turns and twists that came directly from Africa. Porgy and Bess opened in New York to mixed reviews on October 10, 1935. Sponsored by the State Department, the American National Theater and Academy performed the opera on tour in Europe and Africa during 1954 and 1955. After the tour, the opera was performed in the Eastern Bloc countries and received rave reviews.

While performing his Concerto in F in concert with the Los Angeles Philharmonic in February, 1937, Gershwin had a momentary mental lapse. This was the beginning of a series of headaches and feelings of dizziness. On July 11, 1937, he was operated on for a brain tumor and died.

Gershwin, the son of Jewish immigrants, left America a legacy of rich, melodic music.

81

Stella Adler

Teacher, Actress & Stage Director

Stella Adler was the most outstanding personality on the American stage this century. For almost 19, she was involved in theatre, including a successful career in acting, directing and teaching.

She was born on February 10, 1902, into one of the most distinguished and celebrated acting families in theater. Her mother, Sarah, was a successful actress-manager, while her father, Jacob B. Adler was a noted tragedian, who had immigrated to America at the turn of the century. By 1939, there were fifteen members of the Adler family contributing to the Yiddish Theater and the Group Theater in New York.

Adler made her stage debut with her father in "Broken Hearts" when she was four years old. While growing up, she performed in her father's repertory theater. She would play the parts of boys as well as girls. This theatrical group would put on classical plays, translated into Yiddish, of Shakespeare, Ibsen, and Tolstoy, as well as other modern and classical playwrights.

She attended New York University and later studied with Maria Ouspenskaya and Richard Boleslavski, both former members of the Moscow Art Theater.

168   She made her debut in London, in 1919, in the role of Naomi, in

Elisha Ben Avia. Adler returned to New York to star in a number of plays. She toured Europe and South America with the Yiddish Art Theater of New York. From 1927 through 1931, Adler played over a 100 roles in various productions.

Her association with the Group Theater began in 1931. This famous organization was formed by Harold Clurman, Lee Strasberg and Cheryl Crawford. Adler won high praise for her performances in Success Story, by John Howard Lawson, and later in two seminal Clifford Odets plays: Awake and Sing and Paradise Lost.

She married Harold Clurman in 1943, having previously married and divorced Horace Eleascheff. Her marriage to Clurman ended in divorce in 1960.

She stayed with the Group Theater for a decade and lamented and deplored the fact that there was a dearth of good roles for women. She felt that the theater was geared for men and that the plays were written for men only. However, she credited the company for bringing the best out of her and for revitalizing her life in theater.

Adler appeared in the movies with her roles in Love on Toast, 1938, Shadow of the Thin Man, 1941, and My Girl Tisa, 1948. In between films, she appeared in many stage plays which included an engagement in London.

She founded the Stella Adler Conservatory of Acting in New York City in 1949. She taught here for a decade. Some of her most famous students were Marlon Brando, Robert De Niro and Warren Beatty.

She later became an adjunct professor of acting at the School of Drama at Yale University. She wrote a book, "Stella Adler on Acting," which defined her theories of acting.

Adler died on December 21, 1992, of heart failure in her home in Los Angeles, California. For over ninety years her theories on acting have been the center of controversy and stimulation in developing new and talented performers. She will always be remembered for her contributions to the theater and the arts.

82

Eugene Isaac Meyer

Donated Business Expertise to his Country

ugene Isaac Meyer responded to our country's call for help in World War I by selling his business and becoming a dollar-a-year-man in Washington, D.C. He served on many committees dealing with the war effort. Meyer was born on October 31, 1875, in Los Angeles, the son of Harriet and Marc Meyer. He studied at the University of California for a year. His family then moved to New York City, where his father accepted a partnership in the banking firm of Lazard Freres, a prestigious international institution.

Eugene received an A.B Degree from Yale. His father gave him $600 to stop smoking, a lofty sum at the time. Eugene quit smoking and shrewdly invested his money until he had accumulated $50,000, which he used to buy a seat on the New York Stock Exchange.

Meyer was quick to take advantage of investing opportunities. In the stock market crisis of 1901, he started buying stock at cheap prices, making millions by taking advantage of many panic-selling situations. By the time he was 40, Meyer had accumulated about $60 million.

Meyer was one of the major organizers of Allied Chemical Co. He also exerted great influence in the copper mining and automobile industries.

On February 12, 1910, he married Agnes Elizabeth Ernst. One of their five children was Katherine Meyer Graham, who managed his communications empire, which included WTOP-TV, The Washington Post, and Newsweek.

Meyer's reputation for getting things done reached President Woodrow Wilson, who appointed him director of the War Finance Corporation in 1918. When the war ended, he continued in this position, using the agency to help farmers who were experiencing a postwar depression. In 1927, President Calvin Coolidge asked Meyer to clean up the Federal Farm Loan Board, which was wracked with scandals. President Herbert Hoover recognized Meyer's ability, and in 1930 he appointed him a governor of the Federal Reserve Board.

Meyer left public office in 1933 because he did not approve of President Franklin D. Roosevelt's policies. In the same year, he bought The Washington Post. His inexperience at publishing cost him money at first, until he learned the business and the newspaper became a money-maker and a proud institution.

He became the first president of the World Bank in 1946 at the urging of President Harry Truman. However, he was very unhappy in this role and when he completed his task of setting up the bank he resigned the post to return to his communication group, becoming chairman of The Washington Post.

Meyer expanded his communciation investments with the purchase of WJXT-TV, in Jacksonville, Florida, and the Washington Times-Herald in 1954. He died on July 17, 1959, in Washington, D.C.

83

Lena Levine
Gynecologist, Psychiatrist &
Marriage Counselor

Lena Levine was a pioneer in the birth control movement and marriage counseling. She worked very closely with Margaret Sanger and travelled with her to many world conferences.

She was born on May 17, 1903, in Brooklyn, New York, to Sophie and Morris H. Levine, a successful clothing manufacturer. Her parents were Russian Jews from Lithuania, who immigrated to the United States in the 1890s. Levine went through the public educational system, graduating from Hunter College in 1923 with an A.B. Degree. She received her medical degree from Bellevue College, in 1927. Levine married Louis Ferber, a fellow student and they both did their residencies at the Brooklyn Jewish Hospital.

She became a gynecologist and an obstetrician and her husband was a general practitioner. She retained her maiden name in her professional life. They had two children: Ellen Louise (1939) and Michael Allen (1942). Unfortunately, Michael, as an infant, became retarded from an illness and later in life was institutionalized.

Tragedy confronted her again, when in 1942 Louis Ferber died of a heart attack. She was deeply affected and decided to give up obstetrics. She became very close with her daughter and with her housekeeper, Pearl Harrison, who remained with the family until Levine died.

172

Levine met Margaret Sanger and became involved with birth control and planned parenthood. Planned parenthood and marriage counseling became the focus of her life. She became the medical secretary of the London-based International Planned Parenthood Federation.

She was active in marriage counseling in New York with Hannah and Abraham Stone. When Hannah died in 1941, she and Abraham Stone organized a group counseling program on sex and contraception under the sponsorship of Planned Parenthood. This was the first program of its kind in the United States.

Levine offered group therapy for sexual problems and she ran a special consultant bureau for pregnant women. As a physician and psychiatrist, she helped women with their physical and emotional problems and counseled them on the use of contraceptives.

Levine was the author and co-author of five books on marriage and sex problems. She also wrote many pamphlets and papers on women's med- ical and psychological problems for the lay readers and professionals. She lectured widely in America and abroad on sex education, planned parenthood and marriage. She frequently appeared on national television and radio discussing the topics that she wrote about.

She was a supporter of President Franklin Delano Roosevelt's New Deal and other social reform and legislation that affected women. In 1964, she was invited by Sargeant Shriver, Director of the Peace Corps, to meet with 100 other women in Washington, D.C. for a conference on the anti-poverty program.

Levine believed that women's sexual enjoyment, free access to birth control and frankness about sexual techniques contributed to stronger marriages and psychologically healthier children. She advocated "an annual checkup on marriage," like a medical checkup, declaring that an annual re-evaluation was beneficial to new and old marriages. Pre-marital training was another important step to a successful marriage.

Lena Levine died of a stroke on January 9, 1965. Her pioneer work in planned parenthood, sex education and marriage counseling was the precursor of the expanded educational programs that are available today, from puberty to old age.

84

Herbert H. Lehman

A Soldier, Banker and Statesman

Herbert Henry Lehman served in World War I, volunteering as a textile procurement specialist with the Navy Department, where he developed a close friendship with Franklin Delano Roosevelt. In September, 1917, he was commissioned a captain in the Army and left the service two years later with the rank of full colonel.

Lehman was born on March 28, 1878, in New York City, the son of Barbara and Mayer Lehman, who were German Reform Jews. After graduating from college, he entered the business community and joined Lehman Brothers, an investment banking house that had been transformed from a cotton brokerage firm by his brother, Arthur. In 1910, Herbert Lehman married Edith Louise Altschul, the daughter of the head of the New York branch of Lazard Freres, a respected Paris-based banking house.

Lehman's oldest son, Peter, was killed in World War II after flying 57 combat missions in Europe. Prior to serving in the U.S. Air Force, he was on active duty with the Canadian Air Force because the United

States was not in the war and he felt very strongly about defeating Hitler. Peter Lehman received the U.S. Air Force Medal with three clusters and the Dinstinguished Flying Cross was awarded to him posthumously.

Lehman's daughter and other son also served overseas in the armed forces. His son, Captain John Lehman, served with the 20th Armored Force, and his daughter, Hilda Lehman de Vadetzky, served with the Women's Army Corps in Algiers.

Herbert Lehman became active in politics in 1920 and supported Alfred E.Smith.When Smith won the Democratic Party nomination for president in 1928, Lehman became chairman of the finance committee of the Democratic National Committee. It was in that year that he was elected lieutenant governor of New York on a ticket headed by Franklin Delano Roosevelt.

Lehman became Governor of New York in 1932, the year that Roosevelt became a candidate for president. Lehman served four terms. In 1940, his brother, Irving, was elected chief judge of the New York Court of Appeals, the first time in the history of New York that brothers headed the executive and judicial branches of government.

Herbert Lehman ran twice for the U.S. Senate, losing the first time to Irving M. Ives and winning the second time against John Foster Dulles, in a special election to fill the unexpired term of Senator Wagner. In 1950, he was elected to a full term in the Senate.

Lehman was one of the earliest politicians to refute Senator Joseph R. McCarthy and his witch-hunts. He died on December 5, 1963, after receiving the Presidential Medal of Freedom.

85

Henrietta Szold

A Role Model who Helped to Found Hadassah

Henrietta Szold is considered to be one of the most outstanding Jewish women in American history. Her determination and tenacity to uplift the status of Jews in America and abroad made her a role model for all Jewish women.

She was born in 1860, one of eight daughters of Rabbi Benjamin and Sophia Schaar Szold. A year later, the family moved to Baltimore from Europe. At the age of 16, she graduated from Western Female High School in Baltimore.Her father continued her education by instructing her in Bible studies, philosophy, history and in languages (Hebrew, French, and German).

Her mother developed in Henrietta a strong sense of domesticity, duty and order. Encouraged by her mother, she became a teacher at the Miss Adams School in Baltimore, where she taught for 15 years. She also taught children and adults at her father's congregational school.

Szold became interested in writing for Jewish publications and, at the age of 19, she became the Baltimore correspondent for the Jewish Messenger, a weekly published in New York. In 1888, she became involved in the education of newly arrived immigrants, teaching them to read, write and speak English. When her father died in 1902, Szold and her family moved to New York City. That same year, she became the editor of the Jewish Publications Society of America, a post she retained for 23 years. She was also the editor of the American Jewish Year Book from 1904 to 1908.

Interested in Zionism, Szold became involved in the Hadassah Study Circle in 1907. She traveled to Palestine and was greatly impressed with its beauty. In 1912, she and 38 other Jewish women formed the Haddasah Chapter of the Daughters of Zion. The name was later changed to Hadassah and she was elected its first president.

She was very active in raising funds for Hadassah and the American Zionist Medical Unit. In 1919, she became the representative of the American Zionist Organization. The following year, she moved to Palestine, where she was made the director of the Nurses Training School and also directed the health programs in the Jewish schools. The Nurses Training School was about to go bankrupt when Nathan Straus and Hadassah came to its rescue with badly needed funds.

Szold returned to the United States in 1923 and once again became the president of Hadassah. In 1926, she resigned and was named an honorary president. She returned to Palestine the following year as a member of a three-member executive committee of the World Zionist Organization. Szold was responsible for health and education.

She returned to the United States in 1933 and immediately embarked on a program to rescue Jewish children from Hitler, making several trips to Germany. Her efforts resulted in 30,000 Jewish children being saved from the Nazi death camps. This was her greatest accomplishment, in a life that had so many accomplishments.

Henrietta Szold was 84 when she died at Hadassah Hospital in Jerusalem, where she is buried on the Mount of Olives.

86

Margaret Arnstein

Nursing Educator & Public Health Nurse

Margaret Arnstein felt strongly about making the nursing profession aware of the many important and dramatic changes that were taking place in health care. To seek these changes, she stimulated many field studies in public health nursing.

She organized and developed field studies to analyze and systematize the observations and insights of nurses. She hoped to find ways of modernizing the nursing profession. This was a major priority throughout her life.

She was born on October 27, 1904, in New York City, to Elsie and Leo Arnstein. Her parents were second-generation Americans of German-Jewish descent. She was one of four children and the family life was steeped in Jewish cultural activities and tradition. Her father was a graduate of Yale who found success in business. He was later to become the New York City Commissioner of Welfare and the president of Mount Sinai Hospital.

Margaret was greatly influenced by Lillian Wald, of the Henry Street Settlement, who was a close friend of her father. Lillian Wald encouraged and supported Margaret's interest in public health and nursing. She graduated Smith College with an A.B. Degree, in 1925, earned a diploma from the New York Presbyterian Hospital School for Nursing, in 1928, and received a Masters Degree in Public Health Nursing from Teachers College, Columbia University, in 1929.

After earning another Masters Degree from John Hopkins University, she began working as a consultant nurse in the Communicable Disease Division of the New York State of Public Health. She left in 1937. Her career as an educator began in 1938 as a teacher of public health and nursing in the University of Minnesota's Department of Preventative Medicine. She left her teaching position and returned as a consultant nurse in the New York Department of Health in 1940.

Because of her advocacy in using applied research in the public health field, she worked very closely with physicians. It was while doing a study on the contributing factors in the incidence of respiratory infections that she co-authored with Gaylord Anderson the text Communicable Disease Control, in 1941. This book became a standard where public health and nursing was taught.

After a two-year leave to work with the United Nations to advise nurse and training programs in the Balkan countries, she returned to the U.S. She joined the U.S. Public Health Service and remained there for 20 years, later becoming chief of the Division of Nursing.

She wrote A Guide for National Studies of Nursing Resources, in 1953, for the World Health Organization. She conducted the first international conference on nursing studies in France, 1956, and she became the first person to receive the Annie W. Goodrich Chair of Nursing at Yale, in 1958.

Margaret Arnstein received many honors and awards for her contributions to public health nursing throughout the world. She led a very active life and was relatively free of illness. However, she became ill in 1971 from cancer, which slowed her down until she passed away on October 8, 1972.

In her obituary in the New York Times, she was referred to as "a distinguished and outstanding educator and leader in public health nursing in America." The many contributions of Margaret Arnstein will always be remembered in the fields of medicine and public nursing.

179

87

Rabbi Stephen Wise

A Leader in Zionism & Social Reform

Rabbi Stephen Samuel Wise was a leader in the Zionist movement and a social reformer who created the bridge between the old established American Jewish community and the eastern European immigrants who came here at the beginning of the 20th century. Wise was born March 17, 1874, in Budapest, Hungary, the eldest son of Sabine and Rabbi Aaron Weiss. His family came to the United States when he was an infant. His father became the religious leader of Congregation Rodeph Shalom in New York City, and the family decided to change its name to Wise.

Stephen Wise was educated in New York City and entered City College at the age of 15. His Jewish education was provided by his father and later he studied under other rabbis, including the chief rabbi of Vienna, Adolph Jellinek. In 1893, Stephen Wise was ordained a rabbi. He married Louise Waterman in New York City in 1900 and they had two children, James and Justine. He worked as an assistant rabbi at Congregation B'nai Jeshurun while attending

Columbia University, where he received his doctorate in 1901. He became interested in social causes and supported a Brooklyn transit strike, fought against prostitution and gambling, and supported reform candidates.

Wise found himself in the national spotlight when he refused an offer to become the rabbi of the prestigious Temple Emanu-El in New York City because the congregation denied his demand for a free pulpit. A year later, in 1907, Wise founded the Free Synagogue in New York City, where there were no restrictions of any kind on the pulpit. He served there for 43 years.

Wise was a co-founder of the National Association for the Advancement of Colored People in 1909. He also became involved in mediation and arbitration of labor disputes. In 1911, he was greatly affected by the Triangle Shirtwaist Company fire, in which 146 women lost their lives. He fought against sweatshops and unsafe factories.

Wise became interested in Zionism, and in 1897, he and others formed the Federation of American Zionists. He traveled abroad to attend Zionist conferences and pledged to Theodor Herzl that he would devote his life to Zionism. In 1918, Wise was elected president of the newly formed Zionist Organization of America. In 1925, he was chosen to become president of the American Jewish Congress, a position that he held until his death in 1949.

When Hitler came to power in 1933, Wise organized Jews and non-Jews against Nazi Germany. Wise held a rally at Madison Square Garden, at which he called for a boycott of German goods. The fight against Hitler led to the formation of the World Jewish Congress.

88

Lillian Florence Hellman

Playwright & Author

L illian Florence Hellman is regarded as one of the major play-wrights in America during the twentieth century. Her plays were dominated with social justice themes that provoked controversy. Her skilled craftsmanship in writing was compared to Ibsen and Chekov.

She was born on June 20, 1905, in New Orleans, Louisiana, the only child of Julia and Max Bernard Hellman. Her father was of German Jewish ancestry, who struggled to make a living as a shoe merchant. Financial losses forced the family to live six months in New York and then back to New Orleans with her father's two sisters.

Her education was fragmented with different cultures as she went to various schools. She graduated high school in New York and she attended New York University and Columbia University. Her formal education ended in 1924.

Hellman went to work as a manuscript reader for a New York City publisher. After work, she found herself attending many publishers' parties where she was introduced to the antics and reckless life of the literary world of the 20s. She was in her twenties and enjoyed the bohemian and adventurous life of the writers' world.

She married Arthur Kober, a theatrical press agent, on December 1, 1925. They went to Europe. In 1929, in Paris, she made a side trip to Germany where she witnessed the anti-Semitism of the embryonic Nazi movement. This experience appeared in two of her plays that she wrote later in life: Watch on the Rhine and The Searching Wind.

In 1930, she went to work for Metro-Goldwyn-Mayer reading movie scripts. It was here that she met Dashell Hammett, a mystery novelist and film writer. They became lifelong companions and he was one of the greatest influences on her life. In 1932, she had an amicable divorce from her husband.

She wrote many successful plays, including: *The Children's Hour, The Little Foxes, Another Part of the Forest, Montserrat, The Autumn Garden, The Lark, Toys in the Attic and My Mother, My Father and Me*. Hellman wrote the book that served as the basis for Leonard Bernstein's musical Candide. She also wrote many screen plays and books, and she contributed to numerous anthologies and magazines.

Hellman was subpoenaed in 1952 to appear before the House Un-American Activities Committee. Her famous response to the committee's questions was "I cannot and will not cut my conscience to fit this year's fashions." She was blacklisted and forced to sell some of her holdings to meet financial obligations.

Lillian Hellman received many awards during her life: New York Drama Critics Circle Award for Watch on the Rhine, 1941, and for Toys in the Attic, 1960; Academy Award nominations for the screenplays The Little Foxes and The North Star, and she received many honorary degrees from various universities.

Lillian Hellman died of cardiac arrest on June 30, 1984, at her summer home in Martha's Vineyard. Her four-million-dollar estate was placed in two funds: One was named for Dashell Hammett to promote writing from a leftist, radical viewpoint and the other was named after herself to promote "educational, literary, or scientific purposes to aid writers regardless of their national origin, age, sex, or political beliefs." Lillian Hellman was not intimidated by controversial themes. She was very outspoken and her writings place her in the forefront of America's greatest twentieth century writers.

183

89

Lillian D. Wald, M.D.
A Pioneer in Public Health Concerns

Lillian D. Wald was the founder of the Henry Street Visiting Nurse Service and of the Henry Street Settlement. She was also responsible for the instruction of nurses in the public schools and for insurance companies providing free visiting nurses for their policy holders.

She was born on March 10, 1867, of German-Jewish parents, Minnie and Max Wald, in Cinncinati, Ohio. Wald's family sent her to private schools. Her father was a successful merchant in optical goods in Rochester, New York. She became interested in nursing when her sister was sick and had a private nurse.

Her interest in nursing persisted, and when she was 22 years old she enrolled as a student in the New York Hospital Training School for Nurses. Two years later, in March, 1891, she graduated as a nurse. Wald took postgraduate courses where her assignment was to organize a plan for home nursing to meet the needs of the poor immigrant families on the Lower East Side of New York.

After seeing firsthand the miserable conditions that existed, she decided to move to that neighborhood so that she could be a visiting nurse there. Her friend, Mary Brewster, joined her and in the fall of 1893 they set up their office on the top floor of a tenement on Jefferson Street. Wald managed to get financial support from sponsors who recognized the importance of her work. It didn't take long for her to win the confidence of the people in the neighborhood. As the patients increased, so did her staff. She soon had four nurses, and in 1895 she moved to 265 Henry Street, which was her base for 40 years.

Wald's staff dispensed help to all who needed it regardless of race or religion. By 1913, her staff had grown to 92. When she thought about children's absences from school because of illness, she arranged for a member of her staff to provide nursing service in a public school. It was enthusiastically received and the success that it enjoyed soon led to the New York Board of Health organizing and staffing the first public nursing system in the world.

Wald went to the insurance companies to sell them on the idea of providing free visiting public health nurses to their policy holders. Metropolitan Life Insurance Company was the first one to do so in 1903, and it did not take long for other insurance companies to follow.

She recognized that the area mothers and their daughters had to be educated on home nursing, cooking and sewing. She founded the Henry Street Settlement for their education and also to provide recreation and activities for the family and the children. In 1915, Wald founded the Neighborhood Playhouse on Grand Street to help meet the cultural needs of the Lower East Side. Throughout her life she worked very hard for social reform.

Today, the Henry Street Settlement and the Visiting Nurse Service are institutions in New York City. They are testimonials to Lillian D. Wald, who only wanted people to have healthy lives. She died in 1940.

Simon Flexner

Pioneer in the Study of Pathology

S imon Flexner was a fighter against all diseases. He probed and pushed to find the causes and cures for human ailments. As a result of his work, he became the director of the Rockefeller Institute for Medical Research. He was born on March 25, 1863, in Louisville, Kentucky. Simon was the fourth of nine children of Esther and Morris Flexner. His brother Bernard became a famous lawyer and an ardent Zionist. Another brother, Abraham, was the first director at the Institute for the Advanced Study at Princeton.

Simon went to the University of Louisville to study medicine, and received his M.D. in 1889. Finding that the laboratories at the school had very few supplies, he acquired a microscope and taught himself how to use it.

He then went to Johns Hoskins Hospital in Baltimore to study pathology. He soon began to publish papers on pathology and in 1892, he became an associate in pathology in the newly opened Johns Hopkins Medical School.

He became involved with many epidemics, including one of cerebrospinal meningitis in western Maryland in 1893. In 1899, he was in Manilla where he found the strain of dysentery bacillus that became known as the Flexner type.

In 1901, the Rockefeller Institute for Medical Research was created and he was chosen to be one of seven members on the board of scientific directors. He was asked to organize and direct the laboratories on medical research.This concept of research was new to America and it was financially secure through the Rockefellers' endowments.

In 1905, New York City was hit with a severe epidemic of cerebrospinal meningitis, which Flexner had encountered 12 years before. He experimented with monkeys until he found a serum to conquer the disease.

In 1907, he found himself trying to fight an epidemic of poliomyelitis which had spread through the eastern states. He was able to isolate the infectious agent but he couldn't find a cure, since the disease was caused by a filterable virus rather than a bacterial organism. His discovery laid the basis for others to find polio vaccines some 40 years later.

Simon was the only editor of the Journal of Experimental Medicine for 19 years. During this time he wrote many articles on public health, research and education. In World War I, he was commissioned a lieutenant colonel in the Army Medical Corps and went to Europe to inspect and establish the medical facilities of the expeditionary forces. After the war, his role in the Rockefeller Institute became greater, and now included involvement in the animal pathology department at Princeton.

Flexner was active in many organizations and became an officer of quite a few. He retired from the Rockefeller Institute in 1935 and a year after was appointed an Eastman Professor at Oxford University. He died in 1946, leaving behind a legacy in the field of pathology.

91

Molly Picon

A Star of Many Stages

Molly Picon was a petite woman with many talents in the entertainment sector. Picon was a star of the Yiddish and English-speaking stages, motion pictures, radio and television. She wrote almost 100 songs and skits for the stage. She performed for the sick, the American troops in World War II and the surviving Jews in Europe. Picon also took children into her home through the Foster Parents' Plan for War Children.

Picon was the elder of two daughters of Lewis and Clara (Ostrow) Picon. She was born in a tenement in New York City on June 1, 1898. Her father was from Warsaw, Poland, and worked in the needle trades. Her mother had come from Kiev, Russia, and worked as a seamstress.

The family moved to Philadelphia when Picon was three years old. At the age of five, she sang at an amateur night for children and won five gold dollars. She made the rounds of all children's amateur nights and won many prizes and had coins tossed to her by the audience.

Picon's mother was a dressmaker for actresses. One of the actresses told her about an opening in Mike Tomashefsky's Yiddish stock company. At the age of six, Picon began playing children's parts in Tomashefsky's company. Picon toured with a vaudeville act called "The Four Seasons" in 1919. When members of the act came to Boston, they found the theaters closed due to an influenza epidemic. Out of work and out of money, Picon went to the local Yiddish theater in search of a job or to borrow money. Jacob Kalich, manager of the Grand Opera House, gave her a job. The two were married on July 29, 1919.

Kalich recognized his wife's talents. He took her to Europe to perfect her Yiddish and to star in his operetta Yankele. Picon played the role of a small boy. The tour was very successful. After they returned to the United States in 1923, the theater was sold out. Many Europeans had written to their American relatives about the greatness of Picon in Yankele.

Through the years, Picon starred in many Yiddish plays on Second Avenue. She made a Yiddish film in Warsaw called Yiddle With His Fiddle in 1936. She starred in another Yiddish film, Mamale, in 1938. She toured the American vaudeville circuit in the early 1930s. Picon's first Broadway English-speaking role was in Morning Star. She completed 19 years of radio with General Foods as its sponsor in 1951. She starred in a 13-week television show in 1948.

Picon and her husband were among the first entertainers to go to Europe after World War II to entertain the surviving Jews. They brought 700 gift packages of cosmetics and costume jewelry for women who had survived the concentration camps and candy for the children.

Picon was a member of: The Jewish Theatrical Guild, Hebrew Actors Union, Jewish Theatrical Alliance, American Actors Association, Yiddish Composers Guild, American Federation of Radio Artists, American Guild of Variety Artists and Actors Equity. She died on April 6, 1992.

92

David Sarnoff

A Radio and Television Pioneer

David Sarnoff epitomizes the American saga of "rags to riches." He rose to become a giant in the field of telecommunications after immigrating to America from Russia with his family.

He was born in a Jewish community outside of Minsk, Russia, in 1891, to Lena and Abraham Sarnoff. He was the oldest of five children. His father departed alone to the United States in 1900. His mother, who wanted him to be a scholar, sent Sarnoff to his uncle, a rabbi, where for five years he studied the Talmud for 15 hours a day. In 1905, he and his family joined his father in America.

Two days after he arrived, he was selling newspapers on the street, an endeavor he soon expanded into a newsstand. He supplemented his income by singing as a boy soprano in a synagogue choir. His father died when Sarnoff was 15, at which time he had to leave school to take a job as a messenger boy for Commercial Cable Company.

While working, he studied hard and brought himself a telegraph so that he could get a job as an operator. He was hired by the Marconi Wireless Telegraph Company as an operator, and utilized their technical library to further his studies in telecommunications.

Sarnoff then went to work as an operator for John Wannamaker, who had built a powerful radio station on top of his New York store. It was on April 14, 1912, that Sarnoff made a name for himself. He was alone at his telegraph when he picked up a message that the ocean liner TITANIC was sinking after running into an iceberg. He remained at his telegraph for the next 72 hours, receiving and sending out the names of the survivors. Marconi Wireless Company rewarded him by making him an inspector and instructor at their institute.

Sarnoff submitted the idea of transmitting music and voice over the air waves, demonstrating the concept in 1921 when he borrowed a Navy transmitter and helped give a blow-by-blow account of the Carpentier-Dempsey world championship fight. The Radio Corporation of America (RCA) management, which had put up $2,000 for this venture, made him a vice-president. Sarnoff came up with the idea of having combination phonograph and radio sets in one cabinet, which made tremendous profits for RCA.

He was a television pioneer and had a demonstration of this new technology in 1939. Sarnoff was commissioned a lieutenant colonel in the Army Signal Corps Reserve in 1924 and was promoted to full colonel in 1931. He was called to active duty in 1944 and was General Eisenhower's communication consultant in World War II.

Sarnoff was commissioned a brigadier general for his World War II service and received many decorations, including the French Legion of Merit.

In July, 1947, Sarnoff was elected chairman of RCA. He pursued his pioneering in television until he saw the successful use of color.

Sarnoff was the recipient of many honors in peacetime, too. He was on the board of directors at the Metropolitan Opera Association and Chatham Square Music School and was a trustee of New York University and Pratt Institute. David Sarnoff will be remembered as the pioneer in American communications.

191

93

Barbara W. Tuchman
Noted Historian and Journalist

Barbara Wertheim Tuchman was awarded two Pulitzer Prizes for non-fiction in her historical books on men of war and on the brink of war. She was awarded her first prize for her fourth book, The Guns of August, a study of World War I, released in 1962. Her second Pulitzer Prize was for her book Stillwell and the American Experience in China, 1911-1945, in 1971, a biography of General Stillwell, who played a major role in China in World War II.

Barbara Wertheim was born on January 30, 1912, in New York City, to Alma and Maurice Wertheim, both of their families were distinguished. Her father was a banker, publisher, philanthropist and was president of the American Jewish Committee, 1941-1943. Her maternal grandfather, Henry Morgenthau Sr., was ambassador to Turkey, and her uncle, Henry Morgenthau Jr., was Secretary of the Treasury under President Franklin D. Roosevelt.

She graduated from the Walden School and in 1933, she received a B.A. degree from Radcliffe College. She was always interested in history and her honor thesis was titled The Moral Justification for the British Empire. Tuchman went to work for *The Nation*, a magazine owned by her father. In 1937, she went to Madrid to report on the Spanish Civil War. She also reported other events for other magazines. In 1939, she married Dr.Lester

Reginald Tuchman, a New York Internist, and they had three daughters.

Tuchman wrote eleven books: *The Lost British Policy,* British policy toward Spain and the Western Mediterranean, 1938; *Bible and the Sword,* Relations between Britain and Palestine, 1956; *The Zimmermann Telegram,* a 1917 diplomatic message and its international repercussions, 1958; *The Guns of August,* the background and beginning of World War I, 1962; *The Proud Tower,* the quarter-century preceding World War I, 1966; *Stillwell and the American Experience in China,* 1911-1945, a biography of General Joseph W. Stillwell, 1971; *Notes From China,* A Trip to China, 1972; *A Distant Mirror,* The 14th Century, 1978; *Practicing History,* a collection of her shorter writings, 1981; *The March of Folly: From Troy to Vietnam,* some historical mistakes, 1984; and *The First Salute,* the American Revolution placed in an international perspective, 1988. In many of her books, Tuchman prepared herself by traveling to the areas where the events took place. Prior to her writing *The Guns of August,* she went to Europe for an on-the-spot survey of the areas where the early land battles of World War I had taken place. She followed the routes that the German armies had taken through Luxemburg, Belgium, and northern France in their attempt to reach Paris. She tried to personally familiarize herself with the history that she was writing.

Tuchman had a good hold and feeling of her vocation in history and biography. She once told an audience that "the writer's object should be to hold the reader's attention. I want the reader to turn the page and keep on turning until the end. This is accomplished only when the narrative moves steadily ahead, not when it comes to a weary standstill, overloaded with every item uncovered in the research."

Barbara W. Tuchman died of complications of a stroke on February 6, 1989, at her home in Cos Cob, Connecticut. She left behind a better understanding of what preceded and followed the men preparing for war and war itself. She made history an enjoyable readable experience.

193

94

Sylvia Porter

Great Financial Writer

S ylvia Porter was one of the most successful financial columnists and writers in America. At the height of her career, she had over 40 million people reading her syndicated financial column.

Porter was born in Patchogue, Long Island, New York, on June 18, 1913, to Rose and Louis Feldman. Her parents were Russian-Jewish immigrants and her father became a successful physician.

Her father died of a heart attack in 1925 which caused many changes in the family. Her mother changed their name to Field and built up a successful millinery business. Porter was in her freshman year in college when the stock market crashed in 1929. The shock of her mother and other people losing large sums of money raised many questions for her. She switched her major to economics so that she could understand how this all happened.

She applied for and won every cash prize that was available for economic students. She earned her Phi Beta Kappa Key in her junior year and she graduated CUM LAUDE with a B.A. Degree in 1932. A year before she graduated, she married Reed R. Porter, a bank employee who encouraged her with her work.

After college, she worked for a number of investment counseling firms and she soon became an expert in government securities. She began to write a column for the American Banker. In 1935, she went to work for the New York Post to cover Wall Street.Three years later, she became their financial editor.

During the years, her column carried the byline of S.F. Porter. She wrote her financial column in a language that was understood by her readers. Her popularity rose and she didn't shirk at exposing corruption or unethical behavior in the financial community.

She attacked Secretary of the Treasury Henry Morgenthau Jr. for his handling of the bond market and she attacked U.S. Senator Edwin Johnson, of Colorado, for his silver policy. It wasn't until 1942 that the readers discovered that S.F. Porter was a woman. The New York Post felt that the readers would accept a woman with Porter's reputation and expertise as a financial advisor and writer. Her column was syndicated throughout the country and she was in great demand for speaking engagements. In 1978, she left the Post to go to the New York Daily News where she wrote five columns a week.

Porter wrote a number of books which included: *How to Make Money in Government Bonds*, 1939; *If War Comes to the American Home*, 1941; and working together with tax expert Jacob Kay Lassser, they wrote *How to Live Within Your Income*, 1948; *Money and You*, 1949; and *Managing Your Money*, 1953. She also wrote *Sylvia Porter's Income Tax Guide*, 1960, which became an annual guide; *How to Get More for Your Money*, 1961; and in 1975, *Sylvia Porter's Money Book: How to Earn It, Spend It, Save It, Invest It, Borrow It and Use It to Better Your Life*.

Sylvia Porter has received many tributes from civic and business organizations, which included fourteen honorary doctoral degrees. She was the leading force that made it possible for women to enter the field of business and financial journalism. Her expertise combined with her ability to make business and financial language understandable for all people established her as an authority in a field dominated by men.

195

95

Jews Serve in World War II

When the Japanese bombed Pearl Harbor on December 7, 1941, and the United States declared war on Japan and Germany, American Jewish men and women responded to their country's call for the armed forces. Over 550,000 served in the Armed Forces of the United States during World War II. About 11,000 were killed and over 40,000 were wounded. There were two recipients of the Congressional Medal of Honor, 157 received the Distinguished Service Medal and Crosses, which included Navy Crosses, and 1,600 were awarded the Silver Star. About 50,242 other decorations, citations and awards were given to Jewish heroes for a total of 52,000 decorations.

Jews were 3.3 percent of the total American population but they were 4.23 percent of the Armed Forces. About 60 percent of all Jewish physicians in the United States under 45 years of age were in service uniforms.

President Franklin D.Roosevelt praised the fighting abilities and service of Jewish men and women. General Douglas MacArthur in one of his speeches said, "I am proud to join in saluting the memory of fallen American heroes of the Jewish faith." At the 50th National Memorial Service conducted by the Jewish War Veterans of the United States, General A. Vandergrift, Commandant, U.S.Marine Corps, said, "Americans of Jewish faith in the Marine Corps have served with distinction throughout the prosecution of this war. During the past year, many Jewish fighting men in our armed forces have given their lives in the cause of freedom. With profound sympathy and respect, I join you in paying homage to them at this memorial service."

The recognition of the bravery, dedication and sacrifice made by Jewish men and women in combat was expressed by the military leaders of the American Armed Forces. General Mark W. Clark, Commander, 15th Army Group, said, "Thousands of Americans of Jewish faith are serving under my command, carrying their share of the burden in the battle in Italy. Many of them have been killed in the service of their country. To American soldiers of Jewish faith go my most sincere thanks for their faithfulness, diligence and bravery in battle. To those who have passed on must go a nation's gratitude."

The role of Jews in the Navy was best expressed by Admiral Harold R. Stark, Commander, United States Navy in Europe: "The officers and men of the United States Naval Forces in Europe join to honor those gallant Americans of Jewish faith who, during the past year, have laid down their lives for their country...We mourn them as brothers-brothers who cannot be with us to share this European triumph toward which they gave their lives."

The comments made extolling the sacrifices and bravery of Jewish men and women by the military leadership of the United States in World War II were based on their exploits in the field.

96

Jewish Heroes
At Pearl Harbor

hen the Japanese attacked Pearl Harbor on that Sunday morning, December 7, 1941, Jewish fighting men stationed there quickly responded to the call to repulse the attack. Ensigns Nathan Asher and Miton Moldane were aboard the U.S.S. BLUE, a destroyer that was at sea protecting the shores of Pearl Harbor. That morning, the blue was docked for refueling. The skipper of the destroyer was on shore and Ensign Asher was in charge of the ship.

Ensign Moldane was a graduate of the Washington University Law School and a native of St. Louis. Ensign Asher was a graduate of the Naval Academy at Annapolis. Both men were having breakfast when they were informed that the Japanese had attacked the battleships anchored at Ford Island in Pearl Harbor and that they were to take the BLUE out to sea.

Asher directed the crew in heading the BLUE out. Moldane took charge of the forward machine guns and watched the ARIZONA, a battleship, take a direct hit and sink. He describes what he saw as the BLUE battled its way out to sea:

"I could see Japanese planes coming down about 30 or 40 feet over our heads, dropping bombs and shooting at anything that happened to come along. Our ship kept firing at the planes as it headed out to sea. I went out to the bridge to help Asher when we both saw a Japanese plane that the BLUE's guns had hit go into a pineapple field. The men gave out a cheer when they saw the plane burst into flames. It took the BLUE one hour and a half to reach the open seas."

At Hickam Field young Private Louis Shleifer, U.S. Army Air Corps, of Newark, New Jersey, was on his way to breakfast when he heard the sounds of airplane motors. He looked out his window and saw Japanese planes dropping bombs on the field and strafing American planes.

Schleifer grabbed his helmet and his .45-caliber revolver and dashed onto the field to help the other men move some of the planes into hagars. As he was moving the planes, he saw Japanese planes headed his way strafing the men and planes before them. He drew out his revolver and kept firing at the planes until he was mortally wounded. There is a memorial fountain for Private Louis Schleifer in the garden of Temple Beth Shalom, Livingston, New Jersey.Every year on December 7, the Pearl Harbor Survivors Association holds services at this fountain.

Lee Goldfarb, Jersey City, New Jersey, was a 3rd Class radioman on the U.S.S. Oglala. He had just finished his watch at 7 a.m. and was preparing to get some sleep when he heard the sounds of aircraft motors. He looked out of his porthole and he saw Japanese planes attacking the seven battleships tied up at Ford Island, one ship after another getting hit with torpedoes. He went to his battle station to defend his ship agaisnt the enemy, when it was struck by a torpedo and sank.

There were many other Jewish fighting men at Pearl Harbor. Radio Mechanic 3rd Class Rosenthal gave his life aboard the U.S.S. California. From Philadelphia, there were Alex Sherman, of the U.S.S. New Orleans, Ben Lichtman, of the U.S.S. West Virginia, and Irvin Greben, at the Naval Air Stationin Kaneohe Bay. From Overland Park, Kansas, Stan Levitt was aboard the U.S.S. Rigel, and Bernard Rubien, of Rancho Mirage, California, was at Hickam Field.

Jewish fighting men served, fought and died at Pearl Harbor when the Japanese attacked the United States. The heroism that these men displayed has been recorded in the military records of our country. We can be proud of them!

97

Three Jewish Heroes
of World War II

Many Jewish men and women emerged as heroes during combat in World War II. At times they sacrficed their lives and at other times, they suffered serious wounds. Whether on land, or in the air or at sea, Jews were there fighting alongside their fellow Americans.

It was on the first day of the war that Sergeant Meyer Levin and his teammate, Captain Colin Kelly, gave America something to cheer about. They were flying off the coast of the Philippines when they spotted the Japanese battleship Haruna. Captain Kelly flew his bomber over the Haruna. At that moment, Levin, who was the bombardier, launched his bombs scoring a direct hit to sink the Haruna. They were recognized for their bravery in America and songs were written about them.

In the Battle of the Coral Sea, in the Pacific, Levin launched the bombs that destroyed a large transport filled with enemy troops. In January 1943, Levin had flown more than 60 missions. It was on the way back to his base from a mission that Levin once again became a hero in an incident which cost him his life.

His plane found itself in a severe thunderstorm and the fuel tank was reading empty. The pilot tried to gain altitude but couldn't and he landed the plane on the rough seas. Levin climbed out of his bomb bay and started to unhook the life rafts for the men to use. The plane was struck by a large wave which broke the plane in two, trapping Levin. The crew in their rafts watched in horror as they saw the plane go down with Levin in it.

Sergeant Meyer Levin was only 25 when he was killed. In the few years that he served, he was awarded the Distinguished Flying Cross, the Silver Star and Oak Leaf Cluster, the Purple Heart and the Certificate of Merit.

Fighting on land in the Pacific was a Marine named Barney Ross, who was a world champion in three classes of professional boxing-lightweight, junior-welterweight, and welterweight. When Pearl Harbor was attacked, he was an old man in boxing-33 years. He appeared at a Marine recruiting station to enlist. While his fighting days were over, they weren't over in fighting his country's enemies.

It was on Guadalcanal, in the Pacific, on November 20, 1942, that Barney Ross was on a patrol when he and his attachment ran into an advance party of Japanese. A hard fought skirmish began with close quarter combat. The Japanese had wounded most of his patrol. After tending to the wounded, Barney Ross began attacking the enemy by himself. The fighting lasted until the morning when help arrived. He had used up his ammunition and had to use what was left by the wounded. He received the Silver Star for his bravery.

Sergeant Theodore Billen was a gunner on a bomber. He was in the Pacific and flew over 250 missions under enemy fire. He helped evacuate men and equipment from Northern Australia and Java. His plane was in combat over Rabaul where he was credited with shooting down two Zeroes.

Sergeant Billen was in many combat missions. He received the Distinguished Flying Cross, the Air Medal, two squadron citations and a third citation signed by Generals MacArthur and Kenney. He was one of the many Jews to be recognized in the Pacific for their bravery in combat.

98

Two Jewish Medal of Honor Recipients in World War II

Isadore S. Jachman and his parents came to this country from Berlin when he was two years old. They settled in Baltimore, where he graduated from Baltimore City College. After Japan attacked Pearl Harbor, he enlisted in the Army.

Sergeant Jachman was a paratrooper who saved his company from annihilation at Flamierge, Belgium. There was a fierce and bitterly fought engagement there on January 4, 1945. Jachman, without regard for his own safety, pushed through the enemy's wall of concentrated fire and single-handedly saved the day.

He received the Congressional Meal of Honor posthumously. The citation reads as follows:

Sergeant Jachman, Company B, 513th Parachute Infantry Regiment, distinguished himself by conspicuous gallantry and intrepidity above and beyond the call of duty at Flamierge, Belgium, on the fourth day of January 1945. When his company was pinned down by enemy artillery, mortar and small arms fire, two hostile tanks attacked the unit inflicting heavy casualties.Sergeant Jachman, seeing the desperate plight of his comrades, left his place of cover, with total disregard for his own safety, dashed across open ground, through a hail of fire and seizing a bazooka from a fallen comrade, advanced on the tanks, which concentrated their fire on him. Firing the weapon alone, he damaged one and forced both to retire, Sergeant Jachman's heroic action, in which he suffered fatal wounds, disrupted the entire enemy attack, reflecting the highest credit upon himself and the Parachute Infantry.

Second Lieutenant Raymond Zussman was the other Congressional Medal of Honor recipient in World War II. He was raised in Detroit and he entered the Army when he was 23 years old. He was killed in France, several days after the engagement that won him the Congressional Medal of Honor. He was 26 years old.

Zussman was a tank officer and it was in a street-fighting battle at the village of Noroy-le-Bourg, in the Rhone Valley, that he displayed his heroism. He was the officer in charge of a tank which became disabled in the field. He took a carbine and on foot proceeded in front of another tank to guide it through the village streets. With his own weapon, while directing the tank's fire as they went through the streets, he killed 19 enemy soldiers, took 93 prisoners and captured two anti-tank guns, a flak gun, two machine guns and two trucks.

Zussman guided the tank through booby traps that were setup by the Germans and directed its fire to destroy the enemy machine gun positions. When his carbine ran out of ammunition, he picked up a Tommy gun to use. Fearing a trap at one intersection, Zussman went in alone to seek out the enemy. When the tank came around the corner of the intersection, he had 30 prisoners and two anti-tank guns that they were using.

Jachman and Zussman, noncommissioned officer and officer, exemplified the bravery and courage of Jewish fighting men in World War II. Their stories of valor are the answer to those who would question the fighting ability and courage of Jews serving in the armed forces of America.

99

Captain Ben L. Salomon

World War II Soldier-Dentist
Recipient of the
Congressional Medal of Honor

It took 58 years for Captain Ben L. Salomon to receive the Congressional Medal of Honor (CMOH) due to a technical error, which was finally corrected.

Salomon was born on September 1, 1914, in Milwaukee, WI, as the only child of Bess and Ben Salomon. In his youth, he was involved in Scouting. Salomon worked his way through the ranks to become an Eagle Scout. He graduated from the School of Dentistry, University of Southern California in 1937.

After graduation, he first tried to enlist in the Canadian and the United States Armies, but they had no need for a dentist. He then opened a dental practice in Los Angeles. In 1940, President Roosevelt signed the Selective Service and Training Act and Ben Salomon registered for the draft. He was one of the first to be called and he became a private in the infantry. After a year and a half as an enlisted man, his commission came through and he became the regiment dentist for the 105th Infantry in Hawaii.

The citation gives the details of the bravery of Captain Ben L. Salomon:

"Captain Ben L. Salomon was serving in Saipan, in the Marianas Islands on July 7, 1944, as the Surgeon for the 1st and 2nd Battalions.The Regiment's 1st and 2nd Battalions were attacked by an overwhelming force estimated between 3,000 to 5,000 Japanese soldiers. It was one of the largest attacks attempted in the Pacific Theater during World War II. Although both units fought furiously, the enemy soon penetrated the Battalions' combined perimeter and inflicted overwhelming casualties.

In the first few minutes of the attack, approximately 30 soldiers walked, crawled or were carried into Captain Salomon's aid station and the small tent soon filled with wounded men. As the perimeter began to be overrun. it became increasingly difficult for Captain Salomon to work on the wounded. He then saw a Japanese soldier bayoneting one of the wounded men near the tent. Firing from a squatting position, Captain Salomon quickly killed the enemy soldier. Then, as he turned his attention back to the wounded, two more Japanese soldiers appeared in the front entrance of the tent. As these enemy soldiers were killed, four more crawled under the tent walls.

Rushing them, Captain Salomon kicked the knife out of the hand of one, shot another and bayonetted a third. Captain Solomon butted the fourth enemy soldier in the stomach and a wounded comrade then shot and killed the enemy soldier.

Realizing the gravity of the situation, Captain Salomon ordered the wounded to make their way back as best they could back to the regimental aid station, while he attempted to hold off the enemy until they were clear. Captain Salomon then grabbed a rifle from one of the wounded and rushed out of the tent. After four men were killed manning a machine gun, Captain Salomon took control of it.

When his body was later found, 98 dead enemy soldiers were piled in front of his position. Captain Salomon's extraordinary heroism and devotion to duty are in keeping with the highest traditions of military service and reflect great credit upon himself, his men and the United States Army."

205

100

Rabbi Alexander Goode

Chaplain/Hero of World War II

On February 3, 1943, the S.S. Dorshester, carrying 900 American servicemen headed for combat, was working its way through the icy churning waters off Greenland when it was struck by a U-boat torpedo. It was forced to leave the convoy and it didn't take long before a second torpedo scored a direct hit killing 100 men in the hull of the ship.

Throughout the ship there was confusion, terror and chaos as men scrambled about to get their life jackets and in many cases to get dressed. Trying to calm the men were four chaplains: Rabbi Alexander D. Goode; John P. Washington, a Roman Catholic priest; George L. Fox, a Methodist minister; and Clark P. Poling, a minister of the Reformed Church of America.

The extra life jackets were handed out but there were still many servicemen without them. Standing in front of the four chaplains were four men without life jackets. They were cold and afraid. The four chaplains took off their jackets and gave them to these men. The ship was quickly sliding into the sea. Many lifeboats were filled with men in the water and others were being launched.The four chaplains went about the deck helping the men get into lifeboats and comforting those that were terrified. Finally, all the lifeboats were on the waters filled with the remaining troops.

The last sight that these survivors saw of the Dorshester was the four chaplains clinging to each other on the slanting deck as it slowly went into the sea. Their arms were linked together with their heads bowed as they prayed to their God: "Shma Yisroel Adonai Elohenu Adonai Echod...Our Father...which art in heaven...Hallowed be Thy name...Thy kingdom come...Thy will be done."

Benjamin Epstein, a survivor of New York, recalls that fateful night. He personally knew each of the chaplains and he will never forget watching them go down with the ship. Of the 900 men aboard, only 229 were saved.

Rabbi Goode was the son of a rabbi in Washington, D.C. He won many medals for tennis, swimming and track while going through Eastern High School in Washington D.C. While he was studying to be a rabbi, he was an active participant in the National Guard. Goode married a high school classmate and they had a daughter. He wasn't content in only healing men's souls; he felt he had to also heal their bodies. When he got his first synagogue, he traveled to Johns Hopkins University, 45 miles away, to become a medical doctor.

On February 13, 1951, President Harry S. Truman dedicated the Chapel of the Four Chaplains on the corner of Broad and Berks streets in Philadelphia, Pennsylvania. This inter-faith chapel is a memorial, for these four chaplains who gave their lives to save others. There are three altars: Catholic, Jewish, and Protestant. Above the entrance burns an eternal light which calls all men to the unity these four chaplains heroically demonstrated. The Chapel of the Four Chaplains has been relocated to Valley Forge, Pennsylvania.

Rabbi Goode was one of 309 rabbis to be commissioned in World War II. He was one of many to give his life.

207

101

Lt. Frances Slanger

Jewish Nurse in World War II

On the morning of October 21, 1944, Lieutenant Frances Slanger of the U.S. Army Nurses Corps mailed a letter to STARS AND STRIPES telling the GIs how proud she was of them. That evening her unit was the target of a German artillery barrage when one of their shells burst near her. She and three other nurses were hit by shell fragments. While she lay there dying, she never uttered a word of complaint. She was concerned about the other nurses who were hit and she was worried about the grief her death would bring to her family back in Boston. That evening, she died. Her letter was published on November 7, 1944.

Slanger was raised in Roxbury, Massachusetts. She was commissioned a lieutenant in the U.S. Army Nurses Corps and was stationed in the U.S. field hospital.

She was short and a brunette and she was one of the first nurses to land in France, wading ashore with the hospital platoon. She had to hold on to the belts of the soldiers to keep from being swept off her feet in the waves. Once she landed, she started to take care of the wounded and sick soldiers who were sent to the back lines for medical treatment.

It was while taking care of the wounded that Slanger began to appreciate the sacrifices that these men were making. She felt that she had to express this feeling and she decided to write her letter to STARS AND STRIPES, the newspaper for the GIs:

I'm writing this by flashlight. The GIs say we rough it, but we in our little tent can't see it. We wade ankle deep in mud. You have to lie in it. We are restricted to our immediate area, a cow pasture or a hay field, but then who is not restricted? We have a stove and coal. We even have a laundry line in the tent. Our GI drawers are at this moment doing the dance of the pants, what with the wind howling, the tent waving precariously, the rain beating down, the guns firing...Sure we rough it. But you, the men behind the guns, driving our tanks, flying our planes, sailing our ships, building our bridges and the men who pave the way and the men who were left behind—it is to you we doff our helmets. To every GI wearing the American uniform, for you we have the greatest admiration and respect.

Slanger was buried in a military cemetery in France. Her grave was flanked by the fighting men that she admired and respected. Over her grave was the Star of David telling the world that here lies a Jewish heroine who died fighting for her country. Years later, her grave was moved to a Jewish cemetery in Boston area. Jewish women veterans formed an all female chapter of the Jewish War Veterans of the USA, and named it Lieutenant Frances Slanger Memorial Post in honor of the first Army nurse to lose her life in World War II.

102

Two Jewish Heroes in the Pacific

Heroes are not born; they are made when confronted with a situation that calls for action beyond the expected. So it was for two young Jewish fighting men in the Pacific fighting the Japanese in World War II. Army medical aide Hyman Epstein of Omaha, Nebraska, and Marine Corporal LeRoy Diamond of New York City, are two such heroes.

Epstein's outfit was in New Guniea, fighting the Japanese alongside the Australians. George Weller, an American war correspondent, wrote about the last 12 hours of Epstein's life as it was related to him by his commanding officer, Major Bert Zeeff.

Epstein's unit was sent to the front lines to bring supplies and to take care of the wounded of a platoon that had been pinned down by the enemy. The Japanese had staked out their snipers in the trees and set up two machine guns that would give them crossfire. When Epstein's unit arrived, the Japanese opened up with their machine guns, while the snipers gave them additional support. A number of Americans were killed; Major Zeeff woudn't let his medics risk their lives to go out to help the wounded.

Epstein decided that he would help the wounded and started to crawl toward them, becoming the target of the Japanese machine guns. He went from one wounded soldier to another applying sulfanilamide and bandages to their wounds. This continued all night until a bullet found its mark and he was mortally wounded. He was buried the next day by his men who had felt that he had gone beyond the call of duty.

Guadalcanal was the beginning of the American counter offensive to retake the islands that the Japanese had captured after Pearl Harbor. It was here, in August 1942, that Marine Corporal LeRoy Diamond, along with Privates Albert A.Schmidt and Johnny Rivers, were in their machine gun nest next to a stream, waiting for the Japanese to stage a counter attack.

A few scattered shots from the enemy built up to a crescendo as hundreds crossed the stream, firing their guns. Johnny Rivers was killed immediately. Schmidt kept firing his machine gun as Diamond kept feeding it belts of bullets. The fighting was fierce; Japanese bodies kept falling from Schmidt's gun. Diamond kept feeding the gun until he felt a burning sensation in his arm and he knew that he was wounded. He picked up Rivers' automatic weapon, firing it with his good arm.

The Japanese managed to get a few snipers in the trees behind them and one of them shot Schmidt in the face, blinding him. Diamond verbally told him what direction to keep firing the machine gun and they continued to shoot down the enemy.

When they were finally rescued, there were about 200 Japanese dead in front of them. The heroism displayed by Diamond and his squad became the plot of a great war movie, The Pride of the Marines.Diamond received the Navy Cross and Purple Heart for his heroism and his name will always be part of that long list of Jewish heroes in America.

103

"Mickey" Marcus

A Hero in both America and Israel

David "Mickey" Marcus is a hero who fought for the two countries he loved, America and Israel, and was recognized for military exploits by both their armies. Born on New York's Lower East Side, he graduated from West Point in 1924. While in the Army, he studied law and when he entered civilian life in 1927, he joined the U.S. Attorney General's Office.

New York Mayor Fiorello LaGuardia admired Marcus and persuaded him to join the city's Department of Corrections in 1934; he was appointed commissioner in 1940. When World War II erupted, Marcus went back to the Army as a lieutenant colonel. Appointed a divisional judge advocate and later division commander, he attended the meetings of the "Big Five" in 1943. When the Allies decided to invade Normandy, Marcus volunteered to join the D-Day airborne assault. With no previous training, he joined paratroopers and parachuted into Normandy.

In 1945, Marcus joined General Lucius D. Clay's staff to help oversee a military government in Germany after the Nazi's defeat. Marcus was awarded the Distinguished Service Cross, Bronze Star, and British decorations. In 1947, he retired from the Army with the rank of colonel.

Marcus couldn't forget entering the Dachau concentration camp at the head of a tank column and seeing the living and dead Jews. He resolved that he would help Israel survive so that Jews would have a place to live there if they chose.

The Hagganah and the Jewish Agency contacted him, asking him to go to Israel to help build up the fledgling army. Using the name of Mickey Stone, he was smuggled past the British soldiers in January 1948. At one check-point, he was stopped and asked to produce his identification. The British sentry, who wasn't too alert, accepted the forged papers with the name of Mickey Stone. If he had looked carefully, he would have seen Marcus' West Point ring. Marcus worked day and night training the raw Israeli recruits, trying to shape them into soldiers. It was expected that the Transjordan Arab League would be attacking at any time in the hope of destroying Israel.

Marcus returned to America briefly, returning to Israel in May 1948. He was appointed commander of the Jerusalem front and was the first officer to receive the new rank of alluf (brigadier general). Marcus was instrumental in organizing schools for officers, writing manuals, teaching the various uses of armament and helping to develop a fighting spirit within the army.

During the early morning hours of June 11, 1948, Marcus was inspecting the perimeter fence of his military headquarters in Abu Ghosh when an Israeli sentry mistook him for the enemy and accidentally killed him. He was honored by the Israeli military for his leadership and contributions to the defense of Israel.

Taken back to the United States, David "Mickey" Marcus was buried at West Point with full military honors. Mishmar Davis is a village in Judea that is named for him. Marcus was a person blessed to become a hero in two countries that he loved.

104

Two Jewish Junior Officers of World War II

Milton A. ("Mickey") Waldor of New Jersey exemplified the Jewish hero in the American junior officer corps. First Lieutenant Waldor was bombardier in the Tenth Air Force in the China-Burma-India Theater of Operation in World War II.

Waldor flew on 68 arduous missions bombing the Japanese installations in captured Burma. Many times his B-24 was the target for enemy fighter planes and anti-aircraft guns. Flying the China-Burma-India hump was always an extremely dangerous mission. For his bravery in action, Waldor was awarded tthe Distinguished Flying Cross, the Air Medal with Oak Leaf Cluster, the Nationalist China Award and other American medals. On his many missions he met and became friendly with General Claire Chennault, the leader of the Flying Tigers, who was later to become the commander of the U.S. Air Force in China.

When Waldor left the Air Force to return to civilian life, he was a captain. He became a successful lawyer and he got involved in politics and in veterans organizations. He was elected national commander of the Jewish War Veterans of the USA in 1965. He served as a senator in the New Jersey Senate and wrote a book which exposed the John Birch

Society called Peddlers of Fear. His younger brother, Jerome N. Waldor, is a retired Major General of the U.S. Air Force and he is a leader in the United Jewish Federation of MetroWest.

In the Pacific, the United States Marines were fighting to regain the major islands that the Japanese had captured in the early stages of the war. Major Irving Schecter of New York, with his assault unit, landed on the beach in Tinian, one of the Marianas islands. They were met with gunfire from the enemy as they established a beachhead to protect the left flank of the invasion force.

After a quiet night, Major Schecter and his Marines were awakened by a barrage of Japanese gunfire and hand grenades. His men quickly responded with their own gunfire to keep the overwhelming force of Japanese from breaking through the lines.The skirmish lasted for many hours, and Major Schecter's fighting Marines were diminishing in number as they suffered many casualties. Finally a relief force came to their rescue and pushed the Japanese back to their own lines.

Major Schecter found himself once again fighting the enemy when the Marines invaded Saipan. He led his rifle company into battle with the Japanese, exposing himself so that he could better guide his men with their rifle fire. His unit suffered many casualties and he directed the evacuation of the wounded until they were relieved by another Marine Corps unit.

Major Schecter was recognized for his bravery when he was awarded the Navy Cross, the Bronze Star Medal, the Purple Heart and a Presidential Unit Citation.

Milton Waldor and Irving Schecter were the prototypes of the many Jewish heroes in the junior officer corps in World War II.

105

Jewish Army Generals who Served with Distinction in World War II

Generaleneral Maurice Rose proved to be a hero in World War I and World War II. In World War I, he was a second lieutenant in the American Expeditionary Force that fought the Germans on French soil. When the war was over, he decided to make the Army his profession. In World War II, he served as chief of staff of the 2nd Armored Division and was promoted to brigadier general in 1943.

The Second Armored Division was shipped to North Africa, where Rose was involved in many tank battles with the Germans. When the German Army surrendered, General Rose negotiated the unconditional surrender of the Germans in Tunisia. He received the nickname of "Old Gravel Face" because he was very brusque in his dealings with the Germans. He was then assigned to command the 3rd Armored Division in Europe. In 1944, he was promoted to major general. He led his tanks in combat against the Germans through France, Belgium and into Germany. It was in a fierce battle in Germany that General Rose was killed.

Rose was awarded the Distinguished Service Medal, the Silver Star Medal and the Purple Heart. The French Army bestowed upon him the Legion of Honor and the Croix de Guerre. The American press mourned his death as they extolled his bravery and feats in combat. *The New York Times* wrote: "The American Army was deprived of one of its most skilled and gallant officers and a man of rare personal charm besides..." *The Chicago Daily News* said: "He had the reputation of a remarkable leader of men. German prisoners talked of him as the only successor of the status of Rommel..."

The North American Newspaper Alliance wrote: "I think in Maurice Rose's death this Army has suffered its greatest single loss—great as the loss of Stonewall Jackson in the Civil War. He was a perfect example of the American soldier at his best..."

General Rose's 3rd Armored Division had many singular feats: it was the first division to cross the German border; the first to breach the Siegfried line; the first to shoot down an enemy plane on German soil; and the first to fire an artillery shell into German soil. Rose was the son of Rabbi and Mrs. Samuel Rose and was born in Middletown, Connecticut, in 1889. He was buried with military honors in 1945.

Brigadier General Julius Ochs Adler is another decorated hero of World Wars I and II. In World War I, he was the commander of a battalion of infantry on the Western Front in France. He was in many battles with the Germans and was gassed.

In World War II, General Adler commanded the 77th Infantry Division, responsible for the defense of Hawaii from 1941 to 1944. For his leadership and bravery in World War I, he received the Distinguished Service Cross, the Silver Star with Oak Leaf Clusters, the Purple Heart, the French Legion of Honor and the Croix de Guerre with Palms. In 1948, he was appointed as major general in the Army Reserve.

After World War II, he joined *The New York Times* as vice-president, later to become general manager. He was also the publisher of the *Chattanooga Times*. He and 17 other newspaper executives were invited by General Eisenhower to visit the liberated concentration camps in 1945. This visit inspired him to write a series of articles for *The New York Times* describing his experience and feelings.

Generals Maurice Rose and Julius Adler are typical of the many Jewish general staff officers who served their country with distinction and bravery in the U.S. Army.

106

Jewish Naval & Marine Corps Officer Heroes in World War II

In World War II the Japanese propaganda featured the myth that their fighting men are never taken as prisoners. The purpose was to create an illusion that they were invincible. Major General Melvin Krulewitch, the highest-ranking Jewish officer in the U.S. Marine Corps, was one of the first to destroy that myth. He personally captured Japanese prisoners in one of his engagements. Major General Krulewitch was the first to fly the American flag on Japanese territory.

Fighting in World War II to defend America from its enemies was nothing new to Major General Krulewtich. In World War I, he enlisted in the U.S. Marine Corps as a private. His outfit went to France to fight the German Army, and he proved himself to be a hero in Belleau Woods. After World War I, he returned to civilian life to raise a family and establish a successful law practice. When the Japanese attacked Pearl Harbor, he rejoined the Marine Corps as an officer.

Major General Krulewitch was awarded the Bronze Star with Clusters, the Purple Heart, a Presidential Unit Citation and the Naval Unit Citation. He also received a Special Commendation Ribbon of the Secretary of the Navy. During the Korean War, he was sent on special assignment.

When the nation of Israel was born and needed skilled military officers to instruct and develop its fledgling army, Major General Krulewitch joined other World War II Jewish heroes in going there to be of service.

When Admiral Ben Moreel received his fourth star, he became the highest-ranking Jewish officer in Navy history. Admiral Moreel was another hero who fought in two wars for his country. In World War I, he enlisted in the Navy and was commissioned to be a lieutenant (junior grade). He was assigned to the Civil Engineering Corps and promotions followed swiftly. In the 1930s, he served as public works officer at Pearl Harbor, and then became chief of civil engineers of the Navy. He was promoted to the rank of rear admiral and in 1944, President Roosevelt made him a vice admiral.

Admiral Moreel, starting with 3,000 men, formed the Seabees when World War II erupted. It had grown to about a quarter of a million men when the war ended. His Seabees developed airfields, roads and housing in undeveloped islands in the Pacific.

Rear Admiral Louis Dreller was a veteran and hero of World Wars I and II. In June 1918, he was commissioned a lieutenant (junior grade) in World War I and he was assigned for engineering duty. After the war, he remained in the Navy and rapidly rose through the ranks to become a rear admiral in 1943. In World War II, he saw action as a member of the staff of Commander Amphibious Force, Pacific (April 10 to May 7, 1942).

Returning to the United States, he reported to Headquarters, Fourth Naval District, Philadelphia, designing destroyers which were built there for the Brazilian Navy. Admiral Dreller was recognized for his services for many assignment by being awarded the Legion of Merit.

From the Revolutionary War through World War II, Jews have distinguished themselves in the United States Navy, from seamen to a four star admiral, in serving our country.

107

Staff Sergeant Max Warshaw

Highly Decorated Hero of World War II

Staff Sergeant Max Warshaw was awarded 11 medals and a Combat Medic Badge in World War II and he never carried or fired a firearm. He was an Army medic attached to the 26th Infantry Regiment of the First Division, nicknamed "big red one."

Warshaw was born in December 1913, in Korbin, Poland. He was the son of Blanche, nee Pollack, and Jacob Warshaw.They came to the U.S. in 1923 seeking freedom and the opportunity to earn a living. He was educated in the public schools of New York City and later became a linen supply salesman.In March, 1941, he entered the Army.

When Pearl Harbor was attacked by the Japanese and the United States was at war with Japan and Germany, his division was sent to North Africa. As a medic, Warshaw never carried a firearm. The only apparatus he carried was medical to help the wounded.

Warshaw always volunteered for the dangerous assignments. As a Jew, he felt that he had to show the others that Jews weren't afraid to face danger. He received his first Bronze Star medal on November 8, 1942, in the North African Campaign. His regiment was fighting the Germans in Oran, Algeria. He risked his life by exposing himself to the enemy to help his regiment's wounded lying in open areas.

Two days later, on November 10, in Algeria, Warshaw was wounded by shrapnel. "An artillery shell blew up right near me," he recalled, "it didn't knock me out and I didn't require hospitalization. However, for many years I would still need to have artillery shrapnel removed."

Warshaw received his first Silver Star medal for gallantry in action in the vicinity of El Guettar, Tunisia, March 25, 1943.The citation reads, "...when a heavy enemy artillery barrage had compelled two drivers to abandon their vehicles, Sergeant Warshaw fearlessly entered this area and removed the vehicles, thereby saving valuable equipment from destruction." On D-Day, he landed with his outfit in Normandy, where he was one of the first to hit Omaha Beach. It was for his heroism on June 14 and 15, 1944, that he received his second Bronze Star medal.

His division kept pushing the German Army back to its own country. It was in Aachen, Germany, on October 13, 1944, that Warshaw received his third Bronze Star medal. He constantly exposed himself to the enemy to administer first aid to the wounded. Three days later, on October 15, 1944, he was again awarded the Silver Star medal for heroism and gallantry beyond the call of duty.

On November 25, 1944, Staff Sergeant Max Warshaw was captured by the Germans. They gave him a medical kit to care for the other prisoners of war. He was liberated five months later and sent to England for medical care.

Max Warshaw returned to civilian life after the war and he became active in many veterans' organizations. In 1956, he and his wife, Evelyn, moved to Fair Lawn, New Jersey, where he held many positions in the Jewish War Veterans of the USA.

Warshaw is one of the most highly decorated Jews who served in World War II. He has two Silver Star medals, three Bronze Star medals, the Purple Heart, the Ex-Prisoner of War Medal, the Pre-Pearl Harbor Medal, the European Theater of Operations Medal with six campaign clusters, the Victory Medal, the New York State Conspicuous Cross Medal (for highly decorated veterans), and the Army Combat Medic Badge. Max Warshaw is not only a hero, but a legend in the Jewish heroes in America.

108

P.F.C. *Charles Feuereisen*

A Hero Talks with General MacArthur

P.F.C.Charles Feuereisen's unit in the 511th Parachute Infantry Division had a fierce battle with the Japanese in 1945 in Leyte, Philippines, during World War II.The unit overran the enemy and captured many of them.

In a dead Japanese officer's briefcase, a map of California with Japanese site marks for their invasion was found by the unit. Feuereisen and P.F.C. Ralph Merisiecki were assigned to take the map back to the 11th Airborne headquarters near Buraueng. They delivered the document and proceeded to Tacioban, where General Douglas MacArthur had established his headquarters and where they were to get an airlift back to their unit. "Ralph, we'll never get this close to General MacArthur again," Feuereisen said to his friend, "Why don't we visit him?"

Merisiecki thought that Feuereisen was crazy, but he decided to go along with him. They came to the Price House, where MacArthur had his headquarters. It was full of bullet and shrapnel marks.The two worked their way through a maze of officers and reporters, finally reaching Lieutenant Colonel Roger O. Egeberg, the supreme commander's physician and aide, and explained their purpose for being there.

Before long, MacArthur appeared and warmly greeted them with a smile and handshake. He took them into his private office to talk about the military actions of the 11th Airborne paratroopers. Feuereisen was surprised to find how much information the general knew about his outfit. MacArthur spent about 10 minutes talking with them. Before leaving, Feuereisen asked him why the paratroopers were not jumping behind the enemy lines. MacArthur assured him that they would be jumping soon.

Feuereisen made 38 jumps with the 511th Parachute Infantry Division. He joined the division in 1942 and rose through the ranks to become a sergeant. He led a patrol to find the enemy on April 6, 1945, in Lipa, Philippines. As the patrol members proceeded, a booby trap went off, killing the lead man. Feuereisen was wounded by a sniper in the back of the neck, paralyzing his legs and his left arm. He was hospitalized for nine months before he was able to overcome the paralysis.

Feuereisen received many decorations, including the Silver Star Medal, the Bronze Star Medal, the Purple Heart Medal and the Asiatic Pacific Medal with Oak Leaf Clusters.

He was born on May 18, 1918, in New York City, to Regina, nee Fuchs, and Henry Feuereisen. His mother had emigrated from Vienna and his father came from Cracow. Feuereisen's father was in the grocery store business. His young son learned the skills that he used to make a living in the food industry.

After Feuereisen's release from the service, he became involved with veterans organizations. His first love was the Jewish War Veterans (JWV) of the USA. He worked hard and held many JWV chairs. At the JWV convention in August, 1968, Feuereien was elected to be the national commander for one year. Feuereisen has raised hundreds of thousands of dollars for the Jewish War Veterans Memorial Museum in Washington, D.C. He says he feels that this museum, located in the heart of the nation's capital, is a beacon that reminds America that Jews have served, fought and died for their country from colonial days to the present.

223

109

"Hank" Greenberg

A Baseball Great & War Hero

Henry "Hank" Greenberg was one of the first men in baseball to seriously challenge Babe Ruth's record of 60 home runs and Lou Gehrigs' league record of 184 runs batted in.

Greenberg had a chance to shatter Ruth's home run record of 60 in 1938. He had hit 58 home runs and still had five games to play. But the weather was dismal and he faced several erratic pitchers. He failed in his attempt to hit a home run. Greenberg batted in 183 runs in 1937, falling one short of tying Gehrig's record. He did set a major league record of hitting two or more home runs in one game (11 in 1938). Greenberg was elected to Baseball's Hall of Fame and was twice named the Most Valuable Player of the Year.

Greenberg was born on New Year's Day in 1911. His parents had immigrated to New York City from Bucharest, Romania. He attended public schools in the Bronx, New York, and was on the baseball and basketball teams of James Monroe High School. Major league teams were interested in having Greenberg play for them. Greenberg's father turned away the baseball scouts since he wanted his son to attend college. He attended New York University on a baseball scholarship. His parents let him play professional baseball in 1930.

Greenberg spent three years in the minor leagues, perfecting his hitting and working on his clumsy movements on the field. He was called up to play with the Detroit Tigers in 1933. He had a .301 hitting average for the season. The following year, at the age of 23, Greenberg had become the star of the team.

The Detroit Tigers were in contention for winning the penant in 1934. An important game was scheduled to take place on Rosh Hashana. After much soul searching, Greenberg decided to play that day. His two home runs made it possible for the Tigers to win. However, when a game was scheduled for Yom Kippur, he did not play. He spent the day at the synagogue praying and fasting. The Tigers lost the game, but they did win the pennant for the first time since 1909. They lost the World Series to the St. Louis Cardinals.

When Greenberg was drafted into the Army in May of 1941, he was the highest paid player in major league baseball. He was discharged two days prior to the bombing of Pearl Harbor because of a new government policy to release those soldiers over the age of 28. Greenberg immediately re-enlisted. For the next four years, he served as a lieutenant and then as a captain in the Army Air Force. He was involved in the fighting in the China-Burma-India area.

Greenberg returned to baseball on July 1, 1945. The Detroit Tigers' ball park was filled to capacity to greet him. He needed to hit one more home run to have a total of 250. After he hit a home run, the fans gave Greenberg a standing ovation as he trotted around the bases.

Greenberg's last year with the Detroit Tigers was 1946. He led the league with 44 home runs and 127 runs batted in. He was waived out of the American League to the Pittsburgh Pirates. Greenberg was with the Pirates for one year and hit 25 home runs and drove in 74 runs during 125 games. In 1947, he was given his unconditional release. Greenberg turned his talents to Wall Street and became a millionaire. On the field, Greenberg demonstrated his playing powers. In World War II, he didn't shirk his duty as an American. As a Jew, he didn't forget his heritage. Greenberg died on September 4, 1986.

110

Paul Muni
Yiddish Theater and Movie Star

D espite his successes in the American theater and movies, Academy Award winner Paul Muni's first love was the Yiddish theater. Muni's acting career started in the Yiddish theater when he as a young boy.

Muni was originally named Mehilem Weisenfeund and was born in Lemberg, Austria, now Lvov, U.S.S.R., on September 22, 1895. He was the son of Salche and Nacham Favel Weisenfreund, itinerant Yiddish entertainers. The Weisenfeunds traveled throughout Austria-Hungary to Yiddish-speaking villages and performed brief plays, songs, and dances.

After a brief stay in London, where their little variety theater failed, they arrived in America in 1901. At the age of 13, Muni was a last-minute replacement for the old man in the play *Two Corpses at Breakfast*. This was the beginning of his acting career. For a long time, he portrayed old men on the Yiddish stage.

In 1919, Muni joined the Yiddish Art Theater at the invitation of Maurice Schwartz, the founder. He performed in many plays. While rehearsing in Sholom Aleichem's *Schver Tzu Sein A Yid*, he met actress Bella Finkel, niece of Yiddish actor Boris Tomashefsky. They were married on May 8, 1921. Two years later, Muni became an American citizen.

Muni's American theater acting career began in 1926 when he replaced Edward G. Robinson in *We Americans*. In 1929, he used the name Paul Muni when he starred in an early talking movie called *The Vallant*.

For a while, Muni alternated between making movies and appearing in Broadway plays. The movie *Scarface* made him a major Hollywood star in 1932. Prior to making *Scarface*, Muni achieved great success in the lead role in *Counselor-At-Law* by Elmer Rice.He appeared in this play many times throughout his acting career.

Warner Brothers signed Muni for three social-consciousness movies. His first was *I Am A Fugitive From A Chain Gang*, which won him another Academy Award nomination. Muni finished his contract with Warner Brothers. His new contract gave him authority over final approval of his films. This was unheard of in Hollywood. In 1935, he starred in movies that launched his career as one of America's greatest actors. He began playing character roles. The title role in *The Story of Louis Pasteur* won him the Academy Award. He portrayed a Chinese peasant in *The Good Earth*. Time magazine proclaimed him the "first actor of the screen" and the New York Film Critics gave him the best actor award for the title role in *The Life of Emile Zola* in 1937. His ability to use disguises for the many characters portrayed gave him the flexibility to play a variety roles.

Muni ended his relationship with Warner Brothers in 1940. He only made eight more films after this breakup.

Muni was always concerned about the European Jews. He strongly felt that Israel was the haven for those Jews needing a place to live. He starred in Ben Hecht's pageant *A Flag is Born*, which helped rally support for Israel. Muni continued to star in Broadway plays and in movies. His failing health and vision ended his activities. Muni performed in 23 movies and 12 Broadway plays. He had more than 300 roles in the Yiddish theater. He died in California on August 25, 1967.

111

Albert Einstein

A Giant in the World of Physics

lbert Einstein was a theoretical physicist whose writings in physics changed the course of science and of history. The articles Einstein wrote in 1905 brought him world recognition and fame. His article on the theory of relativity shook up and caused great excitement in the scientific world.

Einstein was the son of Hermann and Pauline Koch Einstein. He was born on March 14, 1879, in Ulm, Germany. When Einstein was a young boy, his father established a small electrical equipment factory in Munich with his uncle. The Einstein family moved to Munich, which had a reputation for being anti-Semitic. Young Einstein was the only Jew in his class and was constantly the target of anti-Semitism by his classmates. He vowed that he would never wear a German uniform if conscripted. In 1894, he received notice that he was to serve in the German Army. The family moved to Milan and gave up its German citizenship.

After many unsuccessful attempts, Einstein was admitted to the Eidgenossiche Technische Hochschule in Zurich, Switzerland.

Einstein wrote a number of noteworthy articles on physics in 1905. The most important was "On the Electrodynamics of Moving Bodies," which is known as the special theory of relativity. For the next 10 years, the physicists of the world gradually recognized the importance of Einstein's work. He accepted a professorship at the University of Zurich in 1909.This preceded many other university appointments.

In 1913, Einstein was elected a member of the Prussian Academy of Sciences in Berlin and was offered the directorship of scientific research at the Kaiser Wilhelm Institute for Physics. He accepted the offer with the condition that he didn't have to become a German citizen. In 1914, he moved to Berlin and remained there until 1933.

Einstein received the Nobel Prize for Physics in 1921. When not involved with his scientific work, he was promoting peace and Zionism. He toured America with Chaim Weizmann and other Zionists and spoke in favor of support for the United Jewish Appeal and Israel.

The Nazis raided Einstein's home in Germany and put a price on his head when he was visiting the U.S. in 1933. He remained in the U.S. and became a citizen in 1940. He worked as a professor of theoretical physics at the Princeton University Institute for Advanced Study.

When Weizmann died, Einstein was asked to be a candidate for president of Israel. He declined since he said he wasn't a political person. He did become a trustee of Hebrew University and donated many of his original manuscripts to the school.

Einstein was constantly opposing Nazi Germany in his speeches and articles. In 1938, nuclear fission, which could lead to the development of the atomic bomb, was discovered in Germany. Einstein was urged by six physicists to write President Roosevelt to make him aware of the inherent dangers of Germany's developing an atomic bomb and to stress the need for America to develop one before the Germans. He did this with a heavy heart since he knew what kind of destruction an atomic bomb could cause. This famous letter helped change the course of history when America did develop the atomic bomb.

Einstein died in Princeton, on April 18, 1955. His contributions to the scientific world are immeasurable. He is also known for promoting Israel, fighting bigotry, fighting against the use of nuclear weapons and loving humanity.

Jesse Louis Lasky

A Film Industry Pioneer

J esse Louis Lasky was a pioneer and giant in the film industry. Together with his brother-in-law, Samuel Goldwyn, and Cecil B. DeMille, Lasky made Hollywood's first full length feature movie, *The Squaw Man*. The film was an instant success. Other full length films followed.

In later years, Lasky wanted his films to depict democracy in action. He felt that films were the best way to sell America to the rest of the world. While at Warner Brothers, from 1940 to 1944, he produced biographical pictures like *Sergeant York, Rhapsody in Blue* and *The Adventures of Mark Twain*. Lasky found Mark Twain, a barefoot boy who grows up to become a writer, to be a perfect example of the opportunities in America.

Lasky's life was not too far removed from that of Mark Twain. His grandfather crossed the plains in a covered wagon in 1850 and settled in California. Lasky was the son of Isaac and Sarah (Platt) Lasky. He was born on September 3, 1880, in San Jose, California. He attended

San Jose High School. In his free time, he helped out in his father's store. He learned to play the cornet during this period. This helped him to earn money when finances became tight.

When Lasky was 20, his father died, leaving the family with little money. The family raised $3,000 to send Lasky to Nome to pan for gold. He was one of the first men from the West Coast to go to Alaska for riches.

Lasky lost all of his money panning for gold. He found a job playing his cornet in a cafe. The miners threw coins and sacks of gold dust at the women.Whatever coins and gold fell in the pit were Lasky's to keep. This was how he made his return fare. He was able to repay $1,500 on his family's investment.

Lasky found work playing the cornet in theaters. This led him to become a booking agent for theater acts. He made a fortune getting engagements for entertainers. He lost $110,000 producing stage musi- cal *Folies Bergere*, in New York. Lasky introduced the word "cabaret" to America with this musical.

He became involved with movies in California in 1914. He formed the Paramount-Famous-Lasky Corporation in 1916. Lasky was a success story for 18 years. The movies industry had collapsed under the weight of its theater chains in 1932. Lasky lost all of his $12 million trying to save his company. The following year, Lasky became an independent producer. He was elected president of the (Mary) Pickford— Lasky Productions, Inc., in 1935. Once again, success was with him throughout the years.

Lasky was married to Bessie Ginzberg on December 11, 1909. They had three children: William Raymond, Bessie Dorothy, and Jesse Louis Jr., a screen writer. Lasky died on January 13, 1958.

Lasky was a pioneer in the film industry who participated in developing it from one reelers to full length movies, from silents to talkies and from black and white to color films. He used his talents to produce films that told the world of the opportunities that existed in America.

113

Flora Lewis

Outstanding Journalist

F lora Lewis is a journalist who is at home in any part of the world writing and analyzing events on the national and international scene. She has gone to places and reached heights in the newspaper industry where few women have been.

She was born in Los Angeles, California, in 1920 to Pauline and Benjamin Lewis, who was a prominent attorney. She was a talented and gifted student, who graduated high school when she was fifteen. Three years later, she received her B.A. Degree, Summa Cum Laude, from the University of California. She went to Columbia University Graduate School of Journalism and obtained her masters' degree in 1941.

Lewis went to work for the Associated Press in their New York office. She was soon transferred to Washington D.C. to cover the Navy and State Departments. In 1945, she was transferred to their London office, two days before V-J Day.

In London, she married Sydney Gruson, a *New York Times* foreign correspondent whom she had met while she was a student at Columbia. Because of their busy schedule, they were married on their lunch hour.

She left the Associated Press in 1946 so that she could go with her husband to Poland where he had been transferred. From 1946 to 1954, she free lanced for *Time Magazine, The New York Times Sunday Magazine, The Economist of London, the London Observer* and *France-Soir* of Paris. During her free lance period, Lewis traveled on assignments throughout Europe, Israel and Mexico.

Her career took off on her return to New York City in 1955. She was an editor with McGraw-Hill Publishing Co., first woman foreign correspondent for *Washington Post,* first chief of *The Washington Post's* newly opened New York City office, she travelled five times to Vietnam during a five year period and in 1972, she joined *The New York Times* as chief of its Paris bureau.

In 1980, she became a columnist for *The New York Times* and she exposed terrorist activities in many European countries. She was the author of four books which were well received.

Flora Lewis has been recognized for her achievements in journalism by many universities, colleges and civic organizations. She has been honored four times by the Overseas Press Club for best foreign-affairs reporting for articles in The New York Times (1957), for best daily newspaper or wire interpretation of foreign affairs (1963 and 1977), for best analysis of foreign affairs in Western Europe (1979), The Edward Weintal Award (1978), The French Government's Cross of the Chevalier of the Legion of Honor, the country's highest award in peacetime (1981),the Matrix Award for Newspapers from New York Women in Communication (1985), and the Elmer Holmes Bobst Award in Arts and Letters from New York University (1987).

During her marriage to Sydney Gruson, they had three children: Kerry was born in Ireland, Shelia was born in Israel and Lindsley was born in Mexico. Her life was like a juggler in trying to balance her role as a journalist, wife and mother.

Flora Lewis is an outstanding woman who achieved in a male dominated profession. She made it easier for other women to enter and to succeed in the newspaper industry.

114

Max M. Novich

The Dean of Sport Medicine

hen contact sports were under attack for being brutal and physically dangerous in the 1960s, Dr. Max M. Novich, an orthopedic surgeon, came to their defense. Novich felt that with proper medical attention, training, and supervision, many of the injuries that were sustained could be avoided. Novich outlined a program for pre-adolescent youngsters. This program advocated progressive education in preparing for contact sports. He stressed this time and again to educators and physicians.

In 1971, Novich founded the Association of Ringside Physicians, which had recently been incorporated by the USA Amateur Boxing Federation.The association was to have boxers medically examined before a bout and have physicians at ringside during every boxing match. In the same year, Novich founded the Sports Injury Center at the Newark United Hospitals Orthopedic Center. He served locally, nationally, and internationally on many committees dealing with sports injuries.

Novich was constantly under fire because of his defense of boxing. Novich felt that there were many steps that could be taken to make boxing a safer sport. He advocated the thumbless glove, which would be the best defense against detached retinas. He wanted certified ringside physicians to be allowed to stop fights when they deemed it necessary. He believed in the octagonal ring and fought for the return of boxing as a scientific sport. Novich was constantly lecturing on "How to Make Contact Sports Safer." He wrote more than 50 medical articles and three books on safety in contact sports.

Novich was born on December 9, 1914, in Newark, New Jersey. After receiving his education in the Newark public school system, he went to the University of North Carolina, where he graduated with an A.B. degree. He received his medical degree at the University of Louisville, in Kentucky. He was always interested in boxing and was captain of the boxing team in college; he won several championships in competition. After interning at Beth Israel Hospital in Newark, he joined the Army and served in World War II.

During his Army training period, Novich also taught boxing to the enlisted men and organized boxing shows. His unit was sent to England to prepare for the invasion of Europe and to fight Hitler's army.

After Novich requested a transfer to an assault unit, he was transferred to the 29th Division. When the Allies invaded Europe on D-Day, Novich found himself in France. He was sent to France to replace a wounded battalion surgeon in the 2nd Battalion, 16th Regiment. Novich received a battlefield promotion to captain as his unit fought the Germans through France, Belgium, Holland and into Germany.

Novich was wounded in Julich, Germany. He received many decorations for bravery: the Bronze Star Medal, the Purple Heart Medal, the Campaign Ribbon with Four Battle Stars, the Victory Medal, the American Theater Medal, the German Occupation Ribbon, the Army Combat Medical Badge and the Croix de Guerre.

Novich is an honoree of both the New Jersey and the World Boxing Hall of Fame. He may well be remembered as a hero in World War II, but his legacy is that he is the "dean" of sports medicine.

115

Anna M. Rosenberg

Assistant Defense Secretary

When Anna M. Rosenberg was sworn in as the assistant secretary of defense under George C. Marshall on November 15, 1950, she achieved the highest post ever held by a woman in the national military establishment. Her task was to coordinate the Defense Department's manpower, which had been divided among many agencies.

Anna Rosenberg was born in 1902, in Budapest, Hungary, to Charlotte and Albert Lederer. Her mother was a talented author and illustrator of children's books and her father was a successful furniture manufacturer. When a very large order for furniture was canceled, her father lost his business and they immigrated to the United States to settle in the Bronx, New York.

The day that she entered school, Anna became involved with economic and social issues. In World War I, she was very successful in selling Liberty Bonds and Thrift Stamps for the war effort. She worked part-time in a base hospital in Manhattan. She married Julius Rosenberg, who was a serviceman, in 1919. In that same year, she became a naturualized citizen.

Anna Rosenberg became involved in politics in the early 1920s. She made many important political connections in the ensuing years. When

Franklin Roosevelt was elected Governor of New York, he frequently consulted her on labor matters.

In the early 1930s, she served the federal government in many capacities, primarily in labor and human relations. In 1937, she was named chairwoman of the New York State Constitutional Committee and, in 1938, she was named by President Roosevelt to a committee to study realtions in Great Britain and Sweden. During those years, she developed a consulting business which was very successful.

She served on many committees and boards during World War II. She was the director of the Office of Defense and regional director of Health and Welfare Services. She was a member of the New York City and state war councils and held the secretaryship of the President's Combined War Labor Board.

In July 1944, Anna Rosenberg was sent to the European Theater of Operations by President Roosevelt as his personal observer. She did the same for President Truman the following summer. After the war, she served on many boards for the City and State of New York.

In the Korean War, Anna Rosenberg was appointed to a 12-person committee to advise former Air Secretary W. Stuart Symington on mobilization policy. After she was appointed the assistant secretary of defense, she worked with Secretary George Marshall on a draft for the Senate Armed Services Committee which became known as the Universal Miltiary Service and Training Bill. Rosenberg received the Medal of Freedom in 1945 and the U.S. Medal for Merit in 1947.

She continued to serve her country through the years. In 1968-69, President Johnson appointed her to serve on the Commission on Income Maintenance, which examined all welfare and income support programs. Rosenberg died on May 9, 1983. She was a model for Jewish women to follow in service and dedication to our country. In her own way she was a Jewish hero.

116

"Sandy" Koufax

A Baseball Legend

S anford "Sandy" Koufax, one of the greatest pitchers in baseball, was referred to as the "man with the golden arm." He
established one record after another as he went through an
11-year career as a pitcher with the Brooklyn Dodgers.

Koufax was born in Brooklyn, New York, to Evelyn and Jack Braun.
His mother divorced his father when he was young and remarried Irving
Koufax, a lawyer who played an important role in raising Sandy and his
stepsister, Edith.He took the children to the Yiddish theater in New York
City and he was very supportive of Sandy's participation in baseball and
baketball in Brooklyn's Lafayette High School.

Koufax, who loved to play basketball, was constantly at the Jewish
Community Center shooting baskets or playing with a team. When he
was 15, he pitched for a team in the Baseball Ice Cream League, where
baseball scouts watched him with great interest. After completing high
school in 1952, he went on a basketball scholarship to the University of
Cincinnati. However, the baseball scouts were still after him and finally he
signed with the Brooklyn Dodgers in 1954.

The first three years were hectic Koufax, who had trouble controlling his fast ball. At times, he would walk two or three batters before getting the next man out.

Koufax convinced Dodger management to let him pitch more often. Under the guidance of pitching coach Joe Becker and Norm Sherry, a Jewish catcher, he learned to throw more curve balls and change-ups. The 1961 season brought him 18 wins; he struck out 269 batters for a league record. But the following year, 1962, was almost a disaster for Koufax. He developed a blood clot in his arm that almost cost him his index finger, but the managed to pull through and, in 1963, won two games against the Yankees in the World Series.

When a 1965 World Series game fell on Yom Kippur, Koufax requested that he not ptich on this holy day. Many criticized Koufax and maintained that his personal beliefs outweighed his professional beliefs.

Koufax, who received the Cy Young Award, was elected to the Baseball Hall of Fame in 1972. During his baseball career he established many records, retiring at the end of the season in 1966 when he was plagued by arthritis. He moved to the west coast and turned to broadcasting baseball games and to selling real estate.

Koufax wil alway be famous for breaking records as a pitcher in baseball and not playing baseball on Yom Kippur and Rosh Hashana.

117

Jules Robert Oppenheimer
A Leading 20th -Century Physicist

Julius Robert Oppenheimer was appointed director of the central laboratory for bomb design and development in Los Alamos, New Mexico, in May 1942, by General Leslie R. Groves, head of the Army Engineers.

Oppenheimer recruited a highly qualified staff of scientists by informing them of the German attempt to create an atomic bomb and of the peacetime uses of atomic energy. His ability to mix with the scientists for open discussions and on-the-spot directions and his ability to apply his knowledge to new situations and theories, were components of his leadership ability.

When the Allies succeeded in removing the threat of a German atomic bomb by their military victories, in 1944, Oppenheimer focused his attention on making the atom bomb to help bring a quick end to the fighting in the Pacific. he also felt that knowledge of the possible devastation from the bomb would force nations to work for peace in the world.

When the atomic bomb was finally used in Hiroshima and Nagasaki, in 1945, Oppenheimer was exhausted and deeply troubled. He resigned as direct of the Los Alamos project. He accepted a professorship at Cal Tech and then in 1946, went to the University of California at Berkeley. He found it difficult to teach as he was constantly being called to Washington for consultation.

He left Berkeley to become the director of the Institute for Advanced Study in Princeton. Albert Einstein was already a member of the nonteaching faculty there. The institute attracted many postdoctoral fellows and it succeeded pre-war Copenhagen as the world center of theoretical physics.

Oppenheimer's prestige grew and he became the spokesman for those who believed that the atomic age demanded a broader understanding of science and technology. He wrote many articles and gave many lectures on this subject. He was largely responsible for the tone and content of the Acheson—Lilienthal plan which was presented to the United Nations as a basis of negotiation for atomic energy control. Together with the Soviet scientists, he concluded that international control was technically realistic and achievable.

Oppenheimer served on many government committees that were related to atomic energy. After the Soviets exploded their first A-bomb, a gap developed between President Truman and his committee. President Truman didn't accept the committee's report negating any ideas of building thermonuclear bombs. This was never made public.

When Oppenheimer's General Advisory Committee appointment expired in July 1952, he remained as a consultant. This was the heyday of Senator Joseph McCarthy with his witch-hunts for communists and he focused in on Oppenheimer, who was not a communist.

Oppenheimer's clearance was taken away. He requested and received a secret hearing which lasted from April 12 to May 6, 1954, during which distinguished scientists and public servants testified on his behalf. The hearing concluded that Oppenheimer's loyalty was not in question but it would be unwise to trust him with official secrets.

Oppenheimer remained as director of the Institute for Advanced Study in Princeton until he resigned in 1966. He died in 1967. Oppenheimer was an outstanding Jewish physicist of the 20th century. His development of the A-bomb and his writings and lectures on atomic energy are a testimonial to his greatness.

118

Jonas Salk & Albert Sabin
Conquer Polio

Drs. Jonas E. Salk and Albert B.Sabin were the pioneers and researchers who discovered the vaccine and serum to combat polio, a crippling and killing disease that affected millions of people throughout the world annually.

Salk was the oldest of three sons born to Dora and Daniel B. Salk in New York City on October 28, 1914. An exceptional student, he graduated from Townsend Harris High School, the school for the talented and gifted, and worked his way through City College. He received his medical degree from the College of Medicine at New York University in June 1939. In 1942, he went to the University of Michigan, where he developed an influenza vaccine to destroy the polio viruses.

Salk worked to develop vaccines that killed each of the three types of polio viruses. After injecting small groups of people, Sal announced in October 1953 that he had injected 600 people with the vaccine. This experimental group would determine the safety of the new vaccine. The next month, the National Foundation of Infantile Paralysis announced it was making plans for large scale testing of Salk's vaccine.

During the next year more than a million children received three injections for the three types of viruses. Salk also injected himself, his wife and children. The testing proved that this was the first answer in combating polio. The new vaccine, however, had one drawback: booster injections had to be given periodically.

Sabin, meanwhile, had been conducting experiments on obtaining a live polio virus pill to be taken orally since 1952. In 1955, he conducted experiments with prisoners who had volunteered.

Sabin was born in Bialystok, Poland, on August 26, 1906, one of four children of Tillie and Jacob Sabin. The family came to America in 1921, settling in Paterson, New Jersey, where Sabin's father was in the silk and manufacturing business. Early in his career, Sabin, who received his medical degree from New York University in 1931, became interested in polio. Many of his experiments on polio virus research were reported to the National Foundation of Infantile Paralysis.

During World War II, he served in the U.S. Army Medical Corps, where he was involved with the development of a vaccine against dengue fever and the successful vaccination of 65,000 military personnel against the Japanese type of polio. After the war, Sabin continued his research on polio. He developed a vaccine that used live virus; Salk's vaccine used dead virus.

Sabin and his associates took the oral live viruses before conducting experiments on select groups of people form 1955 to 1957. During this period, Salk's vaccine was in use, but many virologists throughout the world believed Sabin had a superior vaccine.

From 1957 to 1959, the U.S.S.R. and the other Eastern Bloc nations gave the oral vaccine, with its advantages of oral administration and long-term immunity, to millions of children and adults. Finally, Sabin's vaccine was used in the United States. Sabin died on March 3, 1993. Dr. Jonas Salk died on June 23, 1995.

Drs. Salk and Sabin saved millions of lives and protected many more from the crippling disease. They proved to be Jewish heroes in America by their lifesaving contributions.

119

Arthur Goldberg

Supreme Court Justice

A rthur J. Goldberg served the United States in many ways. He was an outstanding labor lawyer, U.S. Secretary of Labor, Associate Justice of the United States Supreme Court, and our ambassador to the United Nations.

Arthur Goldberg was raised and educated in Chicago's West Side. He was the youngest of 11 children whose parents came here from Czarist Russia. He worked his way through college and law school.

During World War II, Goldberg served with the Office of Strategic Services. In 1948, he became the general counsel for the United Steelworkers of America and seven years later, in 1955, played a major role in reuniting the Congress of Industrial Organizations and the American Federation of Labor. Goldberg was the principal author of the AFL-CIO ethical practices code. He also helped guide the USW negotiations in a 116-day steel strike in 1959-60.

When John F.Kennedy was elected president, Goldberg was appointed Secretary of Labor. He used his new powers to uphold the public's interest in labor-management disputes. Goldberg directed the administration's legislative program to fight the recession and unemployment.

In August 1942, President Kennedy appointed Goldberg to the Supreme Court as an associate justice. He found himself siding with Justices Hugo Black and William O. Douglas on many decisions. As a Supreme Court Justice, Goldberg questioned the constitutionality of the death penalty, which he felt was cruel and unusual punishment. He voted with the majority in a decision that required congressional districts to be of approximately equal populations.

In June 1964, Goldberg wrote the Court's famous five to four decision in Escohedo vs. Illinois, holding that confessions cannot be used in court if police question a suspect without letting him consult a lawyer or without warning him that his answers could be used against him. Goldberg dissented from an October 1964 decision rejecting Senator Barry M. Goldwater's demand for equal free time on the radio and television to reply to an earlier TV speech by President Lyndon Johnson. He joined the majority court in striking down Connecticut's 1879 law forbidding the use of birth control devices.

When United Nations Ambassador Adlai Stevenson died in July, 1965, President Johnson asked Goldberg to resign from the Supreme Court and to accept the UN position. On July 28, Goldberg resigned and accepted his new role as ambassador.

Goldberg found himself involved with, among other issues, the Vietnam War, the voting rights of unpaid UN members, the India-Pakistan War, South Africa, and the 1967 Arab-Israeli War. He supported a British resolution that asserted Israel's right to exist, and delivered many speeches in the UN on possible solutions to the Vietnam War.

Goldberg resigned as ambassador on April 25, 1968. He joined the New York law firm of Paul, Weiss, Rifkind, Warton and Garrison and became active in politics. He was in charge of the New York presidential campaign of Hubert Humphrey and, in 1970, lost to Nelson Rockefeller in a race for the New York governorship.

Goldberg was involved in defending many civil rights issues and causes. He never hesitated to leave his secure position to fill a void that existed and serve the country. He will always be remembered as an outstanding labor lawyer, as Secretary of Labor, as Supreme Court Justice, as Ambassador to the United Nations, and as a defender of civil rights. He died on January 19, 1990.

120

Admiral Hyman George Rickover
Father of the Atomic-Powered Navy

ice Admiral Hyman George Rickover took the Navy into the atomic age with his persistence that the U.S. Navy build the first atomic-powered submarine.

He was born in Russian Poland in 1900 to Rachel, nee Unger, and Abraham Rickover, a tailor who brought his family to Chicago. After completing high school in 1918, Rickover received an appointment to the United States Naval Academy, where he was often confronted with anti-Semitism. He graduated in 1922 and was commissioned an ensign. Assigned to sea duty, he remained there for five years before being assigned to the Naval Academy to do graduate work in electrical engineering. He continued his studies at Columbia University where he received his M.S. degree in 1929.

Rickover's various assignments included his first command post aboard the U.S.S. FINCH in the Philippines. When World War II started, he was placed in charge of the electrical section of the Bureau of Ships in Washington, D.C. in the first of many wartime appointments.

In 1946, he was assigned to Oak Ridge, the site of the development of the atomic bomb. Rickover visited other nuclear research centers and he became convinced ships could be powered by nuclear energy. Almost alone in his belief, he finally convinced the Navy to begin to develop a nuclear submarine in 1947.

Before long he was placed in charge of the project and worked with the Atomic Energy Commission, which was going to build the reactors. The reactors were built in Idaho; the submarine in Groton, Connecticut. Finally, in January 1954, the first atomic-powered submarine, the Nautilius, was launched.

Despite his success, Rickover faced opposition both toward his work and toward his open criticism and remarks. After he had been twice passed over for promotion to admiral (the naval codes require retirement if promotion is twice denied), congressional leaders suspected that he was a victim of "foul play." Following an investigation, he was named a rear admiral in 1953. His many plans for nuclear ships were put aside during the Congressional hearings.

He is often credited with being President Jimmy Carter's mentor, but was a critic of President Reagan's defense budget, which he considered to be wasteful and too large. In 1982, he was forced into retirement at age 82. When Rickover retired, he expressed regrets on the role he played in nuclear proliferation and called for an international agreement to outlaw nuclear weapons and reactors because of the radiation dangers that they pose. He died on July 8, 1986.

121

Rosalyn S. Yalow

Novel Prize Recipient in Medicine & Physiology

Rosalyn S. Yalow became the second woman to ever win the Nobel Prize in medicine, 1977. Her achievement was the development of RIA, an application of nuclear physics in clinical medicine that makes it possible for scientists to use radiotropic tracers to measure the concentration of hundreds of pharmacologic and biologic substances in the blood and other fluids of the human body and in animals and plants. She invented this technique in 1959 to measure the amount of insulin in the blood of adult diabetics.

She was born on July 19, 1921, in the Bronx, New York, of Jewish parents, Clara and Simon Sussman. She attended the New York City public school system and in Walden High School she was encouraged by her chemistry teacher to pursue a career in science. She graduated Hunter College and accepted a teaching fellowship in physics at the University of Illinois. In 1945, she became the second woman to receive a Ph.D. degree in physics from Illinois.

She met A. Aaron Yalow, a fellow physics student who was the son of a rabbi and they were married on June 6, 1943. They returned to New

York where she accepted a lecturer's post in physics, which she held until 1950. During this period, they had two children, Benjamin and Elanna.

After World War II, the Veterans Administration was interested in doing research to explore the possible use of radioactive substances in the diagnosis of treatment and disease. The VA Hospital in the Bronx was chosen as one of the sites where research would be conducted. Dr. Yalow, who was a consultant in this facility, was hired to work on nuclear physics in 1947. In 1950, she was appointed physicist and assistant chief of the hospital's radioisotope service.

Dr Yalow was appointed to higher and more responsible positions at the VA Hospital during the years. In 1976, she became the first woman to win the Albert Lasker Prize for Basic Medical Research. During the years, Dr.Yalow was recognized for her achievements with numerous prestigious awards from organizations, societies, universities, etc.

Dr. Rosalyn Yalow was always aware of her role as a woman and as a Jew. After she received the Nobel Prize, the Ladies Home Journal wanted her to receive a special woman's award. She politely refused the offer, which she considered to be as a "ghetto" citation given her because she was a brilliant woman, not a brilliant scientist.

During her hectic life as a scientist and as the wife and mother of a family, she managed to host a five-part dramatic series on the life of Madame Curie, for the Public Broadcasting Service in 1976. She has put in long hours each week at the V.A. Hospital and then come home to her kosher kitchen to prepare meals for her family. Dr. Yalow displayed energy and enthusiasm at all times for work and family.

Dr. Rosalyn Yalow is the beacon and guide for young women in achieving position and recognition in life. She has demonstrated through her life that it is possible for a woman to be an outstanding professional as well as having a good family in their lifetime.

122

Isaac Bashevis Singer

Statesman & Nobel Prize Recipient

The crowning moment in Isaac Bashevis Singer's life was when he received the Nobel Prize for literature in 1978. This recognition of Singer's writings also glorified the beauty and power of the Yiddish language.

Born in Radzymin, Poland, on July 14, 1904, in a long lineage of rabbis, Singer was one of four children. His parents were Rabbi Pincus Menachem and Bathsheba(Zylberman). Singer's young life in the Jewish shtetls of Poland was steeped in Hassidism. He was educated in the Jewish schools and at one time he was enrolled in a rabbinical seminary. When he was four, his family moved to Warsaw where his father, a Hassidic scholar, established a Beth Din (rabbinical court).

In 1917, Singer moved with his mother to his maternal grandmother, who lived in a small town. Here he learned about Jewish life in the shtetl, which would become a topic for his short stories and novels.

In the early 1920s, Singer went to Warsaw to join his older brother, Israel Joseph, who was to write such works as *The Brothers Ashkenazi* and *Yoshe Kalb*. Singer joined his brother despite the vigorous objections of his parents, who wanted him to become a rabbi. In Warsaw, he obtained a job as a proofreader for a Yiddish literary magazine. Interested in writing, he first tried to do so in Hebrew, but since it was used only for prayer, he switched to Yiddish.

By 1926, Singer was writing book reviews and short stories. In 1932, he became co-editor of Globus, a Yiddish literary magazine. In 1935, he left his first wife, Rachel, and his son, Israel, to immigrate to America to join his older brother in New York City, where he became a freelance writer for the *Jewish Daily Forward*. Many of his novels were serialized in the Forward and, in 1950, his novel *The Family Moskat* was translated into English by Alfred A. Knopf, Inc. Singer became instantly famous and he received the Louis Lamed Prize. An Italian translation, in 1968, won him Italy's Bacarrella Prize.

Many of Singer's writings have reflected his experiences as a youth in Poland. The shtetl, mysticism, folklore, the supernatural and religion were his themes. He also wrote stories for children and was acclaimed for *Zlatch the Goat and Other Stories*, a children's book about animals, children, and supernatural creatures.

After he divorced Rachel, Singer married Alma Heimann, a refugee from Germany. A vegetarian, he and his wife both loved living creatures and spent a great deal of time in the park feeding the birds.

Singer is a member of the I.L. Peretz Writers Union and a fellow of the Jewish Academy of Arts and Sciences, the Polish Institute of Arts and Sciences in America and the American Institute of Arts and Sciences. Singer, whose writings have been translated from Yiddish into Hebrew, French, Italian, German, Dutch, Norwegian and Finnish, stands as a giant and legend of our Yiddish writers of our time.

Benny Goodman
The "King of Swing"

Benny Goodman was unofficially crowned the "King of Swing" at new York's Paramount Theater on March 10, 1937. The theater's sunken stage slowly rose as Goodman and his band played its theme song and the packed house burst into a tremendous crescendo of approval. Throughout the show, many audience members were doing the jitterbug in the aisles.

Twenty-five years later, Goodman took his band to the Soviet Union on an official United States government mission.The band's 32 concerts were attended by more than 180,000 Soviets, including Premier Nikita Krushchev. Goodman was hailed as a "true poet of the clarinet" by Sovietskaya Kultura, a cultural newspaper.

Goodman was the eighth of 11 children of David and Dora, nee Grinsky, Goodman. He was born on May 30, 1909. His father was a poor tailor, who had emigrated from Warsaw, Poland.The family lived in Chicago. Surviving was always a tremendous struggle for the Goodmans. The Goodmans learned that Kehelah Jacob Synagogue was giving music lessons and lending instruments to the students for only 25 cents a week. Benny and his two older brothers went to the synagogue for lessons.Harry, the oldest, was given a tuba. Freddie got a trumpet. Benny, the smallest and youngest, was given a clarinet.

Goodman learned to play the clarinet so well that he was able to make money by doing imitations of Ted Lewis when he was 12 years old. He played in many Chicago bands.Ben Pollack, a leading band leader in California, asked the 16-year-old Goodman to join his band. He accepted Pollack's offer and went to California. He was with the Pollack band until 1923, when he left to go out on his own.

Goodman had built up a reputation with the recordings that he had made. He ws in great demand and was kept busy as a freelance musician. In 1933, he met John Henry Hammond Jr., a promoter, who was a socially prominent jazz fan and critic. Hammond arranged recording dates for Goodman with some of the outstanding black musicians of the time. In later years, Goodman would be the first white bandleader to have black musicians in his band.

Goodman formed a permanent band in 1934 with the help of Hammond. He had a Saturday night radio program called Let's Dance, which brought him national fame. He started a cross country tour after he finished the radio series.The tour's reception was dismal until he came to the Palomar Ballroom in Los Angeles. Here, the crowd came up to the bandstand to listen and applaud instead of dancing. This event is considered to have marked the begining of the Swing era.

His success in the popular music field was not enough to satisfy him. He loved classical music and was always performing the classics when he had the opportunity. He commissioned Bela Bartok, Paul Hindemith and Aaron Copland to compose clarinet concertos for him.

Over the years, he found time to make movies. He appeared in The Big Broadcast of 1937, A Song is Born, Powers Girl, Hollywood Hotel and Stage Door Canteen. In 1955, Universal-International produced **The Benny Goodman Story.**

Goodman had a sellout tour of the Far East in the winter of 1956-57. In the following years, he toured the world with his band as a goodwill ambassador. In 1942, he married Alice Hammond, a sister of John Hammond.They had two daughters, Rachel, a concert pianist, and Benjie. Goodman died on June 13, 1986. He gave the world a rich heritage in music.

124

Lydia Rapoport

Educational Leader in Social Work

Lydia Rapoport was a leading educator in developing social worker curriculum for colleges, examining and defining the necessary skills for the social work practitioner and educator and examining the theoretical basis for social casework.

She was born on March 8, 1923, in Vienna, Austria, the youngest of two children of Eugenia, nee Margolies, and Samuel Rapoport. Her father immigrated to New York City in 1928 and worked as a translator. The family remained in Vienna until 1932 so that her brother could finish his education. Lydia attended the New York City public school system and majored in sociology at Hunter College.

She was a brilliant student and she took accelerated programs at Smith College School for Social Work. She was twenty-one when she received her master's degree in 1944.

Rapoport accepted a position as a child guidance counselor at the Institute for Juvenile Research, in Chicago, Illinois. She then became the supervisor at the Children's Guidance Clinic at the Bobs Roberts Hospital of the University of Chicago. She continued to diversify her experience in this field and she became the supervisor of the Jewish Children's Bureau of the Michael Reese Hospital.

Lydia Rapoport was recognized for achievements when she won a Fullbright Fellowship in 1952. She went to study at the London School of Economics in England. It was here that she met Richard Titmuss, a leading architect of the national health service, and Dame Eileen Younghusband, an outstanding English social work scholar and educator. They both became her lifelong friends and advisors. In 1954, Rapoport returned to the United States and went to California to become the supervisor of the California State Mental Health Clinic for students of the School of Social Welfare at the University of California. She joined the faculty and by 1969, she became a full professor.

During her years of teaching, she was doing major research and writing. Her work as on the central concepts of personality stress, learning theories and the preventative orientation of public health rather than the medical model of treatment.

Lydia Rapoport was a major developer in helping to formulate a theoretical basis for defining consultation and supervision and distinct social work functions. She also defined and spelled out the role of the social worker as a consultant and supervisor in education and in social work practice.

In 1963, she became a visiting professor at the Baerwald School of Social Work of Hebrew University in Jerusalem, Israel. She helped to develop an undergraduate curriculum in the country's schools of social work. Her visit to Israel rekindled in her a close identity to her Jewish heritage.

In January, 1971, she went to New York to become the first United Nations Inter-Regional Adviser on Family Welfare and Family Planning. A few months later, she became ill and underwent emergency surgery. She died on September 6, 1971.

Lydia Rapoport's contribution to social work education made an impact on the country's schools in raising it to its highest level. Her refining and updating the thinking and curriculum in social work was her legacy to the American people.

125

Henry Alfred Kissinger
Statesman & Nobel Peace Prize Winner

Henry Alfred Kissinger, who served as Secretary of State under Presidents Nixon and Ford, seemed to be the invisible president during those eight years. Foreign and domestic leaders sought him for guidance and advice or blamed him for the American policy failures.

Born on May 23, 1923, in the Bavarian city of Furthh, he was the second son of Paul (Stern) and Louis Kissinger. The elder Kissinger was a school teacher and after Hitler's rise to power, the family immigrated to London in 1938. After a short stay, they moved to Washington Heights in New York City. Kissinger attended high school at night and he worked in a shaving brush factory during the day. While attending City College of New York, in 1943, he was drafted into the Army and became a German interpreter for the 970th Counter-intelligence Corps. When Germany surrendered in May 1945, Kissinger held various positons in the military government.

After his discharge, he went to Harvard, where he earned his B.A. Degree *Summa Cum Laude* in 1950. He then went on to earn his M.A. and his Ph.D. by 1954. He used his doctoral thesis as a basis for his first book, *A World Restored: Castlereagh, Metternich and the Problems of*

Peace (Boston, 1957), where he saw history as a struggle between revolutionary and conservative forces.

By 1962, he became a professor at Harvard University and he associated himself with the Council on Foreign Relations and with Governor Nelson Rockerfeller. He wrote a book, *Nuclear Weapons and Foreign Policy* (New York, 1957), in which he took the position that America's survival and victory depended not only on its strength, but also on its ability to recognize and fight aggression in all of its forms. The publication of this book established his reputation.

When Richard Nixon was elected president in 1968, Kissinger was brought into the administration, later to become Secretary of State. During the presidencies of Nixon and Ford, he emerged as a very powerful man. Kissiniger initiated shuttle diplomacy, played a major role in negotiating the Middle East peace treaty, and in negotiating a Vietnam peace treaty after many ups and downs in the fighting. He initiated detente with the Russians and established relations with China.

Kissinger was awarded the Nobel Prize for Peace in 1973. He shared this award with Le Duc Tho, a North Vietnamese peace negotiator. Henry Alfred Kissinger has always been the target of political criticism for he had the courage to follow-up on what he thought was the best course to take at the given time. Time will place Henry Alfred Kissinger in his proper place in American history.

126

Leonard Bernstein

Conductor, Composer & Pianist

Leonard Bernstein has his aunt to thank for introducing him to music. When he was 10 years old, his aunt gave his family her piano. He was so fascinated with it that he began to play by ear and to compose simple pieces for it. Despite his father's apprehensions about musicians, he soon began formal piano lessons.

Born in Lawrence, Massachusetts, on August 25, 1918, Bernstein was the son of Russian immigrants, Samuel Joseph and Jennie, nee Resnick, Bernstein. His father was in the hair goods and beauty supply business. Bernstein attended Boston Latin School, where he received a well-rounded early education. He graduated from Harvard in 1939 with a degree in music. He continued his studies at the Curtis Institute of Music in Philadelphia, where there were many leading musicians on the staff.

When World War II broke out, Bernstein was just beginning his career. His first work, the Clarinet Sonata had been published and he was busy producing operas for the Boston Institute of Modern Art. He received his first major opportunity in September 1942, when he was appointed as the assistant conductor at Tanglewood, Massachusetts.

This position gave him entree to many other opportunities. In the 1942-43 season, he conducted concerts in New York and in 1943, he was appointed as the assistant conductor of the New York Philharmonic. On November 13, 1943, Bernstein was asked to conduct the Philharmonic in place of Arthur Rodzinski, who had become ill. His success was instantaneous. *The New York Times* praised his debut on its front page and he received the plaudits of his colleagues.

Bernstein was very sensitive to the feelings of people. When he was a guest conductor with the Israel Philharmonic, he was asked by parents in the audience to write a work to honor their 19-year-old son, a flautist, who had fallen in the 1973 Yom Kippur War. Bernstein said, "I never knew Yadin Tannenbaum, but I knew his spirit." He wrote "Halil," which he dedicated to the flautist and his fallen brothers. Bernstein wrote many pieces dealing with the world's cruelty and injustices. His feelings were expressed in his works the *Jeremiah Symphony, the age of Anxiety, Candide, Mass, and Kaddish.*

Bernstein was also known for his popular music. He composed music for *Fancy Free, Wonderful Town, West Side Story* and *The Dybbik.* He also composed a one-act opera, *Trouble in Tahiti,* a piano piece, *Touches,* and a piece in memory of Andre Kostelanetz titled A *Musical Toast.*

Bernstein was a leader in introducing music to the youth through his television program, the Young People's Concerts. He displayed much enthusiasm and vigor in these concerts. Bernstein resigned as director of the New York Philharmonic in 1969, following the death of his Chilean born wife, Felicia Montealegre Cohn. The New York Philharmonic honored him by giving him the title conductor laureate.

Bernstein's contributions cannot be measured. He will always be a giant in American music. He died on October 14, 1990.

127

Jews who Fought in World War II and Korea

Many Jewish veterans of World War II didn't rest on their laurels for long. They joined the American Armed Forces to fight in the Korean conflict. One of these men was Major Melvin Garten.

Garten was a highly decorated hero of World War II. He had received the Silver Star Medal, the Bronze Star Medal, a Presidential Unit Citation, and the Purple Heart Medal with Three Oak Leaf Clusters for having been wounded four times in battle.

Garten was the captain of K Company, 312th Infantry Regiment, U.S. Army, when he was hailed for extraordinary heroism in action against the armed enemy. This action took place on October 30, 1952, near Surang-Ni, Korea. Garten observed that the assault elements of companies F and G were pinned down by a withering fire on a dominant hill. He voluntarily proceeded alone up the rugged slope to help them. When he reached the besieged troops, he found that the key personnel had been wounded and that the men were without command.

He took command of the remaining troops by rallying eight men. He assigned four to machine guns and distributed hand grenades. Employing the principle of fire and maneuver, the troops stormed the enemy trenches and bunkers. These men, led by Garten, displayed such tenacity and heroism in attacking that the enemy was routed and the objective was secured. He directed and coordinated a holding action until reinforcements arrived.

Garten was awarded the Distinguished Service Cross for gallantry in Korea. The end of his citation sums up his heroism: "Major Garten's inspirational leadership, unflinching courage under fire and valorous actions reflect the highest credit upon himself and are in keeping with the cherished traditions of the military service."

Another World War II veteran who fought in Korea was Major Joseph I. Gurfein of Brooklyn. Gurfein was a West Point graduate. He was involved in months of combat in World War II. His fearless and calm leadership under enemy fire in Korea earned him the Silver Star Medal.

Gurfein was a parachute-engineer liaison officer attached to a battalion that had the mission of breaking through the enemy lines. In the winter, the battalion was moving through a mountain on a narrow trail. A booby-trap exploded and wounded several men at the point of the column.

The soldiers in the front became confused. Those behind started to move back toward where they came from. Gurfein stopped the soldiers' withdrawl, reorganized them and started moving them ahead. A few hours later, the enemy attacked. Again, confusion set in. Gurfein again acted to steady them. By this time, the snow was falling and the temperature had dropped below zero. Without regard for his safety, Gurfein moved among his troops. He tried to inspire them to continue the attack. He finally restored order. His men moved forward to engage the enemy.

Garten and Gurfein exemplified the Jewish fighting men in the Korean Conflict. Not only were they heroes in Korea, but they were also heroes in World War II.

128

Corporal Abraham Geller Heroic in Korea

When the North Korean forces invaded South Korea on June 25, 1950, the United Nations authorized its member nations to give support to South Korea. Fifteen nations responded, including the United States. General Douglas MacArthur was appointed as commander of the United Nations fighting forces. As in the past, Jews in America responded to their nation's call to arms.

Billy Rose, in his widely syndicated column, "Pitching Horseshoes," tells of the heroism of U.S. Marine Corporal Abraham Geller of New York City's Lower East Side. Geller was the son of a rabbi. The family lived near Delancey Street. In the Marine Corps, Geller always awakened a half-hour earlier before the others so that he could go through the ritual of Orthodox morning prayers.

His regiment had been pushing the enemy back. The regiment had crossed the Han and cut the Seoul-Haesong Road. The soldiers bedded down in hastily dug foxholes to get a few hours sleep. They knew that in the morning they were going to fight their way toward the Korean capital.

An hour before dawn, the only ones awake were the sentries: Captain George O'Connor, who was figuring out strategies to use when the regiment moved ahead, and Geller, who had started his morning prayers. When Geller finished praying, O'Connor told him to get a cup of coffee from the chow truck.

"Thanks, Captain," said Geller, "But today is Yom Kippur, and I'm not supposed to eat until sundown."

O'Connor was amazed that Geller wouldn't eat until the day was over. Geller fasted and observed his holiday as well as a Jew can when in combat.

That morning, the regiment moved forward. The advance moved slowly as the enemy put up stiff resistance. The casualties were high for both sides. Dead bodies were all over the field. One of the badly wounded North Koreans was playing dead as Geller's company moved forward. Geller was standing a few feet from O'Connor when he saw the North Korean move. He pulled out his bayonet and made a dive for the enemy soldier. Geller managed to kill him. But, he also stopped three bullets that were intended for O'Connor.

The fighting was so heavy that it was three hours before Geller received a shot of penicillin. He was then carried into the operating room. The surgery lasted an hour. O'Connor waited for it to be over. When the surgeon came out, he was there to greet him.

"How is he doing?" O'Connor asked.

"He is doing well. The bullets went through his abdomen and the penicillin was a factor in preventing peritonitis. In a manner of speaking, Geller owes his life to the fact that when he was shot there was hardly any food in his stomach."

O'Connor shook his head as he started to understand a little bit more about the meaning of fasting on Yom Kippur.

129

Tibor Rubin
An Unusual Hero of The Korean War

Tibor Rubin's bravery during the Korean War is probably unparalleled in the history of America's fighting heroes. That is why many organizations and individuals are involved in a major campaign to have Congress award him the Congressional Medal of Honor.

Rubin, a Hungarian Holocaust survivor, lost his parents in a Nazi concentration camp in the latter part of World War II. He managed to stay alive and he was liberated. He came to the United States a year and half later and enlisted in the Army to fight in Korea.

While in Korea, he had broken his leg and was shipped to an Army hospital in Japan. Although his leg was not completly healed, he was assigned to Company I, 8th Cavalry Regiment, which was engaged in fighting the enemy. Former Sergeant Randall J.J. Briere wrote in a letter to the President of the United States, "Although his leg was not completely healed, Tibor went about his everyday chores, always helping others who needed a boost, never concerned for his own health or safety. I warned him to be more cautious since the enemy was out in front of us, but when a cry for help was heard, Tibor managed to be the first one on the scene..."

On November 1, 1950, Tibor was wounded with shrapnel from a grenade in the left hand and chest. He and others of his company were captured by the Chinese, who were fighting with the Korean Communist government. The Chinese forced the captured American soldiers, including the wounded and the sick, to march hard and tedious distance to their prisoner of war camp. Tibor and Father Emil Kapaun, who later died in the prison camp, were both wounded but were carrying stretchers and assisting others who could not walk.

Tibor and Chaplain Kapaun were risking their lives when during rest breaks, they went up and down the line to console the tired soldiers, urging them to continue the march.Those who lagged behind were shot by the enemy. The death rate in the prisoner of war camp was running between 30 and 40 men a day. There were shortages of food, medical attention and medicine.The soldiers were still wearing their summer clothes with temperatures between 30 and 40 degrees.

Rubin, who had learned to survive in a Nazi concentration camp, applied his experience to sneak out during the night to steal food from the Chinese. He would give this food to the other prisoners, especially the sick and dying. Everytime he went out for food, Tibor was risking his life. He felt that this way his way of getting back at the enemy as they were short on food themselves.

Tibor was a prisoner for two and one-half years. His fellow prisoners credit him with saving 35 to 40 lives with his daring, almost nightly ventures of stealing food for his comrades. Tibor turned down a number of offers from the Chinese to send him back to his native Hungary.

Tibor Rubin and the others were finally released and sent back to the American hospital in Freedom Village, Korea. He was a stretcher case, suffering from his wounds without complaints. He has been recommended for the Congressional Medal of Honor by the Jewish War Veterans of the USA, Korean Prisoner of War Association, many of his comrades in the prisoner of war camp, individuals and others.

Many heroes receive their awards and recognition through an action that could take minutes, hours, and even a few days.Tibor's heroism and bravery was to be over a two and a half year period, never knowing when he would be caught and executed.

Tibor Rubin resides in California. The campaign to have him receive the Congressional Medal of Honor for his heroism and bravery is stronger than ever.We must give full recognition to heroes like Rubin.

130

Judith Raskin
A Great Lyric Soprano

Judith Raskin was one of America's greatest lyric sopranos of the twentieth century. She was not only famous for her voice but also for her acting.

She was born on June 21, 1928, to Lillian and Harry A. Raskin. Her mother was a grade school teacher and her father was a high school music teacher. It was her father who aroused Judith's interest in music. As a child, she studied the violin and piano. Later, singing became the focus of her musical interest.

She graduated Roosevelt High School in Yonkers, New York, in 1945, and then entered Smith College in Northhampton, Massachusetts where she majored in music. She started taking singing lessons while at college. After graduation, she continued taking lessons as her voice displayed great warmth and artistry. She won the Marian Anderson award for 1952 and 1953. She began making appearances on the concert stage throughout the country.

Raskin first received national recognition when in 1957 she sang in the televised American premier performance of Poulenc's "Dialogues des Carmelites." In July of 1957, she performed a concert version of Puccini's *"La Boheme"* with the Symphony of the Air in New York City's Central Park. After many concerts, she joined the New York City Opera Company and made her debut in Mozart's *"Cosi Fan Tutte"* in 1959.

In February, 1960 she sang the title role in Douglas Moore's *"Ballad of Baby Doe"* for the New York City Opera. The Herald Tribune reviewer thought that her beauty, acting and great voice made it hard to believe that she could be the "sweetheart" of miners on Colorado.

The pinnacle of her career came on February 23, 1962, when Raskin made her debut at the Metropolitan Opera House in the role of Susanna in Mozart's "Marriage of Figaro." She was hailed by the critics for her outstanding performance.

Through the years she continued singing in concerts, ensembles and in operas. She felt that Strauss and Mozart roles were the best for her voice. During this period, she campaigned for more opera companies in the cities. She was quoted as saying "What we get is well trained American singers with no place to go. The only way to become professional is to perform."

She married Dr. Raymond A. Raskin on July 11, 1948. They had two children, Jonathon, who became a medical internist, and Lisa, who was an associate professor of psychology at Amherst College. Through careful planning, Judith Raskin managed to have a happy marital and family life as well as a career.

She became an instructor at the Manhattan School of Music. In 1979, she taught at the 92nd Street YM-YWHA, where she sang the role of Pearl, the rabbi's wife in the new Opera "The Golem."

Raskin was active in many music advisory boards, the Young Concert Artists, the National Opera Institute and the National Endowment of the Arts. During her career, she recorded for Columbia, London, Decca, RCA Victor and CRI Records.

Judith Raskin died on December 21, 1984, after a long struggle with cancer. Services were held at the Stephen Wise Free Synagogue in New York City where she was eulogized as being one of the finest artists of our time who could be emulated by other future Jewish aspirants of the concert and opera stage.

131

Colonel Jack H. Jacobs
Medal of Honor Recipient in Vietnam

Thousands of Jews responded to America's call to arms to fight in Vietnam. Jack H. Jacobs was one of them. Jacobs entered the Army in 1966 as a lieutenant and served until 1987, when he retired as a colonel and a hero. Colonel Jacobs received the Congressional Medal of Honor in 1969 for saving the lives of 12 soldiers and stopping an ambush of his unit in Vietnam.

It was on March 9, 1968, in the Province of Kien Phong, in the Republic of Vietnam, that Jacobs' actions in combat were beyond the call of duty and at the risk of his life. At the time, Jacobs was a first lieutenant serving as assistant battalion adviser, Second Battalion, 16th Infantry, 9th Army Infantry during an operation in the Kien Phong area. The Second Battalion was advancing to make contact with the enemy when it came under intense heavy machine gun and mortar fire from a Viet Cong battalion positioned in well-fortified bunkers. American casualties were high as they became disorganized. Jacobs was with the command element of the lead company. He called for and directed air strikes against the enemy positions so that the Americans could hope to regroup for a renewed attack.

The enemey continued to shower them with mortars and machine gun fire. Jacobs had to take command since the senior officers were either dead or seriously wounded. He had been wounded in the head by a mortar fragment and was bleeding profusely. His vision was imparied by the flow of blood from his head.

He saw a wounded man out in the open. Despite his wounds and poor vision, he went out to bring the man in under intense enemy fire. His administration of first aid saved a man's life. Jacobs then went out again to bring in the wounded company commander. He made repeated trips into the field to bring in the wounded and weapons while the enemy continued to rake the area with mortar and machine gun fire.

On three seperate occasions, he contacted and drove off the enemy patrols that were looking for the allied wounded and weapons. Jacobs single-handedly killed three Viet Cong soldiers and wounded many more.

Jacob's Congressional Medal of Honor citation tells the rest of the story:

His gallant actions and extraordinary heroism saved the lives of one U.S. adviser and 13 allied soldiers. Through his efforts, the allied company was restored to an effective fighting unit and prevented defeat of the friendly forces by a strong and determined enemy. Jacobs, by his conspicuous gallantry and intrepidity in action in the highest traditions of the military service, has reflected great credit upon himself, his unit and the United States Army.

Jacobs also received two Silver Stars, three Bronze Stars, and two Purple Heart Medals.

Jacobs is a resident of New Jersey and is involved with investment banking. He is designated as a brigadier general in the event of mobilization in the defense of his country. Jacobs is one of the seventeen Jews to receive the Congressional Medal Honor. His heroism and gallantry in battle follows a long line of Jewish heroes who have given themselves to defend this country from its enemies.

132

John L. Levitow

The Only Air Force Enlisted Man Awarded the Congressional Medal of Honor in the Vietnam War

John L. Levitow was the only Air Force enlisted man to be awarded the Congressional Medal of Honor. He was a sergeant in the Air Force 3rd Special Operations Squadron in the Vietnam War.

John L. Levitow was born on November 1, 1945, Hartford, Connecticut. After he left the Air Force, he worked for over 20 years in the federal and state veteran affairs agencies.

Levitow was very proud of being a Jewish veteran. In 1997, he became a member of Connecticut Post 45 of the Jewish War Veterans of the USA,the oldest veterans organization in the country

In a ceremony, in January, 1998, at Long Beach, California, the Air Force named a C-17 Globemaster for him. On the fuselage it read: "The Spirit of Sgt. John L. Levitow."

He died on November 8, 2000, and is buried in Arlington Cemetery. His Citation is the following::

"For conspicuous gallantry and intrepidity in action at the risk of his life above and beyond the call of duty. Levitow (then A1c.), U.S. Air Force, distinguished himself by exceptional heroism while assigned as a loadmaster aboard an AC-47 aircraft flying a night

mission in support of Long Binh Army post. Sgt Levitow's aircraft was struck by a hostile mortar round. The resulting explosion ripped a hole 2 feet in diameter through the wing and fragments made over 3,500 holes in the fuselage. All occupants of the cargo compartment were wounded and helplessly slammed against the floor and fuselage. The explosion tore an activated flare from the grasp of a crew member who had been launching flares to provide illumination for Army ground troops engaged in combat. Sgt. Levitow, though stunned by the concussion of the blast and suffering from over 40 fragment wounds in the back and legs, staggered to his feet and turned to assist the man nearest to him who had been knocked down and was bleeding heavily. As he was moving his wounded comrade forward and away from the opened cargo compartment door, he saw the smoking flare ahead of him in the aisle. Realizing the danger involved and completely disregarding his own wounds, Sgt Levitow started toward the burning flare. The aircraft was partially out of control and the flare was rolling wildly from side to side. Sgt. Levitow struggled forward despite the loss of blood from his many wounds and the partial loss of feeling in his right leg. Unable to grasp the rolling flare with his hands, he threw himself bodily upon the burning flare.Hugging the deadly device to his body, he dragged himself back to the rear of the aircraft and hurled the flare through the open cargo door. At that instant the flare separated and ignited in the air, but clear of the aircraft. Sgt. Levitow, by his selfless and heroic actions, saved the aircraft and its entire crew from certain death and destruction. Sgt. Levitow's gallantry, his profound concern for his fellowmen, at the risk of his life above and beyond the call of duty are in keeping with the highest traditions of the U.S. Air Force and reflect great credit upon himself and the Armed Forces of his country."

133

P.F.C. Stewart Burr

A Hero of Vietnam

Private First Class Stewart S. Burr of the United States Marines received the Silver Star Medal for his bravery in Vietnam. He was killed while bringing much needed supplies to his unit.

Burr was serving as a rifleman with Company E, Second Battalion, Ninth Marines, Third Marine Division, in connection with operations against the enemy in the Republic of Vietnam. Burr's squad was maneuvering to reinforce an adjacent unit which had become heavily engaged in battle with the enemy in the Cam Lo area on April 23, 1969.

As his squad moved forward, it also fell under attack from a well entrenched enemy force in a bunker-complex. The enemy was using automatic weapons and mortar against Burr's squad, which was sustaining heavy casualties. The Marines fought back by firing into the enemy bunkers. Soon, the ammunition supply was nearly depleted. The squad could get more ammunition from an adjacent Marine squad. However, there was an open field between them which was being swept with enemy bullets.

Without regard for his own safety, Burr fearlessly dashed across the fire-swept terrain to the other unit to obtain a supply of ammunition. He started maneuvering back with precious supply of machine gun rounds when he was wounded by enemy fire. Ignoring his painful wounds, he continued moving forward with the ammunition. As he reached his unit, he was mortally wounded by grenade fragments.

His Silver Star Medal Citation issued by the President of the United States summed up his action: "His heroic and timely actions inspired all who observed him and contributed significantly to the accomplishment of his unit's mission. By his courage, bold initiative and unwavering devotion to duty, Private First Class Burr upheld the highest traditions of the Marine of the United States Naval Service. He gallantly gave his life in the service of his country."

Burr was raised in Passaic, New Jersey, where he graduated from Passaic High School. He was on the high school's track and cross country teams. He had been at college for two years when he decided to enlist in the Marine Corps to fight in Vietnam.

His family received the Silver Star Medal posthumously at a Passaic City Hall ceremony. Rabbi Solomon Weinberger of Tifereh Israel in Passaic remembered Burr as being a leader of youth who unselfishly gave of himself to help others. In addition to the Silver Star Medal, Burr received the Purple Heart Medal, the Vietnam Campaign Medal, Vietnam Service Medal and the National Defense Medal.

Burr is one of the many Jews who have fought and died for this country. His name will always be among those of the Jewish heroes in America.

134

Two Jewish Generals
of the Vietnam-Era

I n every war in which the United States was involved, there were Jewish generals in leadership roles. Vietnam was no exception. Major General Stanley H. Hyman and Robert B. Solomon had major roles in the Vietnam War.

Hyman was a major when he received the Legion of Merit by the direction of the President of the United States. He was attached to the Military Intellgence of the U.S. Army in Vietnam from August 1968 to August 1969. It was for his excellent work during this period that he received his decoration. Utilizing his extensive intelligence experience, Hyman was able to acquire a voluminous amount of information.

Hyman was able to use his intelligence information to predict the enemy's intentions and plans which helped American commanders fight the enemy. His citation reads: "Through his initiative, resourcefulness, adaptability to change and readiness to resort to the expedient, he has contributed immeasureably to the Free World effort in the Republic of Vietnam. Major Hyman's professional competence and outstanding achievements are in keeping with the highest traditions of the military service and reflect great credit on himself, his unit and the United States Army."

Hyman quickly rose through the ranks to become a major general. He was born on June 25, 1936, in Long Branch, New Jersey. Hyman is married to the former Rosala Carol Mersky and they have four children. He holds the Distinguished Service Medal, Legion of Merit with Two Oak Leaf Clusters, Defense Meritorious Service Medal, Meritorious Service Medal with Two Oak Leaf Clusters, Department of the Army Staff Badge and the Organizations of the Joint Chiefs of Staff Badge.

Solomon is another Jewish officer who served his country in Vietnam. He made many notable contributions to the war effort in the Republic of Vietnam. He served as chief of the Command Information Division for the United States Military Assistance Command in Vietnam and was active there from July 1968 to July 1969. After his tour of duty in Vietnam, Solomon was sent to Europe to command the 1st Battalion, 35th Armor, 4th Armored Division. He has had many responsible positions throughout his military career.

He was promoted to major general in January 1982. His decorations include the Legion of Merit, Defense Superior Service Medal, Meritorious Service Medal with Oak Leaf Cluster, Joint Service Commendation Medal and the Army Commendation Medal with two Oak Leaf Clusters.

Born on December 14, 1930, in Baltimore, he has a master of science degree from Johns Hopkins University, Baltimore. He is married to the former Frances Nathanson and they have three children.

Hyman and Solomon have contributed to the legacy of Jews who have served their country in war.

135

Three Jewish Heroes
of The Vietnam War

I n the National Museum of American Jewish Military History in Washington D.C. there is an exhibit that makes a comparative examination of Jewish contributions to World War I and the Vietnam War. The exhibit compares three Jewish fighting men of each war. Roger Steven Briskin, Fred Zedeck, and Joseph Ira Goldstein are the heroes of the Vietnam War.

Briskin was a corporal in the United States Marines. He was born in 1947 and attended public school in Ardmore, Pennsylvania. Briskin was a quiet and conscientious student who took things seriously. He had planned to become a medical doctor. When he graduated from high school, the Vietnam War was in progress. Briskin felt he had a responsibility to help his country. He enlisted in the U.S. Marine Corps. He went through basic training and displayed leadership ability. It didn't take long before he was promoted to corporal. After Briskin was sent to Vietnam, his unit was immediately pressed into battle.

It was in the Da Nang Quong Nam Province, on March 31, 1967, when he was in the thick of a fierce battle with the enemy, that Briskin saw one of his men wounded by the mortar attack against them. While attempting to rescue him, Briskin was killed by mortar fragments. He was recognized for his bravery and was awarded many citations posthumously.

Captain Zedneck served with the U.S. Air Force, 388th Tactical Fighter Wing, in Korat, Thailand. He was born in Brooklyn, New York, in 1946. He went to public schools and to New York University, from which he graduated in 1968. Zedneck was commissoned a second lieutenant in the Air Force. He earned his navigator wings in 1969 at the Mather Air Force Base in California, after he finished his flight training. Later, he was to be certified as an Air Force weapon systems officer on the F-4 Phantom fighter plane.

In the Southeast Asia area of operations, Zedneck flew 165 combat missions and logged more than 450 combat hours. His many decorations include the Air Force Distinguished Flying Cross and the Air Medal with Ten Oak Leaf Clusters. He retired from the military as a colonel and had a productive career in the Federal Aviation Administration's Office of Emergency Operations. Zedneck and his wife provide a home for foster babies prior to their placement in a final foster home.

Lieutenant Joseph Ira Goldstein, U.S. Navy, Fighter Squadron VF154, was born in Roosevelt, New Jersey, in 1942. Goldstein graduated from Rutgers University in 1964. He enlisted in officers' training school in Pensacola, Florida, where he became a Naval flight officer. He was sent to Vietnam, where he flew about 110 combat missions. He received the Navy Unit Commendation Medal, the Vietnam Gallantry Cross, five air medals and other medals.

After the Vietnam War, Goldstein taught ROTC courses at the University of Michigan until 1971. He then went into government service in Washington, D.C.

Briskin, Zedeck and Goldstein are three of the thousands of Jews who fought for our country. Some died. Some were wounded. Some brought the mental scars of war back with them. Again, as in America's past wars, Jews responded to their country's call for fighting men.

136

Aline B. Saarinen

Art Critic and Correspondent

A line Bernstein Saarinen was one of the nation's best know art and architecture critics, a television journalist and commentator and author.

She was born on March 25, 1914, in New York City, to Irma and Allen Milton Bernstein, who were both amateur painters. Her parents encouraged her interest and participation in artistic and cultural activities. Allen Bernstein was the head of an investment firm and he considered his family to be "high brow."

Aline graduated from the Fieldstone School in New York City in 1931.She went to Vassar College where she took art courses and became interested in journalism. In her junior year, she was elected to Phi Beta Kappa, received a Vassar College Fellowship and graduated with an A.B. degree in 1935.

Following her graduation, she married Joseph H. Louchheim, a public welfare administrator, on June 17, 1935. In the same year she enrolled at the Institute of Fine Arts at New York University and graduated in 1941 with an A.M. degree in the history of architecture. While going to N.Y.U., she had two sons, Donald, in 1937, and Harry, in 1939.

In 1944, Aline Louchheim joined the staff of Arts News magazine in New York City and she was its managing editor from 1946 to 1948. The magazine sponsored a book, 5000 Years of Art: A Pictorial History, with commentary by Aline Louchheim. The press, including The New York Times gave it excellent reviews.

In 1951, her marriage ended in divorce. It was the same year that she received The International Award for Best Foreign Criticism at the Venice Bennale. In 1953, she received the American Federation of Arts Award for best newspaper criticism. After interviewing Eero Saarinen, the noted Finnish-born architect, they were attracted to each other and were married in 1954.

She became the associate art editor and critic at The New York Times from 1948 to 1953 and associate art critic from 1954 to 1958. She also published a number of articles on art and cultural trends for The New Times magazine and other major magazines.

Her years with Eero Saarinen were happy and productive. They had a son Eames, named for the designer Charles Eames, December, 1954. She received a Guggenheim fellowship in 1957, and she wrote The Proud Possessors, a biographical study of major American art collectors. It became a best seller and Aline became a public personality.

In 1962, she started her third career in television at age fifty. She was invited to appear on television to discuss art. She was an immediate success and she made documentaries such as The Art of Collecting for NBC. In 1964, she became the third woman correspondent for NBC News and she was the moderator of For Women Only show. In this program she dealt with the sensitive issues of abortion and birth control.

She was named to become chief of the NBC's Paris News Bureau in 1971. She was the first woman to become the head of an overseas news bureau. She held this position until her death on July 13, 1972.

Aline Saarinen demonstrated in her writings about art and architecture that it can be interesting, exciting and understandable for the public to read. Her success and fame was built on this style of writing.

137

Dore Schary

Film Writer and Producer

Dore Schary was one of the first producers to make a film dealing with anti-Semitism. He made the film Crossfire, which was enthusiastically acclaimed by critics. Critic Bosley Crowther wrote, "It boldly comes out and names a canker which festers and poisonously infects the very vitals of American democracy." Many of Schary's films would be about real life in America.

Schary was born on August 31, 1905, in Newark, New Jersey with the name Isadore, which he shortened to Dore when he entered show business. Dore was the son of Herman Hugo and Belle (Drachler) Schary, immigrants from Europe engaged in the hotel and catering business. Schary attended Central High School in Newark, but dropped out of school when he was fourteen. He tried his hand at many jobs before realizing that his educational handicap was preventing him from moving ahead. He returned to Central High to finish his education.

In the middle 1920s, Schary was playing bit parts in New York stage plays with such stars as Paul Muni and Spencer Tracy. When he wasn't working on stage, he was teaching himself to master play writing. His first play to be produced onstage was Too Many Heroes, in 1938. It had a brief run.

Schary had submitted some of his plays to movie producers which resulted in a one-year (1932-33) contract with Columbia Pictures. During this year, he wrote eleven screenplays and established a reputation of being a steady, imaginative and reliable writer. After his contract expired, Schary freelanced for the next seven years. He was the author or co-author of 35 screenplays which included the Oscar-winning script for the Metro-Goldwyn-Mayer production of Boys Town.

In 1941, MGM made him an executive producer. Schary had a theory that "B" pictures were badly made not because of the lowbudget, but because of the poor quality of the story and script. He proved this when he made such hit "B" movies as Journey For Margaret, Bataan, Lassie Come Home and Joe Smith, American.

In the coming years, Schary would be involved in producing many movies which dealt with social issues and problems. He was producing the movie The White Tower, in 1948, when it was suspended after the House Un-American Activities Committee probed alleged communistic influence in the movie industry. Schary was called to testify before the committee. He stated that he would hire people on the basis of ability, regardless of their political ideology, unless the ideology was legally defined as inimical to the state. Most socially conscious pictures being made in Hollywood were all put on hold for many years.

Dore Schary produced or supervised over 250 films in his life. He wrote the Tony Award-winning play Sunrise at Campobello. He was the national chairman of the B'nai B'rith Anti-Defamation League, 1963-69. He received the Thomas Jefferson Award from the Council Against Intolerance in America, in 1948. Schary also received the Golden Slipper Club Award for humanitarianism, 1947.

Dore Schary married Miriam Svet, an artist, on March 5, 1932, and they had three children, Jill, Joy and Jeb. He died on July 7, 1980, in New York City. His achievements in the entertainment industry have earned him many accolades, but he will also be remembered as a fighter against anti-Semitism and for standing up for his principles.

138

Judith Martin

Director and Playwright

Judith Martin is an innovator and creator of the Paper Bag Players, a theatrical group that performs for children. She pioneered a new form of children's theater.

Martin was born in Newark, New Jersey, in August, 1918, where she grew up and received her education.

Her grandparents were poor working class Russian-Jewish immigrants and her parents were upper-middle class.

Martin would commute to New York City for dance and drama lessons while attending the Newark public schools. When she graduated high school, she attended for two years the Neighborhood (Playhouse) School Theater. Maria Ouspenskaya, a noted actress of stage and films, taught her the Stanislavsky method of acting. Martin then enrolled in the New Theater School where she studied under Larry Galpern. He had studied the Russian method of dramatizing fairy tales with song, dance and fantasy. Martin was able to capitalize on this method in the development of the Paper Bag Players.

Martin became the director of the dance project of the National Youth Administration in New York. She choreographed American dances for them which toured for two years throughout the metropolitan New York City.

With Diana Merliss, a former classmate, they founded the New York Theater for Children. The productions were based on the original stories written by Martin, such as "The Runaway Horse." The productions were very professional and well received, but a shortage of bookings, forced them to end their venture.

Her initial professional success was in dance. She had studied modern dance with Martha Graham and then performed with many new innovative dance companies, including the Anna Sokolow Dance Company. She joined the Merce Cunningham Company where Martin was a choreographer, director and lead dancer.

Her career was interrupted in 1956 when she married Solomon Miller, an anthropologist, who taught at Hofstra University. They left New York to travel to Illinois and on an expedition to Peru.

In 1958, Martin and three women formed an experimental group which became the Paper Bag Players. She was a major force in the group as she directed, designed, wrote and acted in all productions. By 1965, everybody, except Martin, had left and others replaced them.

They toured schools and children's theaters with their performances of dances, sketches and songs. Their fantasy coupled with animation on the stage captivated the young audiences. Martin also interacted the performers with the children by audience participation.

The Paper Bag Players used people of all sizes, ages, and physical characteristics in the performances. They felt that children could more easily identify with people who look and act normal. It was not unusual to have performers go into the audience to involve the children.

Their stories were about the life that surrounds the children. "Hot Feet" deals with the problems and joys of urban living; "Dandelion" is about the evolutionary theory in nature; "I Won't Take A Bath" is involved in children's fantasies; "Grandpa" depicts the life process of growing, changing and growing old.

Judith Martin and the Paper Bag Players reflected the realities of life designed to educate and entertain children through the fantasy and the magic of the theater. She also brought to many children the only theater that they will ever see.

139

Gregory Goodwin Pincus

Father of "The Pill"

Dr. Gregory Goodwin Pincus and Dr. M.C. Chiang, his collaborator, developed the first practical oral contraceptive birth-control pill after being persuaded to do so by Margaret Sanger, a leader in the American birth-control movement, and Katherine Dexter McCormick, an heir to the International Harvester fortune. He received a grant from the Planned Parenthood Federation in 1951. Pincus and Chiang began to look for a progestin or a synthetic progestin that could be used as a birth control agent.

After much experimentation with more than 200 substances, the two derived the steroid compunds from the roots of the wild Mexican yam. The steroids were found to be successful in inhibiting ovulation in laboratory animals and appeared to be harmless.

Pincus started conducting field tests for the steroids in pill form with hundreds of women in Brookline, Massachusetts; Puerto Rico; and Haiti in 1956. They proved to be effective. The only side-effects were brief feelings of nausea.The United States Food and Drug Administration (FDA) authorized the marketing of steroids for limited use in 1957. Three years later the FDA licensed Enovid, a birth-control pill produced by G.D. Searle Company.

Soon after the success of the birth-control pill, Pincus and Chiang started work on a new pill which would prevent implantation after fertilization. The two were still working on this new pill when Pincus died on August 22, 1967.

Pincus was the son of Joseph William and Elizabeth Florence (nee Lipman) Pincus. He was born on April 9, 1903, in Woodbine, New Jersey. His father was a teacher, the editor of the Jewish Farmer and an agricultural consultant. Pincus' father was also a leader in a community of Russian Jews who hoped to turn refugees from the czar's pogroms into American farmers in the late 19th century.

Pincus went to Morris High School in the Bronx, New York, after his family moved there. He received his B.S. degree in biology from Cornell University, Ithaca, New York, in 1924. While in his first year of graduate school at Harvard University, he married Elizabeth Notkin, a social worker he had met when she was a boarder in his family's home. They had two children. Pincus received his doctorate of science in 1927.

Pincus was recognized many times for his work. He received the Lasker Award from Planned Parenthood, the Oliver Bird Award (London) in 1960, and the Modern Medicine Award in 1964. He was elected to the National Academy of Sciences in 1965.

140

Judy Blume

Author of Juvenile & Adult Novels

After the rejections notices stopped coming to Judy Blume, she became one of the most popular writers of young adult novels. Her ability to understand and relate to the problems and human foibles of kids brought her this success.

Blume was the daughter of Esther and Rudolph Sussman, a dentist, who was born in Elizabeth, N.J., on February 12, 1938. After graduating high school, she entered New York University. Her two goals in attending college were to obtain a degree and to find a husband. She met John Blume, a young ambitious lawyer, and married him in her junior year. After graduating NYU, she had a daughter, Randy, and a son, Larry. Her marriage ended in divorce in 1975.

While she was comfortable being a suburban housewife and mother, Blume felt that something was lacking in her life. After a few attempts at other activities, she began writing stories and books for children.

After a few rejections and some writing courses at N.Y.U., she started selling her short stories to magazines while working on her novels. In 1969, she sold The One in the Middle is the Green Kangaroo to Riley and Lee, which was the beginning of a successful and long writing career.

Blume's early novels were written for younger children. As she matured, she expanded her audience to include adolescents and adults. She wrote two adult novels and others for the adolescents.

Her ability to discuss openly and realistically, with sincere feelings, about many sensitive subjects facing and effecting adolescents, attributed to her popularity. For example, in *Iggie's House*, racial prejudice was the main issue; first love was the topic in *Forever...*; menstruation was the subject in *Are You There God? It's me Margaret*; divorce and family breakups was in *It's Not the End of the World*; masturbation was involved in *Deenie*; and social ostracism was in *Blubber*.

Blume displayed sensitivity, humor and insight in capturing the joys, fears, uncertainty and anguish of these adolescents which enabled her to establish this affinity with them through the use of the first-person in her writings. This technique established a closeness and identification between her characters and her audience.

Blume felt very strongly about the lack of communication between children and their parents. She did something about this lack of communication with the establishment of the KIDS Fund in 1981. She financed it with the royalties from Judy Blume Diary: The Place to Put Your Own Feeling. The fund has been contributing about $40,000 a year to various non-profit organizations who help young people communicate with their parents.

Judy Blume has received many prestigious awards and honors for her stories and novels; including Are You There God? It's Me Margaret? as the best book for children in 1970 by The New York Times.

Judy Blume has been able to communicate with her readers through her writings. Her ability to discuss and deal with the sensitive issues facing young people has earned her the readership of millions. Her work has shown young people that reading can be meaningful and fun. Judy Blume is today considered to be the foremost writer of children's novels; a position that she has worked hard to achieve.

141

Nancy Lieberman
A Great Women's Basketball Star

Nancy Lieberman was the greatest woman basketball star produced in the United States. She broke the professional gender barrier with her debut in the United States Basketball League.

Nancy was born in Brooklyn, New York, and she was raised by her mother after her parents were divorced. She was always to be found in the neighborhood playgrounds playing basketball days and nights. At night she played and practiced "radar ball" because you couldn't see the ball go through the basket, but you could hear it.

Basketball was an outlet for her consuming ambition to be the best in the game and she would always play against the boys' strongest opposition to improve her skills. She did not give an inch against the boys and would sometimes be in a fist fight with them. She did not play against the girls until she was on the girl's high school basketball team. Lieberman went to Old Dominion University where she was the star of the girl's basketball team. She made All-America three times: 1978, 79 and 80. Her asphalt arrogance and hawklike intensity made her the outstanding women basketball player in America. Her style of playing and basketball court personality earned her the name of "Lady Magic" as she was compared to the Los Angeles star "Magic" Johnson. She had his crowd-pleasing passing skills and court demeanor.

One of Nancy Lieberman's ambitions was to play on an American women's basketball team in the Olympics. She was made the United States Olympic squad in 1976 when she was a senior in high school. She was also on the 1980 squad but the United States decided to boycott the games because Russia had invaded Afghanistan.

Lieberman was disappointed as she was at the height of her career. After trying a number of things, she made her debut in the United States Basketball League. She was the first woman to play in a men's professional league. She was twenty-seven years old when she joined the Springfield Fame's which was short-lived.

She became actively involved in the business world. She managed to arrange for book and film deals, owned two sporting goods stores and owned real estate in Texas and St. Croix. She endorsed many products and there were times that she was wealthier than the owners of the women's professional teams for whom she played.

When she graduated college in 1980, Lieberman received many awards. She received the Wade Trophy for outstanding women's basketball player in America, The Broderick cup, presented annually to the top AIAW athlete of the year, The Maccabee Award for the Jewish Athlete of the Year and she was named for every All-American women's basketball squad during her college career.

Nancy Lieberman rose to stardom along with other women of '70s and '80s. They also achieved the monetary gains that come when you are an exceptional athlete. Nancy Lieberman has made it possible for other Jewish women to become recognized for their athletic skills and abilities.

142

Beverly Sills

Soprano and Opera Director

Beverly Sills' greatness and recognition as a coloratura soprano and as a director of an opera company is the epitome of the American success story. Her singing drew millions to the New York City Opera and her general director's skills of the company kept it flourishing.

She was born Belle Miriam Silverman on May 25, 1929, in Brooklyn, New York, to Shirley and Morris Silverman, of Russian-Jewish descent. When she was three years old, she won a beautiful-baby contest after singing *The Wedding of Jack and Jill.*

Her mother was convinced of Beverly's musical talents, and she provided her with lessons in dance, voice and elocution. In the thirties, she performed professionally on radio (Uncle Bob's Rainbow House-WOR) and in the 1938 film *Uncle Sol Solves It.* In 1936, Beverly Sills began taking lessons with Estelle Liebling, a famous singing teacher, who encouraged her to audition on CBS' radio's *Major Bowes' Amateur Hour.* She became a member of his company and she was heard every Sunday across the nation.

Beverly Sills launched her full-time career in 1945 when Broadway producer J.J. Shubert was determined to make her a star. She starred in the Gilbert and Sullivan national touring company and the following year appeared in other operettas. When her father died in 1949, she and her mother lived in a one-bedroom apartment where her singing in a private club just about supported them.

For years, Beverly Sills tried to become a member of the New York City Opera. Finally, she was hired and she made her debut on October 29, 1955, as Rosalinde in Johann Strauss's *Die Fledermous* which drew raves from the newspaper critics. In 1958, her appearance in the premier performance of the "Ballad of Baby Doe" in 1958, fully established her as a leading soprano.

Beverly Sills married Peter Buckley Greenough, whose family owned the Cleveland Plain Dealer, on November 17, 1956. Upon her marriage, she was confronted with a twenty-five room French chateau on Lake Erie and two small children from her husband's previous marriage. The children, Meredith, was practically deaf, and Peter Jr., was mentally retarded. Sills took time off from the opera to spend more time with her children. She resumed her career when she sang the *Queen of the Night* in Mozart's *The Magic Flute*, in January, 1964.

In the late sixties, Sills went abroad and captivated the opera audiences with her singing. She returned home and concentrated on mastering the high coloratura roles repertory. On April 8, 1975, she made her debut at the Metropolitan Opera as Pamira in Rossini's *The Siege of Corinth* and received an eighteen-minute ovation. She continued to sing here until she announced her retirement from professional singing to become the co-director of the New York City Opera.

On a national televised PBS program from Lincoln Center on October 27, 1980, celebrities from the stage, screen, television and opera made appearances bidding her farewell and wishing her the best of success in her new role. Sills, as general director, turned around a debt-ridden New York City Opera into a financially self-sustaining organization.

Beverly Sills is one of the few women who has achieved success as a general director of an opera company and as a coloratura soprano.

143

Mark Spitz

An Olympic Swimming Star

The 1972 Olympic Games in Munich, Germany, were filled with a mixture of emotions for the participating Jewish athletes. Mark Spitz won seven gold medals and established many world records for swimming. Terrorists murdered eleven Israeli athletes. The world was elated over Spitz's achievements in swimming and was stunned and angered by the cold-blooded murder of the athletes.

At the games, Ameican security guards quickly formed a shield of protection around Spitz since they were fearful that the terrorists might strike at him because he was a Jew. Spitz was angry and saddened by the loss of the Israeli athletes. However, he was too stunned and protected to do anything symbolic against the terrorists.

Spitz was the oldest of three children and was born on February 10, 1950. His parents, Lenore and Arnold Spitz, introduced him to swimming as soon as he could walk. When he was two years old, his father, a steel company executive, was transferred to Honolulu, Hawaii. Spitz swam at Waikiki Beach every day. "You should have seen that little boy dash into the ocean. He'd run like he was trying to commit suicide," Lenore Spitz told a reporter for *Time* (April 12, 1968).

After a few years, the family moved back to California. Spitz's father was always teaching him about the importance of being first. At the age of 15, at the Maccabiah Games in Tel Aviv in August 1965, Spitz won four gold medals and was named the most outstanding athlete. This was the beginning of his long list of victories. By the spring of 1972, Spitz had set 23 world swimming records and 35 United States records. He won two gold medals, one silver medal and one bronze medal in the 1968 Olympics. Many expected him to do better, but a bad cold had prevented him from doing so.

Spitz set his first world record in June of 1967 at a small swim meet in California. He swam the 400 meter free-style in four minutes, 10 and six-tenths seconds. After this meet, he went on to other meets. His list of swim records became larger and larger.

Spitz won his first gold medal in the 200 meter butterfly in two minutes and seven-tenths of a second for a world record at the Munich Olympic Games on August 28, 1972. That same night, he won a second gold medal when his team established a world record for the 400 meter free-style relay. The following day, he won his third gold medal. Again, he established a world record when he swam the 200 meter free-style in one minute and 52.78 seconds.

He swam the 100 meter butterfly in 54.27 seconds to earn a world record and a gold medal on September 1.He then went on to anchor the United States 800 meter free-style relay team to victory for another gold medal. He won the 100 meter free-style in 51.22 seconds and swam the butterfly leg on the victorious United States team in the 400 meter medley relay for his seventh gold medal on September 3. He set another world record with his seven gold medals when he surpassed the record held by Italian fencer Nedo Nadi, who had won five Olympic gold medals in 1920.

After the '72 Olympics, Spitz made movies and commercials and went into business. He lives in California with wife Suzy, and his son.

293

144

Barbara Walters
Noted Interviewer & Star of Television

Barbara Walters has become a television superstar through her state of the arts form of questioning of celebrities and journalistic instinct. She achieved this status the hard way as she broke through "the man's world of television journalism."

She was born on September 25, 1931, in Boston, Massachusetts, to Dena and Lou Walters, who was the owner of New York City's famous nightclub, The Latin Quarter. She was raised in Miami and New York as her father's business of being an impresario took them to these two cities during the year. Because she was surrounded by celebrities who worked and socialized with her father, she was not intimidated by their presence.

She attended public schools in New York and Miami and then entered Sarah Lawrence College, in Bronxville, New York. She received her B.A. degree in English in 1953. After graduation, she moved to New York City where she wanted to pursue a career in television.

She was hired by RCA-TV, the local affiliate of NBC, to do some writing, producing and public relations. Her talent was recognized by Dave Garaway, an early host of the Today Show, who invited her to become a writer on his staff. It was not long before she was given on-air assignments. The choice news stories were assigned to the men and Walters had to break through this wall of sexism. Her popularity rose because of her unique ability to interview celebrities.

They gave her a regular spot on the show for her interviews. She was able to schedule members of the Kennedy family, the widow and children of the late Dr. Martin Luther King, Jr., and other important and well known people. This was also a period where television learned how to become an important media in reporting breaking news as it was happening. In 1976, ABC hired her from NBC, as a co-anchor woman for their prime news time at a record breaking one million dollars a year. In November, 1977, Walters scored her biggest scoop when she interviewed Egyptian President Anwar Sadat and Israeli Prime Minister Menachem Begin.

Walters has continued to conduct interviews with such well know personalities as Princess Diana of England, General Colin Powell, Hillary Rodham Clinton, wife of President William Clinton, Robert Shapiro, famous defense attorney, etc. Her ability in drawing people out, understanding the situation and to make it as clear as possible during interviews has attributed to her success. The year 1996 marks the twentieth anniversary of her relationship with the American Broadcasting. Her 20/20 television show is always in the weekly top ratings according to the polls. Walters has substituted many times for a vacationing Ted Koppel on his Nightline program and has her own special programs throughout the year.

Barbara Walters was married and divorced. She has an adopted daughter, Jacqueline, with whom she enjoys the mother-daughter relationship. Jacqueline once complained to a friend, "My mommy can't drive and she can't make meat loaf. All my mommy can do is television."

Barbara Walters is a television superstar who broke through the male dominated news broadcasting. Her success as a television newscaster and host of magazine programs and special shows proves that women can achieve stardom in television when given the opportunity.

145

Barbra Streisand

Concert Star, Actress, Director & Producer of Movies

B arbra Streisand, a superstar with many talents, by the age of twenty, was a Broadway star. During the years, she has enjoyed success as a concert star, actress, writer, director and producer receiving many awards for her work.

She was born on April 24, 1942, in Brooklyn, New York, to Diana and Emanuel Streisand, who was a high school English teacher. Unfortunately, he died when Barbra was fifteen months old. Her mother maintained a kosher home and she went to a Jewish religious school. After graduating Erasmus High School, Brooklyn, with high honors, Barbra Streisand began her career, singing in Greenwich Village bars and clubs.

David Merrick, a Broadway producer, saw her performing at the Blue Angel, a nightclub, and he immediately signed her to play Miss Marmelstein in "I Can Get It for You Wholesale." While the show lasted nine months, Barbra Streisand became an instant star, who was in demand for many roles. In 1964, Barbra Streisand accepted the starring role of Fanny Brice in *Funny Girl* which became one of the most successful musicals in the theater. She won an Oscar for the film version of *Funny Girl*.

Two contemporary songs *People* and *Don't Rain on My Parade*, became her signature songs which sold millions of records. She had many Gold Record Albums selling over a million: *People*, 1965; *My Name is Barbra*, 1965; *Color Me Barbra*; 1966, *Stoney End*, 1971; *The Way We Were*, 1974; *A Star is Born*, 1976; *Superman*, 1977; and the list goes on.

Her films after *Funny Girl* included *Hello Dolly*, 1969; *On A Clear Day Your Can See Forever*, 1970; *The Owl and the Pussycat*, 1970; *What's Up Doc*, 1972; *Up the Sandbox*, 1972; *The Way We Were*, 1973; *For Pete's Sake*, 1974; *Funny Lady*, 1975; *A Star Is Born*, which she co-produced, 1976; *The Main Event*, 1978; *All Night Long*, 1981; *Yentl*, which she directed, co-wrote and co-produced, 1983; *Nuts* 1987; *The Prince of Tides*, 1991, which won seven Oscar nominations and was directed and co-produced by Barbra Streisand.

Streisand traveled abroad and at home with her successful concert tours attracting capacity audiences. Her T.V. recordings of the concerts expanded the attendance which brought her closer to her audiences.

Barbra Streisand was married to Elliott Gould, actor, and they had a son, Jason. They were divorced, but both were involved in the raising of their son. When it came time for Jason's bar mitzvah, they decided to have it in the small orthodox synagogue in Venice, California. She had recently become involved again with her religion which gave her great comfort and security.

Streisand donated $50,000 in 1981 for the funding at the UCLA Hillel of a Streisand Center for Jewish Cultural Arts which will sponsor a performance by a well known personality in the arts each year.

Barbra Streisand has been very outspoken on women's rights, abortion, aids research, sexism and women's abuse. She established The Streisand Foundation which is committed to women's rights, civil liberties and environmental protection. She received many awards and recognition not only for her artistry but for her contributions to society.

Being a superstar is demanding on a person for their performance and emotional being. Barbra Streisand has demonstrated over the years that you can be a superstar and a "mensch" at the same time if you are concerned about people.

297

146

Ruth Bader Ginsburg
Associate Justice of The U.S. Supreme Court

When Ruth Bader Ginsburg was sworn in as the 107th justice to the United States Supreme Court in August, 1993, she became the second woman to sit in this court (Sandra Day O'Connor was the first woman) and the first Jewish justice since 1969.

She was born on March 15, 1933, the daughter of Celia and Nathan Bader, in Brooklyn, New York. Nathan Bader was a furrier and her mother had a strong passion for reading, language and the love of books. Ruth Bader was one of two daughters, her oldest sister, Marilyn, died of meningitis and she was reared as an only child.

She was an excellent student in school, graduating at the top of her class in grammar school and an academic leader in high school. She was confirmed with honors from the East Midwood Jewish Center. Ginsburg was very active in high school where she played the cello in the orchestra, was a member of Arista, was a cheerleader and a baton twirler and the editor of her high school newspaper. Her mother died the day before she was to graduate from James Madison High School.

After earning her B.A. degree in government, in 1954, she married Martin D. Ginsburg, who had graduated Cornell the year before. He was called for military service the same year and they lived at Fort Sill, Oklahoma, for two years. It was during this period that Ruth Ginsburg experienced sex discrimination.

She applied for a job with the local social security office while she was pregnant. She was appointed to a position and when she told them that she was pregnant, they demoted her three levels in pay. Another woman, who was appointed and never told them of her pregnancy, received no demotion in the pay scale.

After her husband completed his military service, they moved to Cambridge, Massachusetts, where they both enrolled in the Harvard Law School. She transferred to Columbia Law School after her husband graduated Harvard Law School and obtained a job in Manhattan.

Following her graduation, there followed a succession of job experiences. She served as a clerk for Federal District Judge Edward L. Palmieri, spent two years on a Columbia Law School project, became the second woman to join the faculty of Rutgers Law School. 1963, and she tried many cases for the American Civil Liberties Union before the United States Supreme Court.

Ruth Bader Ginsburg was nominated by President Jimmy Carter to the United States Court of Appeal for the District of Columbia. She was sworn in on June 30, 1980 and served for thirteen years.

President Bill Clinton was confronted with a vacancy on the Supreme Court after Judge Byron R. White resigned. After three months of searching for a candidate, he nominated Ruth Bader Ginsburg. During her Senate confirmation hearings, she did not answer any questions concerning issues that were coming up before the court. Her nomination was approved by the Senate by a vote of ninety-six to three and she was sworn in on August 10, 1993.

Ruth Bader Ginsburg had to overcome many obstacles as a woman and as a Jew to achieve her success. She has paved the way for other Jewish women to move up the ladder of success.

147

Barbara Boxer

United States Senator from California

Barbara Boxer and Dianne Feinstein were the first pair of women to be elected together to the United States Senate from the same state in 1992. Boxer's election was another successful step upward in her political career.

She was born on November 11, 1940, to Sophie and Ira Levy, in Brooklyn, New York. In her youth she never contemplated having a career in public office. Boxer went through the public school system and graduated from Brooklyn College in 1962. It was here when she was a senior that she married Stewart Boxer. She went to work so that he could attend Fordham Law School.

Barbara Boxer experienced sex discrimination and sexual harassment as a woman. When in college, her professor gave her a very low mark on an exam and when she saw him in his office about the grade, he made sexual advances towards her. When she wanted to become a stockbroker on Wall Street, she discovered that they only hired men. When she ran for supervisor on the county board in California, she was attacked for not staying home to take care of the home and children which cost her the election.

They had moved to San Francisco, California, when her husband obtained a legal position after graduating law school and passing the bar exam. It was here that she had two children, Doug, a son, and Nicole, a daughter. Her interests became involved in the high school dropout rate and to provide job training for those who left. The program called the Education Corps of Marin worked so well that the county adopted it.

After losing her first election, she went to work for two years as a reporter at the Pacific Sun. She then became an aide for Congressman John Burton and after two years, she ran again for supervisor in Marin County which she won. This was the beginning of her successful political career.

She served as a supervisor for six years and she became the first woman to be president of the Marin County Board of Supervisors. In 1983, she was elected to the United States House of Representatives from California's Sixth District. Here too she was faced with sexual discrimination. When House Speaker Thomas (Tip) O'Neill referred to "the men in Congress", she sent him a letter politely asking him to say "men and women." He answered by telling her that he would not make the mistake again. Also, the house gym for women was totally inferior to the men's facility.

Boxer served for ten years as a congresswoman. In that time she exposed overcharges by Pentagon contractors, one charged $7,600 for a coffee pot. She introduced legislation for more competitive bidding from contractors, fought for military reforms and to protect whistle blowers in government. She exposed mismanagement in the waste program, fought for airline cabin safety and was an advocate for domestic priorities in the areas of health, biomedical research and education.

She was recognized for her achievements with awards from the Anti-Defamation League, National Council of Jewish Women, Planned Parenthood, League of Conservatism, American Police Hall of Fame, etc.

Barbara Boxer's success in the political arena is a model to emulate by every young woman.

148

$\mathcal{D}$ianne $\mathcal{F}$einstein

United States Senator from California

Dianne Feinstein is an astute politician who has successfully climbed the ladder of elective offices in San Francisco and California. She is the first woman elected U.S. Senator from California, (1992), the first woman to be elected president of the San Francisco Board of Supervisors, (1969), the first woman to be mayor of San Francisco, (1978), the first woman to be considered for selection as the vice-presidential candidate of a major political party, and the first woman to be nominated as governor by a major party in California.

Dianne Feinstein was born on June 23, 1933, in San Francisco, the oldest of three daughters of Betty and Leon Goldman. Her father was a nationally known surgeon who was a professor at the University of California. She received a B.S. degree in history in 1955 from Stanford University. While going to college, she modeled clothes on television for her Uncle Morris Goldman, a clothing manufacturer.

Her first election campaign was at Sanford University when she ran for vice-president of the student body. While attempting to give a speech at a fraternity house, one of the hecklers picked her up and put her in the shower and drenched her with water. She won the election and remembered the fraternity by denying them a permit to hold an overnight football game party.

Feinstein began working in the district attorney's office and she met Jack Berman, a prosecutor. After a short courtship, they were married on December 2, 1956. Three years later, they were divorced and she was left with her daughter, Katherine Anne, born on July 31, 1957.

After deciding that politics was her forte, she was appointed by Governor Brown to a membership on the Board of Trust of the California Institution for Women which was later changed to California Women's Board of Terms and Parole, which regulated the prison terms and parole conditions for women convicts.

She resigned from her position on the Board of Terms and Parole to spend more time with her husband Bertram Feinstein, a neurosurgeon, and her daughter. In 1969, she was elected to the board of supervisors and receiving the highest vote which automatically elected her to be president of the board for a two year term. Feinstein held this position for a number of terms and on the morning of November 27, 1978, she was planning to announce her retirement from political life when she received the news that Mayor George Moscone had been fatally shot. Feinstein immediately became the acting mayor. It was during this year that her husband died.

She finished her term as acting mayor and then won the election for mayor in 1979. The law allowed only two terms as mayor of San Francisco, Dianne Feinstein left office in 1988. She married Richard C. Blum, an investment banker, on January 20, 1980, who helped support her losing campaign for governor as candidate of the Democratic Party.

Diane Feinstein set her sights on winning the senate vacancy created when Pete Wilson vacated this position to become governor of California. She easily defeated John Seymour in a special election in 1992. Two years later, she edged out Michael Huffington, a millionaire Republican congressman from Santa Barbara for a full six year term.

Diane Feinstein has demonstrated that Jewish women can achieve politically in a male dominated sexist society if they work hard at it.

303

149

Letty Cottin Pogrebin

Feminist Leader & Magazine Editor

L etty Cottin Pogrebin is one of America's outstanding feminist journalists. She was the founding editor of "Ms." magazine, author of the column "Working Woman" and author of a number of books relating to women in business and non-sexist child rearing.

She was born on June 9, 1939, to Cyral and Jacob Cottin. Her father was a successful attorney and her mother was a known designer. Letty graduated CUM LAUDE from Brandeis University with a B.A. Degree in English and American Literature.

In 1960, she went to work for a book publisher, Bernard Geis Associates, and she soon became the director of publicity, advertising and subsidiary rights for the next ten years. In 1970, her talents were recognized and she was made a vice president of the company. It was the same year that her book, "How to Make it in a Man's World" was published. It was a practical and humorous guide on how a woman can succeed in the male-dominated world of business. Some of the humor can be seen in the chapter titles: *How to Succeed in Business Without Really Typing, Executive Sweets* and *If Your Can't Stand the Heat, Get Back to the Kitchen.*

Pogrebin helped found the pioneering magazine for women Ms. in 1971. She became the editor and she continued to write her column, *The Working Woman*, for the *Ladies Home Journal*. She also wrote articles for other magazines on women and employment, feminism, the psychology and sociology of child rearing, women in politics and the role of the women in the family.

In her book, *In Getting Yours: How to Make the System Work for the Working Woman*, (1975) she writes about how women can get the greatest benefits from union membership, the need for child caring centers for working women, maternity rights, Equal Rights Amendment, sexism in religion and society and many other issues relating to feminism.

In 1980, her book, *In Growing Up Free: Raising Your Child in the 80s*, her main thrust is non-sexist child rearing. She stresses the importance of questioning everything that we do with, to, for and around children.

Pogrebin was one of the founders of the National Women's Political Caucus in 1971. She and the other founders realized the need for political action and clout to achieve legislation gains for women in society.

She worked with actress Marlo Thomas on *Free to be You and Me*, a record, book and television package of non-sexist songs and stories. She is also on the board of directors of Action for Children's television, which monitors children's television programs.

She has been fighting anti-Semitism all of her life. She was outspoken when she encountered it in the feminist movement. In her article in *Ms.* magazine, in June, 1982, she states that Jewish women have two battles to fight: Against sexism and against anti-Jewish beliefs. She wrote that women as Jews within the feminist movement with as much zeal as we identify as feminists in Judaism.

Letty Cottin Pogrebin continues to struggle for the rights of women in society. Her outspoken writings and lecturing on feminism and women's rights display a leadership and courage that will help women achieve their equal place in America.

150

Judith A. Resnik

The Second Woman in Space

Astronaut Dr. Judith A. Resnik once said, "I think something is only dangerous if you are not prepared for it, or if you don't have control over it or if you can't think through how to get yourself out of a problem." In 1984, Resnik became the second American woman to travel in space. Dr. Sally K. Ride flew a mission in 1983. On her first trip into space, Resnick was a mission specialist on the maiden voyage of the space shuttle DISCOVERY.

After the DISCOVERY was in orbit, she radioed back to NASA that "the Earth looks great." Part of her job on the mission was pointing a camera on the craft's robotic long arm to inspect initial efforts to shake a chunk of ice off the craft's side. The crew managed to make the robotic arm knock off the piece of ice. Resnik had logged 144 hours and 57 minutes in space.

Resnik was born on April 5, 1949, in Akron, Ohio. She went to public schools and graduated from high school in 1966. She received a Bachelor of Science Degree in Electrical Engineering from Carnegie-Mellon University, Pittsburgh, in 1970, and a Doctorate in Electrical Engineering from the University of Maryland, College Park, in 1977.

After her graduation, Resnik held a number of jobs before entering the space program. Her first was with the RCA Corporation in

306

Morristown, New Jersey, where she worked on circuitry for specialized radar control systems. While working for RCA, Resnik authored a paper on design procedures for special-purpose integrate circuitry.

Resnik was a biomedical engineer and staff fellow in the laboratory of neurophysiology at the National Institute of Health in Bethesda, Maryland, from 1974 to 1978. Prior to her selection by NASA in 1978, she worked for the Xerox Corporation in El Segundo, California. She was selected as an astronaut candidate by NASA in January 1978 and completed her one-year training evaluation period in August 1979. NASA assigned her to work on a number of projects in support of the Orbiter development, including experiment software, the Remote Manipulator System, and training techniques.

Resnik was determined to do everything she could possibly do. She was the only girl among 16 students to have perfect scores on her SATs in high school. She was a classical pianist and a gourmet cook. Also, she was working on her pilot's license. "I never play anything softly," she said when questioned about her intensity at the piano. She also liked to run and ride her bicycle.

On January 28, 1986, millions saw Resnik on television as she strutted aboard the CHALLENGER wearing a smile and waving her hand. She was joined by Dr. R.E. McNair and Lieutenant Colonel E.S. Onizuka (U.S. Air Force); two civilian payload specialists, G.B. Jarvis and S.C. McAuliffe, a teacher; Commander M.J. Smith (U.S. Navy), the pilot; and F.R. Scobee, the spacecraft commander. The CHALLENGER was launched from Scobee, the spacecraft command. The CHALLENGER was launched from the Kennedy Space Center at 11:38 a.m. Resnik and crew died at 11:39 when the CHALLENGER exploded seconds after it was launched.

Resnik was carrying a ring for her nephew and a heart-shaped locket for her niece when she died. She saw danger as another unknown to be mastered. She will live in the legacy of Jewish women and men who contributed to their country, many of whom died in doing so.

151

Lynn Gottlieb
Rabbi & Jewish Feminist

Rabbi Lynn Gottlieb had a long and tough struggle before she was ordained as a rabbi. She became a major mover in helping other women understand their Jewish heritage so that they could attain a positive role as modern Jews.

Rabbi Gottlieb was born April 12, 1949, in Bethlehem, Pennsylvania, to Harriet and Abraham Gottlieb. Her father was a businessman and her mother was a puppeteer and the director and teacher of a theater school until her death in 1971.

While attending high school in Allentown, Pennsylvania, in 1946, she went to Israel as an exchange student at the Leo Beck High School in Haifa for a few months. This visit to Israel rekindled her desire to become a rabbi. The Jewish establishment still had their doors closed in allowing women to become ordained. She decided that she would get herself educationally qualified to become a rabbi.

After a brief stay as a student in the New York State University in Albany, she enrolled at the Hebrew University in Jerusalem, where received her B.S. Degree in 1972. For the next nine years, her main focus was preparing and studying for the rabbinate. She studied at the Hebrew Union College in New York, at the Jewish Theological Seminary and privately with various scholars and rabbis.

Gottlieb became involved in working with the deaf. She was able to communicate with the deaf through her knowledge and use of the sign language. Her theatrical background enabled her to use pantomime for religious services, story telling and teaching. She became the spiritual leader for a deaf congregation in Hollis, New York.

Gottlieb travelled throughout the United States talking to women's groups on Jewish feminism. She referred to these sessions as "life cycle ceremonies."

Because so many doors were closed to women, she looked for alternative ways of celebrating Judaism. She became involved with the New Jewish Agenda, a movement composed of mostly younger Jews seeking alternative ways to the more conservative policies of organized American Jewry.

Gottlieb continued her struggle to be ordained which was thwarted by the Conservative Jewish leaders. She made some progress when Rabbi Seymour Siegel, a professor of theology and ethics at the Jewish Theological Seminary, came out publicly in support of ordaining women as rabbis.

Gottlieb turned to Rabbis Zalman Schachter, Everett Gendler and Shlomo Carlebach, who were leaders in alternative Judaism. They ordained her as a rabbi in 1981.

Gottlieb still enjoys her reputation as being a Jewish storyteller. She travelled to campuses, hospital, synagogues organizations, etc., across the nation, Many times, she was with Bat Kol, a small troupe of feminist actors, who portrayed biblical women or other heroine of ancient and recent history.

"God has a female presence," she once said, but noted, "the female presence is in exile. It is not until we redeem Her and bring Her home to rest in us that the entire world will be redeemed."

Rabbi Lynn Gottlieb has been joined by other women rabbis like Melanie Aron and Sally Priesand in helping to redeem the world. Her work and struggles are an inspiration to other women who would want to have a more important role in Judaism.

Picture Gallery

Sgt. Benjamin Kaufman- #63

Uriah P. Levy #8

Col. Jack H. Jacobs- #131

Admiral Hyman George Rickover

312

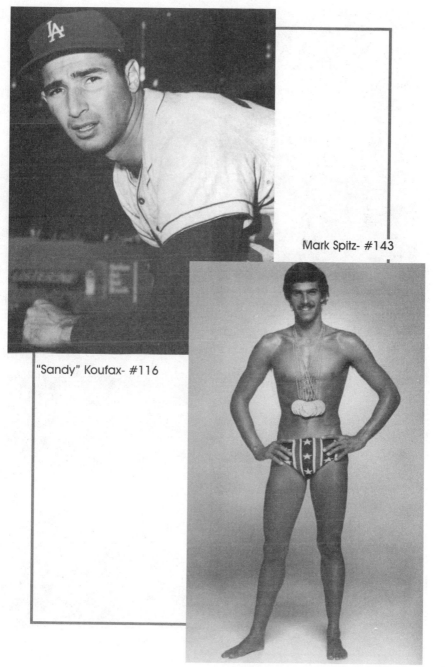

Mark Spitz- #143

"Sandy" Koufax- #116

Barbara Walters- #144

Barbara Streisand- #145

Bennt Goodman- #123

Fanny Brice- #72

314

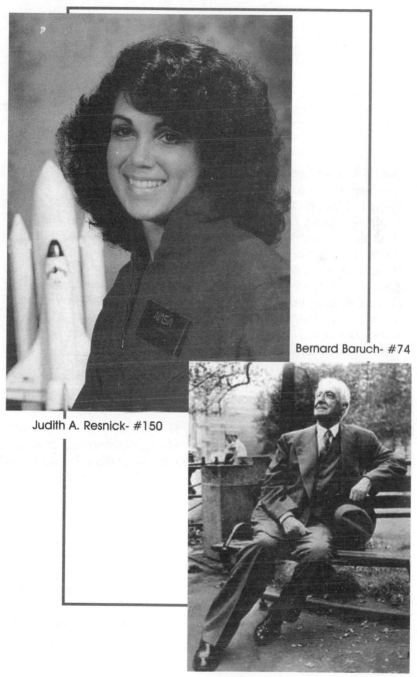

Bernard Baruch- #74

Judith A. Resnick- #150

317